is data human?

Is Data Human?

the metaphysics of star trek

Richard Hanley

Basic Books
A Member of Perseus Books, L.L.C.

Published by Basic Books,
A Member of Perseus Books, L.L.C.

Designed by Elliott Beard

Library of Congress Cataloging-in-Publication Data is available.

Originally published as *The Metaphysics of Star Trek*.

ISBN 0-465-09124-5 (cloth)
ISBN 0-465-04548-0 (paper)

98 99 00 01 02 RRD 9 8 7 6 5 4 3 2 1

To Jo and Brianna, the centers of my universe

contents

acknowledgments

I owe thanks to Robyn Shuster for first suggesting *Star Trek* as a pedagogical tool in philosophy; to the departments of philosophy at the University of Maryland, College Park, and Central Michigan University, for allowing me to teach courses based around *Star Trek;* to Gary Fuller for reading the first draft; to Val Kelly for reading parts of the second draft; to Sam Gates and Steven Glaister for comments on chapter 6 and general suggestions; to Steve Matthews for useful advice; to Ian Mond and David Hull for loaning me videotapes; to Callan Ledsham for encouragement and research assistance; to the staff of Blockbuster Video, Mount Waverley, and Movieland, Ashwood, for their courteous assistance; to the faculty, staff, and students at the University of Maryland, College Park, Central Michigan University, and Monash University for moral support; to my family and friends for always being there; and to those who continue to teach me philosophy—especially Fred Adams, John Bigelow, Michael Devitt, Richard Holton, Jerrold Levinson, Raymond Martin, Michael Slote, and Aubrey Townsend.

This book would never have appeared without the support of Susan Rabiner at Basic Books, who took a suggestion and helped me to turn it into an idea. I turned the idea into a manuscript, but the manuscript was turned into a book by the tireless effort, sharp insight, and firm hand of Sara

Lippincott. Any remaining deficiencies are surely my doing, and not hers. The subtitle, *The Metaphysics of Star Trek,* is partly a pun: the term "metaphysics" gets its meaning from commentary on Aristotle, literally as what comes after *The Physics*. In punning, I express a debt of gratitude to Lawrence Krauss, author of *The Physics of Star Trek*.

Finally, thanks to my wife, Joanne Sampson, for her unflinching support; for indulging my *Star Trek* habit above and beyond the call of duty; and for giving birth to our daughter while this book was in gestation.

> "Space, the final frontier. These are the voyages of the starship *Enterprise*. Her five-year mission: to seek out new life and new civilizations, to boldly go where no man has gone before." —*Captain James Tiberius Kirk*

> "*That* is the exploration that awaits you. Not mapping stars and studying nebulae, but charting the unknown possibilities of existence."
> —*Q to Captain Jean-Luc Picard, "All Good Things . . . "*

The Philosophic *Enterprise*

introduction

Philosophy literally is the love of wisdom, but that definition probably isn't very informative. In my view, philosophy is best thought of as an activity, an enterprise that largely consists in seeking wisdom through exploration. So the philosophic *Enterprise* has a mission not unlike that of the starship *Enterprise.* Metaphysics—literally, "after physics"—is the branch of philosophy that explores the nature of existence.

Why explore at all? Because travel broadens the mind. When we visit other places and other people, we often encounter different ways of living, and this provokes us to examine our own lives anew. If we are objective and reasonable in this examination, sometimes we will conclude that there is more than one way to live, sometimes we will conclude that the way other people do things is not for us, and sometimes we will conclude that we ought to adopt that other way of living. So travel isn't just about exploring other people and places, it's about exploring ourselves and testing our limits. Of course, not everyone who travels is objective and reasonable—sometimes travelers think they already know how to live and that the only possible interaction with those who think differently is to convert them. But in general, travelers are more likely to examine their lives than are those stay-at-homes who presume that home and home ways are best. Nor are stay-at-homes usually enlightened merely by being told about other places. Travel enriches the mind because it makes other places *real*—it enables the traveler (temporarily, at least) to detach himself from the comfortable familiarity of home, to try something different on for size. And as any traveler knows, living away from home works even better, allowing genuine immersion in a different place. It is human nature to want what is familiar and to complain about what is not, and one needs time to get over those prejudices and see the new surroundings as they really are.

Star Trek asks us to imagine with hope a future in which we have thoroughly explored the Earth and learned its lessons. By the twenty-third century, Earth has achieved peaceful, enlightened, worldwide government, with an end to all forms of discrimination based on sex, race, and species membership. Naturally enough, the boundaries of exploration have been extended into outer space. And just as early explorers on Earth discovered other human life and human civilizations, the explorers of outer space discover extraterrestrial life and extraterrestrial civilizations. Exploring this world has broadened the human mind, and we should expect that the exploration of other planets, other worlds, will broaden it further.

There is one significant limitation on the mission of the starship *Enterprise*—it cannot discover what is not actually there. Hence it may be that important alternatives to accepted ways of living and thinking are overlooked, simply because no one has ever tried to live or think that way. This is where philosophy enters the picture: philosophers try to examine all the possibilities. Whereas the starship *Enterprise* traverses outer space, the philosophic *Enterprise* traverses *logical* space, visiting various possible worlds—that is, sets of internally consistent conceivable ways that things might be. It stays as long on each possible world as is appropriate, long enough to get a feel for the place. Its continuing mission: to boldly go where few human minds have gone before. And occasionally to return home, richer for the experience, since the major goal of such travel remains the exploration of ourselves, the exploration of inner space.

This activity is not easy. Not only is it often difficult to discover different possibilities, it is even harder to suspend your home beliefs and customs long enough to engage strange new worlds seriously. Yet that is what philosophers must do, and proper philosophical training is a slow process of release from one's former prejudices. One method that philosophers use to this purpose is that of *thought experiments*—experiments we conduct solely in our imagination. Devising such experiments is something of an acquired skill, as is imagining the experimental situations with sufficient vividness, and that's where appropriate fiction comes in. Good fiction—in particular, good visual fiction—engages our imaginative faculties. This is the role of *Star Trek* in "doing philosophy." Many of the situations in *Star Trek* resemble those in the thought experiments of philosophers, and watching a *Star Trek* scenario unfold forces us to entertain notions that our home prejudices would otherwise blind us to. For fifty minutes or so, we get to live in a different world, to try it on for size.

Looking at philosophy through the lens of *Star Trek* is a strategy I have adopted with success in the classroom, but in this book I turn the tables and look at *Star Trek* through the lens of philosophy. I come neither to praise *Star Trek* nor to bury it. There is much to ponder in the *Star Trek* canon: the original television series (I'll designate it *TOS*), *The Next Generation* (*TNG*), *Deep Space Nine* (*DS9*), *Voyager,* and the motion picture series. My interest is in showing how an introductory grasp of philosophy can lead you deeper into *Star Trek,* since *Star Trek* is by its nature so deeply philosophical.

Two brief remarks about the diverse discipline of philosophy. First, I am part of the *analytic* or "Anglo-American" school of philosophy, and moreover accept *naturalism*—roughly, the view that philosophy is and ought to be continuous with the natural sciences, since both enterprises employ the combination of reason and empirical investigation. Hence the philosophical lens with which I look at *Star Trek,* with particular emphasis on the scientific and technological devices and processes it depicts, is not representative of the whole of philosophy. For example, some philosophers think it's hopeless to take an objective, scientific approach to studying the nature of the mind, that one must start instead from the inside—that is, from the subjective, phenomenological nature of mental experience. Other philosophers would be interested in the mysticism of Vulcans, Bajorans, and the Native American Commander Chakotay. Still other philosophers would be interested in the examination of *Star Trek* as mythology, as "text," or as "cultural icon." I am none of those philosophers. Second, even within the analytic, naturalist approach there is substantive disagreement over many philosophical issues, and I am sometimes in a minority. I shall often present and argue for what I take to be the most defensible position on an issue, but this should not be taken as representative of what all philosophers think. That said, I will consider the important views on an issue even if I must ultimately reject them.

As for metaphysics, it can be relatively pure or relatively applied. *Star Trek* raises some pure metaphysical issues, as in *TNG:* "Where No One Has Gone Before," when young Wesley Crusher wonders whether thought is the basis of all existence. This book focuses instead on applied metaphysics—that is, upon metaphysical issues that matter to the daily lives of persons such as ourselves. It is intended to be relatively easy to read. Thus, for instance, I have avoided footnotes altogether. The result is very much a book about ideas rather than about philosophers or the history of philosophy, and I have tried to keep to contemporary views, especially those at the shifting border between science and metaphysics. Where it is important to do so, I have mentioned those philosophers responsible for various positions and arguments. Readers wishing to research further may consult the recommended readings at the end of the book. The text is, I hope, a useful introduction to the contemporary debates concerning humankind's place in the world, as they apply to the diverse fiction that is *Star Trek*.

New Life, New Civilizations

part i

"Recognizing new life, whatever its form, is a principal mission of the vessel."

—*Jean-Luc Picard,* TNG: *"The Quality of Life"*

Prime Suspects

chapter 1

All fiction concerns itself with the human condition, and *Star Trek* is no exception. The unique contribution of *Star Trek* as popular fiction is the way in which it extends the boundaries of human concerns. In each of the television series, the most interesting characters frequently are those who are like us but also not quite like us. And instead of treating the strange and different as something to be feared—and killed—*Star Trek* encourages us to imagine what life is like from the nonhuman point of view. *Star Trek* thus performs two valuable functions: it teaches us something about ourselves and it exposes to popular consciousness (and so calls into question) the common conviction that members of the species *Homo sapiens* necessarily occupy a special place in the cosmos. Is this conviction warranted, or is it mere hubris? What, if any, are our ethical obligations to those who are like us but not like us? Does a moral principle—the Golden Rule, say—extend to our dealings with nonhumans? How different from humans does a species have to be before the Prime Directive—Starfleet's rule of noninterference—does not apply to dealings with it?

Star Trek forces us to ponder these questions by examining the boundary between human and nonhuman on many fronts, and no more so than in its choice of central characters. In the original series, the *Enterprise*'s first officer is the famously half human and half Vulcan Mr. Spock. Spock seems almost contemptuous of humanity, continually striving to repress his human nature in favor of his Vulcan side. When the ship's medical officer Leonard McCoy suggests, in "Court Martial," that Spock is the most cold-blooded person he has ever met, Spock replies, "Why, thank you, Doctor." And when at the end of "The Devil in the Dark," in the near obligatory light moment on the bridge, Kirk says, "I suspect you of becoming more and more human all the time," Spock replies, "Captain, I see no reason to stand here and be insulted."

A counterpoint to Spock's predilection is provided by three central characters in the later series. In *The Next Generation,* the behavior of the android Data is largely devoted to the mimicry of humans, and if we take Data's word for it (whether or not we should do so is a question we shall ponder at length in chapter 3), then Data's highest aspiration is to become human. In *Deep Space Nine,* Security Chief Odo is a shape-shifter who has spent all his time among humans and adopted their outward appearance; he seems more at home with them than among his own kind, the evil rulers of much of the Gamma quadrant. In *Voyager,* an "emergency medical hologram" is pressed into permanent service when the ship's doctor is killed, and though it cannot leave the holodeck it gradually exhibits aspirations to humanity. But what is the nature of humanity, and why is human nature desirable?

Logic Versus Emotion

> "Only the discipline of logic saved my planet from extinction."
>
> —*Spock to Bele,* TOS: *"Let That Be Your Last Battlefield"*

> "I have no regrets."
>
> —*Spock to Lieutenant Commander Data,* TNG: *"Unification II"*

What has Spock got against humanity? Simply that humans are overinfluenced by emotion and underinfluenced by logic. In their ancient past, the Vulcans were so aggressively emotional that they spent all their time fighting, and in all likelihood would have perished in perpetual civil war. The solution the Vulcans adopted was to suppress their emotions through rigorous training, and to follow the dictates of logic instead (the *Pon farr*—the septennial Vulcan rut—notwithstanding). Dr. McCoy, on the other hand, often indulges in emotion, professing in numerous episodes to reject Spock's logical approach to life. McCoy meets Spock's cool demeanor with a barrage of emotional and instinctual reactions, adopting an air as superior as Spock's. Captain Kirk, perhaps, represents the quintessential human, in his expression of both logic and emotion, but he has his moments of deep sympathy with

McCoy. ("Your logic can be most annoying," he remarks to Spock, in "Tomorrow Is Yesterday.")

Many nonhumans seem largely to agree with Kirk and McCoy that emotion or unreason is worth embracing. Here are just a few examples. In *TOS:* "By Any Other Name," the uppity Kelvans assume human form in order to take over the *Enterprise,* and they quickly come to appreciate some of the baser aspects of humanity, including sex and drunkenness. In *TNG:* "Clues," the xenophobic Paxans decide to destroy the *Enterprise-D* and its crew to protect the secret of their existence, but they are so impressed by the human determination to survive that they change their minds. Q, that omnipotent and immortal being from a different dimension of existence, torments the *Enterprise-D* crew in several *Next Generation* episodes, precisely because he finds humanity illogical and thus endlessly fascinating.

Certainly in the original series we are given the general impression that violent emotions are worth having. In "This Side of Paradise," the entire *Enterprise* crew falls under the influence of delirium-inducing plant spores, and it is only by becoming passionately angry that Kirk is released from this influence. In "The Deadly Years," the landing party visiting Gamma Hydra IV becomes infected with an age-accelerating virus, except for Ensign Pavel Chekov. With Kirk and McCoy near death, it is discovered that Chekov is unaffected because he experienced great fear while on the planet. The adrenal response killed the virus, and McCoy uses this knowledge to manufacture a cure. Coming back to Earth, we can explain our susceptibility to an emotion like fear in terms of evolutionary adaptiveness: presumably, fear prevents a destructible creature from engaging in suicidal behavior in dangerous circumstances; more generally, the adrenal response prepares one for "fight or flight." (It is wise, though, not to rely on adaptation to explain the origin of every one of our present characteristics: often the most we know about a trait is that it hasn't been selected *against.*)

Spock and McCoy represent two different philosophical traditions on the relation between reason (the mental faculty that produces and assesses beliefs) and passion (the mental faculty that produces desires and emotions). According to the ancient Greek philosophers Plato and Aristotle, the human condition is a struggle between reason and passion—a struggle that reason ought to win. According to the other tradition, most closely associated with the eighteenth-century Scottish philosopher David Hume, there is no conflict at all, and passion is preeminent. It is desires and emotions that motivate behavior, and, in Hume's famous expression, "Reason is, and ought only to be, the slave of the passions." Putting it roughly, reason can tell you how to get what you care about, but it cannot tell you *what* to care about.

Who is correct? Spock and the Greeks, or McCoy and Hume? I am inclined to think that the most defensible view of human nature is somewhere in between the two. There is a temptation to think of the passions—emotions and desires—as states that happen to us. We are in some sense the victims of passion, whereas reason, the deliberate application of logic in the formation and assessment of beliefs, is entirely within our control. But I doubt that matters are so simple. Suppose I tell you (and you believe me) that Monash University is in Victoria and Victoria is in Australia. Can you help but come to the conclusion that Monash University is in Australia? Here's some incentive—I'll give you a million dollars if you can bring yourself sincerely to believe in the next five minutes that Monash University is in Victoria and Victoria is in Australia, but that Monash University is *not* in Australia. Surely logic tells you that it's in your interest to do what I ask. (I'll wait while you try. . . . *Whew,* another million saved!) I suspect that reason and passion are both largely beyond deliberate control, but that both can to some extent be cultivated. One can train one's logical abilities, as the Vulcans do, and one can probably train one's desires and emotions, too.

So there is a point in applying logic to try to control the emotions, as Spock does. But is there a point to suppressing the emotions altogether? Or do we need emotions to motivate action, as Hume claims? My hunch is that Hume is at least partly correct. Emotions may provide the key to a puzzle: they may contribute to the average human's ability to solve what cognitive scientists call the *frame problem*. In order to perform an action, a cognitive agent—myself, say—must decide between options. Rational deliberation, at a minimum, seems to require weighing the probable outcomes of a bewildering range of possibilities. This is true of even the simplest task, such as my getting up from my computer to go to the refrigerator. Should I stand up? Lift my arm an inch? Whistle? Sing? Contract my abdominals? Tracking all possible actions even a short way into the future produces a combinatorial explosion of yet more possibilities. In addition, to perform such an action I must access what I know and draw the appropriate inferences from this knowledge concerning what I ought to do in order to complete the task. But I know uncountably many things, so I must somehow eliminate the irrelevancies (for example, that it's Wednesday, or that the Moon has no atmosphere), without the brute force method of accessing each bit of information and deciding whether or not it is relevant to my proposed action. The frame problem is actually a group of many different problems, but we can summarize the difficulty: somehow, a cognitive agent needs to know what to think about without first having to think about what to think about.

A way to solve part of the frame problem is to divide the mind into various subcapacities, or *faculties,* each of which simply gets on with whatever job it's supposed to perform. (When I stand, I don't have to consciously contract my abdominals—somehow this just gets done without "me.") Putting it bluntly, the frame problem is eliminated for certain tasks by taking them out of the clutches of deliberation altogether and farming them off to special-purpose mental devices. But the behavioral flexibility of cognitive agents such as ourselves suggests that this isn't the whole solution. It appears that we have a more general-purpose mechanism for narrowing the focus of our thinking, and perhaps the emotions are implicated here. It is well understood that emotions affect attention; when we love someone, we attend to their virtues and ignore their faults, to use a banal example. So if—and this is an extremely speculative "if"—we did not have emotions, we would be frozen into permanent inaction by the sheer size of even the simplest task.

This explanation of the interdependence of emotion and logic receives a nice allegorical treatment in *TOS:* "The Enemy Within." A transporter accident somehow "splits" Kirk into his cerebral and animal halves. Though physically identical, these two individuals behave very differently: for instance, the animal Kirk, lacking the control of reason, tries to rape a female crew member. The cerebral Kirk at first seems well adjusted, but it becomes clear that without his baser emotions and instincts he is weak and indecisive, incapable of command. Each half is incomplete without the other. Kirk the human being needs both logic and emotion, if he is to be a successful cognitive agent.

Spock might well agree that certain emotions are worthwhile. There is a plausible distinction between what are often called *higher* and *lower* emotions. (It is doubtless more accurate to think of emotions as lying along a spectrum, the lower at one end and the higher at the other, but we can ignore this.) Lower emotions are rooted in the limbic system and the brain stem—the so-called *crocodile brain*—while higher emotions are cortical. We share lower emotions with many other animals—primary examples are fear and anger. Higher emotions typically are missing in other animals, and include hope and regret. In general, we associate very strong feelings—or, to use the technical term, *affect*—with the lower emotions, while higher emotions seem characterized more by their accompanying cognitive states. For instance, if one *regrets* doing something, then one *believes* that doing something else would have been better and *wishes* that one had instead done the alternative.

Vulcans surely display their fair share of higher emotion. For instance, there is little doubt that Spock genuinely cares for his friends (and I don't think this is entirely explained away by his being half human—pure Vulcans do, too). It is Spock's *admiration* of logic and his *hope* of mastery of logic that motivate him. When Spock remarks to Data that he has "no regrets" (see the epigraph at the beginning of this section), he is not claiming that regret is an emotion he does not experience—far from it. Spock has many regrets—arising, for example, from his poor relationship with his father, Sarek—but he does not particularly regret choosing to follow the Vulcan teaching, which is the content of his remark. It is only the lower emotions (in which Kirk, McCoy, and the *Star Trek* writers occasionally revel) that Spock seeks to suppress.

"Human" and "human"—What Is Human?

COLONIST: "You're not human."
DATA: "That is correct. I am an android."

—TNG: *"The Ensigns of Command"*

"Ugly giant bags of mostly water . . . "

—*The Microbrain, referring to the* Enterprise-D *crew,* TNG: *"Home Soil"*

Since Spock genetically is half human, isn't it pointless for him to spurn his humanity? And since Data undoubtedly is not a member of the human species, isn't it pointless for Data to aspire to be human? Yes and no. "Human," as we ordinarily use the term, has at least three distinct meanings. The first is the sense in which one is human if and only if one is a member of the genus *Homo;* in this biological sense, Data will never be human. *Star Trek* suggests that this biological sense may well include extraterrestrial species, such as Vulcans, Klingons, Romulans, Ferengi, Bajorans, and Cardassians. There are genetic similarities among all these species, and in *TNG:* "The Chase" the crew of the *Enterprise-D* learns why. A puzzle planted in the genetic code of various humanoid species leads the *Enterprise-D* to a message from the past: an ancient race planted its genetic seed on various planets throughout the Alpha quadrant, so all humanoid species have a common origin. I shall stick to *Star Trek* language and use "humanoid" to designate the strictly biological sense of "human"—the sense that the colonists in "The Ensigns of Command" have in mind when they remark that Data is not human.

One is human in the second sense if one has roughly the same psychological characteristics as fully developed terrestrial human beings. It is in this sense that Spock struggles to be less human, and that Data aspires to be human. It is in this sense that Kirk accuses Spock of "becoming more and more human," and that Picard, in *TNG:* "The Quality of Life," characterizes a particular decision of Data's—to put Picard's life at risk to prevent the destruction of possibly intelligent machines—as "the most human decision" Data ever made. I shall reserve *human* in italics for this second, psychological sense.

The third ordinary sense of "human" is the most elusive but also the most important: it is the moral or ethical sense of the term. When people speak of "human rights," for instance, it is in this moral sense. Suppose that someone mounts the following argument: a human fetus is human, and all humans have a right not to be killed, therefore a fetus has a right not to be killed. Such an argument seems to trade on the equivocation between different senses of "human." A human fetus unquestionably is humanoid, but one doubts that all humanoids have a right not to be killed. And even if all *humans* have a right not to be killed, a human fetus unquestionably lacks some of the psychological properties of fully developed terrestrial human beings. It is the third, moral sense of "human" that matters to the argument; until we know what being human in this sense amounts to, we cannot judge whether a human fetus qualifies.

Star Trek helps us to investigate this third, moral sense, which the *Star Trek* writers designate by speaking of "sentience." As long as we remain rooted on Earth, it is difficult even to *see* this third sense, since we are so used to the idea that humanoids and *humans* are the only sorts of individuals with (for instance) a right not to be killed. The United Federation of Planets recognizes not terrestrial human rights per se but "sentient" rights, and it is clear that the Federation extends the notion of human rights at least to other humanoids. For instance, it surely would be just as wrong (other things being equal) to kill Spock as it would be to kill McCoy.

Here we must abandon the usage of the *Star Trek* writers, since a sentient individual is simply an individual aware of its sense impressions. While sentience might be necessary for "humanity" in the moral sense, it is unlikely to be sufficient. A chicken is sentient, but I doubt that we intend to include chickens in our discussion of "human rights." A better term—the one philosophers use to capture this moral sense of "human"—is "person." The important philosophical question which *Star Trek* can help us to answer is, What is personhood? Being humanoid is not sufficient, since a humanoid corpse is not a person. And while there is no doubt that being *human* is sufficient for personhood, the example of Spock shows that it's not strictly necessary. But is being humanoid necessary for personhood? *Star Trek,* in its famous search for "new life and new civilizations," shows us that the answer is No.

New Life, New Civilizations, and New Ethics

> "I do not believe it is justified to sacrifice one life-form for another." —*Data to Commander William T. Riker,* TNG: *"The Quality of Life"*

> "If the ship truly is an emerging intelligence, then we have a responsibility to treat it with the same respect as any other being."
> —*Picard to senior officers,* TNG: *"Emergence"*

Star Trek examines the possibility of new life in four distinct categories: extraterrestrial life—that is, life that arises by nonartificial means on other worlds; artificial life; intelligent life; and "sentient" life—that is, personhood. Of course, these categories are not mutually exclusive (you, for instance, are living, intelligent, and a person), and there may be no extraterrestrial or artificial life at all.

In *TNG:* "The Quality of Life," Data remarks to the chief medical officer of the *Enterprise-D,* Dr. Beverly Crusher, "I am curious as to what transpired between the moment when I was nothing more than an assemblage of parts . . . and the next moment, when I became alive. What is it that endowed me with life?" Putting aside for the moment the issue of whether or not Data really is alive, we can ask Data's question about ourselves. For instance, what is it that endowed you with life?

When scientists speak of the possibility of extraterrestrial life, they usually have in mind a purely biological category; the discussion of recent evidence of life on Mars is a case in point. And of course, to determine whether or not something is a form of life, one needs a working conception of just what life—in the purely biological sense—is. Early scientists commonly thought that life was animation of ordinary matter by a special sort of stuff called *élan vital.* So does Picard, to judge from *TNG:* "Datalore," an episode in which the *Enterprise-D* is threatened by a crystalline entity about which little is known except that it has ravaged Data's home planet. Picard notes in the log that this entity is "insatiably ravenous for the life force found in living forms." However, modern science sees life as an arrangement of *élan*-less matter in which the right sorts of events and processes occur. Dr. Crusher appears to agree: when Data asks her for a definition of life, she says, "Life is what enables plants and animals to consume food, derive energy from it, grow, adapt themselves to their surroundings, and reproduce." In *TNG:* "Home Soil," the *Enterprise-D* visits a "terraforming" operation on a planet where yet another crystalline substance exhibits suspiciously lifelike behavior. Dr. Crusher suggests that growth, development, and reproduction may be basic for any definition of life, "organic or inorganic." Later in the same episode, Data remarks of the crystalline substance that "only life can reproduce itself, Doctor. It *is* alive!"

In this episode, then, we have two explicit claims about the relation between reproductivity and life. According to Dr. Crusher, the ability to reproduce is necessary to life, and according to Data the ability to reproduce is sufficient for life. But both claims are implausible. First, there are many hybrid animals on Earth which cannot reproduce but which are nevertheless alive. Second, some simple computer programs can reproduce themselves but hardly seem thereby to be alive.

Dr. Crusher's attempt in "The Quality of Life" is more promising, since it is what philosophers call an *ostensive* definition. Instead of trying to give necessary and sufficient conditions for life, Crusher points to certain features of plants and animals and says that life is what underlies or gives rise to these features. Whether correct or not, both kinds of definition offered by Dr. Crusher leave open the possibility that life might be produced artificially. So both raise the question of whether or not entities like the exocomps in "The Quality of Life"—small machines designed for various engineering purposes and capable of altering their own circuitry—qualify as life-forms. The great irony is that the exocomps' chief defender is Data, itself an artifice, a designed and manufactured entity. But why, after all, should anyone be concerned with whether or not the exocomps are properly said to be *alive?* Because, or so *Star Trek* invites us to believe, whether something is alive or not makes a difference as to how we ought to treat it.

In "The Quality of Life," Will Riker has to decide whether to send the exocomps on a mission that will destroy them, in order to save the lives of Jean-Luc Picard and Geordi La Forge, the *Enterprise-D*'s chief engineer. If the exocomps are just machines, then no problem, but if they're life-forms it would be wrong to sacrifice their lives for those of the two human beings. This is the view forcefully put by Data in the quote at the beginning of this section, and it seems to be a part of the episode's message.

That is, the crew of the *Enterprise-D* appears to have adopted what philosophers call a *life-centered* ethic. According to such an ethic, the entities in the universe that are morally considerable are all and only those entities that are alive. Moreover, all life-forms are of equal moral significance, so it would be wrong to sacrifice one for another. This sounds in turn like the popular "sanctity of life" view captured in the biblical injunction "Thou shalt not kill," but I submit that it is not the same, and neither is it a very plausible ethic. If you took the strictures of a life-centered ethic absolutely literally, then you would be wrong to uproot and cook a plant in order to eat it, wrong to swat the mosquito in your bedroom, wrong to swerve your vehicle to avoid hitting a child if you thereby kill a chicken, and so forth (although such an ethic probably permits killing other life-forms in genuine self-defense).

Undoubtedly the boundary of moral considerability extends beyond humanoids. Animals such as dogs and dormice are morally considerable; other things being equal, one ought not to torture them, for instance. But the life-centered ethic is unconvincing. It's hard to see what is so morally important about the boundary between life and nonlife, nor does all life seem equally morally significant. So what is all the fuss about in "The Quality of Life"? Why is Data willing to sacrifice the lives of Picard and La Forge for machines that may happen to be alive? Perhaps the answer is that the category of life under consideration here is the third mentioned at the start of this section—that of intelligent life. If we focus on terrestrial life for a moment, it seems that we ordinarily draw a moral distinction between intelligent and unintelligent life—between dogs and dormice on the one hand and elms and orchids on the other. One reason is that the intelligent creatures on Earth are capable of suffering, and if a creature is capable of suffering, then it is wrong to inflict suffering upon it unnecessarily.

Philosophers call an ethic which pronounces first that all and only intelligent life is morally considerable, and second that all intelligent creatures are equally morally significant, a *psychocentric* ethic. The quote from Picard which heads this section seems to affirm just such a view. But while the first claim of psychocentrism is plausible, the second is not. A fully developed human being is more morally significant than a typical chicken, even though both are intelligent and both are morally considerable. Why? Briefly, because a fully developed human being has future-oriented mental states: beliefs about how her future life might go, and preferences for how her future life *will* go—preferences that can be frustrated in various ways. She has such preferences because she has a concept of herself as an entity persisting through time. Just as it is wrong, other things being equal, to cause severe pain to a chicken, it is wrong, other things being equal, to severely frustrate the preferences of a human being. But while a chicken has an interest in avoiding pain and suffering, it has no future-oriented preferences to frustrate.

Let us connect this point to the discussion of humanity: a fully developed human being is a person, and a fully developed human being is morally considerable by virtue of having a concept of self and the concomitant future-oriented preferences. A moment's reflection reveals that this is no coincidence. For this reason, philosophers hold that a *person* is an individual with a *concept of self*—a concept of himself or herself as a continuing entity. Persons are more morally significant than intelligent nonpersons like chickens precisely because they have a greater range and depth of preferences. Some philosophers have advocated a *person-centered* ethic, according to which all and only persons are morally considerable, and all persons are equally morally significant. I do not agree with this ethic either. While I agree that all persons are equally morally significant, the person-centered ethic implies that causing extreme unnecessary suffering to a nonperson, such as a chicken, does no wrong *to the chicken*. According to the person-centered ethic, if inflicting such suffering is wrong, it's because of the harm this act causes to persons—perhaps it upsets other persons, or brutalizes the torturer. I suggest instead an ethics according to which all and only intelligent entities are morally considerable, and all and only persons are fully (and equally) morally significant. This is an *extended person-centered ethic,* because some of the direct moral consideration due to persons is extended to intelligent nonpersons.

The extended person-centered ethic is after all consistent with the message in "The Quality of Life." Data and La Forge construct an experimental simulation, in which an exocomp is supposedly threatened with destruction; they are hoping the exocomp will detect the danger and try to avoid it. But they are testing for more than mere intelligence—they are testing whether or not the exocomp forms beliefs about how its "life" might go and acts upon its preference as to how its "life" will go. This sort of behavior in a real situation was what originally convinced Data that exocomps are alive; an exocomp burnt out its own circuits instead of following an order that would have led to its own destruction. So Data and La Forge are testing for personal life, and Data's conviction that the exocomps qualify as persons explains his refusal to sacrifice their lives for Picard and La Forge. As it turns out, Data is vindicated: the exocomp not only passes the test but sees right through it. And when the exocomps realize the danger to Picard and La Forge, all three of them join in a rescue attempt and one is destroyed in the process.

The ethic I have outlined is a relatively conservative one—in the sense that human beings are at its center—but not entirely so. Human beings play no essentially special role in a person-centered ethic, since it is an entirely contingent matter that fully developed human beings are persons. Had our species' development gone differently, we might not have been inside the circle of fully morally significant individuals. Some critics will claim that a person-centered ethic is still too conservative, however. They propose a radical view, which focuses moral consideration not on individuals but instead on large ecological systems, such as the terrestrial biosphere—the Earth itself together with its atmosphere. Among the worthwhile properties of large-scale ecosystems, according to this "deep ecological" view, is biological diversity. But deep ecology has major difficulties, such as settling upon a definition of diversity. If diversity consists in numbers of species, then an ecological system containing only beetles, but one million species of them, is more diverse than a rain forest containing half a million species. Moreover, even if one can give a workable characterization of diversity, to maintain the deep ecological view one needs to explain what is so special about diversity aside from the benefit it bestows upon intelligent and sentient individuals. This is no easy task.

The well-known Vulcan IDIC credo ("Infinite Diversity in

Infinite Combinations") is never clearly explained in the *Star Trek* canon, but whatever its content it seems compatible with the extended person-centered ethic. One can agree that diversity is a good thing without going "deep," by holding that diversity is generally beneficial to those entities that are morally considerable—namely, intelligent individuals and especially persons. (The benefits of diversity might arise in a number of areas—medical, scientific, recreational, aesthetic.) I take it that there is at least no cogent case against the relatively conservative, extended person-centered ethic, and I shall proceed on that basis.

Applying the extended person-centered ethic to nonhumanoid life is a matter of determining which of three categories a living individual or community falls under. (Curiously, the Federation seems to have a classification system for intelligent life, but I don't know how it works. The Sheliak in *TNG:* "The Ensigns of Command" are described as "nonhumanoid intelligent life-form, classification R3.") Starfleet crews must ask themselves of a candidate individual, Is it intelligent or nonintelligent? And if it is intelligent, they must ask themselves, Is it a person or not? If an individual or community is nonintelligent life, then according to the extended person-centered ethic it is not morally considerable. Presumably the new plants discovered by exobotanists fall into this category. Note well that this does not entitle the Starfleet crews to do whatever they choose with such life—it only entails that whatever they do does no wrong *to the plant*. Obviously, removing or otherwise interfering with the vegetation on a planet can have serious effects on the intelligent life and persons there, and so might be morally wrong. Let us call candidates for nonintelligent life *tertiary suspects* (Dr. Crusher's definitions of life appear most helpful in identifying tertiary suspects).

If an individual is intelligent but not a person, it is morally considerable. Suppose that one encounters an alien creature roughly equivalent in intelligence and sensory apparatus to a chicken. If the creature is capable of feeling physical pain, then it would be wrong to inflict pain upon it just for fun. But it would not be wrong to kill it for food, other things being equal (say, as long as dispatching it causes no unnecessary suffering to the creature or to any person—such as its owner). Let us call candidates for intelligent nonpersons *secondary suspects*.

If an individual is a person, then it is morally considerable in the fullest sense. When the *Enterprise* encounters other nonhuman persons, no matter how exotic, the actions of the crew are guided by all the moral considerations that apply in dealing with other *humans*. This includes the application of the Prime Directive. Hence the *Enterprise* needs to be on the lookout for *prime suspects*—individuals that may qualify for personhood and for full moral consideration. But how does one identify prime suspects, given that they may be exotic? I propose that we begin by noting that prime suspects will be secondary suspects, too. Under what conditions should Kirk, Picard, and company suspect that they are dealing with intelligent life?

Secondary Suspects

> "Commander, prove to the court that *I* am sentient!"
>
> —*Picard to Commander Bruce Maddox,*
> TNG: *"The Measure of a Man"*

What qualifies an entity as a secondary suspect, and how should these suspicions be further investigated? Kirk and Spock find themselves with this problem in *TOS:* "The Devil in the Dark." The mining operation on Janus IV is threatened when fifty of the miners are killed by what appears to be a large rock. Spock suspects that the rock is a silicon-based creature—intelligent life, Jim, but not as we know it. In such situations, it clearly would be handy to have some sort of intelligence test at the ready. I don't mean an alien version of an IQ test; IQ tests are administered to subjects already presumed to be intelligent and are supposed to measure the degree of that intelligence. Rather, I mean a test to detect the presence of intelligence—the possession, to whatever degree, of a mind.

Kirk, Picard, and company have an unfair advantage in this regard over the rest of us, given the psychic abilities of Spock, counselor Deanna Troi in *The Next Generation,* and Tuvok (and perhaps Kes) in *Voyager*. In each of these cases, the ability seems to be a form of extrasensory perception. Troi's empathic version of ESP is restricted to discerning the emotional state of a subject and seems to operate all the time, while the Vulcans Spock and Tuvok can initiate a much fuller "mind meld," by making the proper physical contact. (Of course, these abilities pose an occasional disadvantage to the *Star Trek* writers; in *TNG:* "Where Silence Has Lease," the plot requires the crew to be unaware of the presence of an intelligent individual who is manipulating them. The writers get around this by having Troi fail to recognize "an intelligence so vast it eluded me!") Some Starfleet personnel have even more impressive ESP abilities. In *TNG:* "Tin Man," we learn that the Federation's leading expert in alien contact is an exceptional betazoid with full-blown mind-reading powers. (It is noteworthy that all these psychic members of Starfleet are extraterrestrials, because there is no evidence that we terrestrial humans have any ESP abilities, despite frequent claims to the contrary.) In "The Devil in the Dark," Spock uses his ESP shortcut as a kind of intelligence test, performing a mind meld with the rock entity. He discovers that the creature is a Horta, the mother of thousands of rocky offspring which are being destroyed by the mining operation, and that it is dying of wounds inflicted by the crew's phasers. Dr. McCoy does a little masonry work to repair the wounds, a treaty is negotiated between the Horta and the miners, and all ends well.

Another advantage enjoyed by *Star Trek* crews is the existence of life-detecting sensors. In numerous episodes, an officer on the bridge will "scan for life-forms" on a planet below or on a seemingly abandoned space station; and such scanners are also used by landing parties on planet surfaces. In *TNG:* "The Arsenal of Freedom," Data claims to have scanned for *intelligent* life-forms on the planet Minos and found none. This last instance seems more like a convenient plot device than anything else, but even if such an intelligence sensor were possible, why should the crew accept a negative finding (especially given Starfleet's mission of discovery)? Whereas a positive reading might warrant the conclusion that there is intelligent life below, because it's in a recognizable form (whatever that may be), a negative reading surely doesn't warrant the conclusion that there isn't any, since it might not be in a recognizable form.

But how, in the absence of ESP or other special sensors, would Kirk be able to detect the presence of intelligence in the Horta? It may surprise you to know that this is part of a very old philosophical problem, called *the problem of other minds*. Just think about your own mind for a moment. You have states of mind—such as beliefs, memories, hopes, and sensations. But how do you know when you're in a particular mental state, such as pain? The overwhelmingly plausible answer is that you know by introspection (literally, by "looking within"). But if true this raises an obvious problem. In the absence of ESP, you don't have introspective access to other minds (whereas Spock, who actually felt the pain of the Horta during the mind meld, does have introspective access to other minds). Without such introspective access to other minds, how do you know that there are any other minds at all? How do you know that *I*—Richard Hanley—have a mind, for instance? This might seem like a crazy question. When Picard asks a similar question of Commander Maddox in "The Measure of a Man" (see the epigraph), Maddox replies, "That's absurd! We all know you're sentient!" However, unless you can give this "absurd" question—"How do you know that *I* have a mind?"—a satisfactory answer, you are doomed to one of two very extreme views. One is *solipsism,* the view that you alone in the universe are intelligent, and the other is *panpsychism,* the view that absolutely everything in the universe is intelligent. If you wish to adopt the sensibly moderate view that some things in the universe apart from yourself are intelligent, but not everything is, then a justified intelligence test is called for.

Clearly Commander Maddox thinks he knows that Picard is intelligent, since earlier in the episode Maddox cited intelligence as a condition of "sentience" (that is, personhood). We shall delve more deeply into Maddox's position in chapter 3, but of present relevance is the importance Maddox seems to place on humanity in the sense of being humanoid. Maddox might be reasoning as follows: I am intelligent, and I am humanoid. Picard is humanoid, therefore (probably) Picard is intelligent, too.

If this is Maddox's reasoning, then some philosophers have agreed with him. That is, you can argue for the existence of other humanoid minds by an argument *from analogy*. You know in your own case that you have a mind, so by analogy another humanoid probably also has a mind—just as, if your particular make and model of car is economical to run, then you can infer that another car of the same make and model is economical to run, too. But I don't think that this argument demonstrates anything at all. The inference in the car case is strong because of known background facts—in particular, facts about the uniformity of production procedures for vehicles. So what background facts would make the other-minds analogy a strong one? Facts connecting being humanoid with being intelligent. But no such facts are known in advance—indeed, it is the existence of other humanoid minds that the argument is supposed to establish! By way of illustration, if no background facts about car production are known, then concluding that the other car is as economical to run as yours makes just as much sense as concluding that the other car is the same color as yours.

The only plausible intelligence tests are *behavioral* ones, and this is the sort of test regularly employed by the members of Starfleet—which is just as well, since even if the analogy argument worked in the case of other humanoids, it would not be applicable to nonhumanoids. Data decided the exocomps were intelligent because of the way they behaved. And in "Home Soil," when attacked by a laser drill, Data concludes that the machine's behavior is too "dynamic" to be an accident; there was, in other words, "a mind, working against me." Moreover, long before Spock performs the mind meld with the Horta, he suspects that it is intelligent because of the way it behaves (otherwise, why would he try a mind meld with a rock?). Kirk also performs behavioral tests on the Horta, brandishing his phaser and putting it away again and watching the Horta's reactions. Back here on Earth, it is the behavior of animals such as dogs, chickens, and the like which causes us to attribute an (albeit relatively rudimentary) intelligence to them. Just as the Horta retreated whenever Kirk brandished his phaser (having been wounded once already), animals like dogs very quickly learn to avoid further harm from individual humans.

What kinds of entity fail the behavioral test of intelligence? On Earth, plants are considered nonintelligent life (by most people, anyway), and the same goes in the *Star Trek* cosmos, as far as I can tell. No one who practices exobotany (for example, Dr. Crusher in *TNG:* "Clues") assumes anything to the contrary. But is this just prejudice, an inability to see the possiblities of alternative intelligent existence? I don't think so. Here on Earth, we can discern two basic strategies adopted by relatively large living things in competition with others. One is a trench warfare strategy, and the other is a guerrilla warfare strategy (if you'll forgive the militaristic metaphors). Plants have adopted the trench strategy, digging themselves in. The larger the entrenched individual—a tree, say—the more it depends on a stable supply of food and water, and heavy armor for protection. The guerrillas, on the other hand, are mobile, and the larger the individual guerrilla—a cat, say—the more the key to its survival is flexibility of behavior and the ability to learn; such creatures literally *live by their wits*. Thus behavior that is flexible and adaptive is a pretty good indicator of intelligence.

But what about the really dangerous exotics that turn up in *Star Trek?* In *TOS:* "The Doomsday Machine," the *Enterprise* encounters an artificial consumer of entire planets, and in *TOS:* "Obsession," a nonartificial gaseous entity that drains all the red blood cells from its victims. No one on the *Enterprise* seems terribly concerned about whether these entities are intelligent, and both episodes end with their deliberate destruction. However, things are a little different in the *Next Generation* episodes "Datalore" and "Silicon

Avatar," in which the *Enterprise-D* encounters the crystalline entity that lays waste to whole planets. Although the latter episode ends with the destruction of the crystalline entity, this is effected by a civilian with a grudge against it, and Picard strongly disapproves of her action. Why is Picard so upset? Why isn't he just relieved and grateful, as Kirk and the others were in the original series? The likely answer is that in this case the crew has just established *linguistic communication* with the entity.

Surely one of the most impressive behaviors an entity can display is linguistic communication, so linguistic ability seems to be a clear sign of intelligence and perhaps more. This linguistic ability was either lacking or not established in the other cases we have considered so far, and I chose them carefully for that reason (putting aside a small aberration—the Horta somehow manages to etch "No kill I" in a rockface, *before* the mind meld and with no "universal translator" in sight). By far the majority of intelligent life that Starfleet encounters enjoys linguistic ability, and thanks to the device called the "universal translator" Starfleet personnel can usually establish immediate linguistic contact. (Not always. In *DS9:* "Little Green Men," three Ferengi find themselves transported back in time to Roswell, New Mexico, in 1947 and their implanted universal translators go on the blink. When they begin to slap their heads in an effort to jolt the translator back on line, the uncomprehending Earthlings interpret the head slapping as an attempt to communicate, and reciprocate in kind.)

Universal Translation for Fun and Profit

> ZEFRAM COCHRANE: "What's the theory behind the device?"
>
> KIRK: "There are certain universal ideas and concepts common to all intelligent life. This device instantaneously compares the frequency of brain-wave patterns, selects

those ideas and concepts it recognizes, and then provides the necessary grammar."

SPOCK: "Then it simply translates its findings into English."

—*Conversation from* TOS: *"Metamorphosis"*

On one level, Kirk's explanation of the operation of the universal translator sounds rather ridiculous. But on another level, it connects with a popular theory of human language acquisition and the innate psychology that makes it possible. In the relatively new field of psycholinguistics, the received wisdom is that there are cognitive universals among all humans on Earth, hardwired into our brains in the form of a universal grammar. This innate grammar is posited as the best explanation of our substantial ability in early life to learn natural languages. Kirk's first sentence sounds remarkably like this hypothesis, extended to *all* intelligent life, everywhere! (Although the example Kirk gives is tendentious. He says, "The idea of male and female are universal constants," but the J'naii in *TNG:* "The Outcast" are androgynous.)

The universal translator is sometimes invoked to solve an apparent problem in the *Star Trek* canon: as Lawrence Krauss, in *The Physics of Star Trek,* points out, "Almost all alien species encountered by the *Enterprise* are humanlike, and they all speak English!" I have read on the Internet an explanation of the ubiquity of English in the *Star Trek* cosmos: we see and hear things from the perspective of the crew, and because the crew has the benefit of the universal translator they hear alien speech instantaneously translated into English. Thus we, too, hear aliens speak English, although that is not the language the aliens are speaking. If we accept this explanation, then the universal-translator idea certainly makes dramatization easier (much the way that the transporter idea does, obviating the need to land the ship). But it seems to me to be mistaken. Pick just about any Hollywood movie set in a non–English-speaking country: *War and Peace, Dangerous Liaisons, The Unbearable Lightness of Being,* and so on. It is no part of these stories that the characters are speaking English, indeed it is true in most such stories that the characters do *not* speak English. The actors are speaking English, of course, otherwise we likely wouldn't understand them, but this is just the vehicle for the movie to represent what the characters are saying in Russian, French, Czech, or whatever. Moreover, although sometimes we do hear things from the perspective of the *Enterprise* crew (for instance, when we are looking at the viewscreen on the bridge), this isn't the case always. In *TNG*: "First Contact," Riker is stranded on Malcor III and pretends to be a local. Do the Malcorians all speak English, for some unfathomable reason? No. Do we hear them speaking English because we hear their speech from Riker's point of view? No, we hear them speaking English among themselves, too. What's true in "First Contact" is that everyone on Malcor III, including Riker, is speaking Malcorian. If Riker were using the universal translator instead of speaking Malcorian, he would give himself away, since I presume the universal translator does not change one's lip movements. (Riker must have an amazing gift for languages: in *TNG:* "Who Watches the Watchers," he and Deanna Troi infiltrate the Bronze Age Mintakans at very short notice; they may both have been taking Mintakan lessons just in case, since they cannot use the universal translator.) Later in "First Contact," once the game is up, Picard reveals himself to the Malcorians. Since I presume that Picard doesn't speak Malcorian, it must be that the universal translator kicks in.

This is not to say that from time to time there is no way of making sense of a *Star Trek* storyline except by supposing that the aliens speak English. In a number of episodes in the original series, the alien culture parallels that on Earth to a startling degree, and the landing party, concerned about the Prime Directive, must remain incognito. This scenario obtains in "Miri" (general resemblance to Earth), "Patterns of Force" (Nazi Germany), "The Omega Glory" (the United States flag and Constitution and the Communist menace), "Bread and Circuses" (the twentieth century, but the Roman Empire never fell), and "The Paradise Syndrome" (Native Americans). In "Bread and Circuses," the *Star Trek* writers explicitly note that the locals speak English—"twentieth-century colloquial English," what's more. We hear an interesting if dubious explanation of this from Kirk: "They are creatures of a heavily industrialized twentieth-century-type planet, very much like Earth—an amazing example of Hodgkin's Law of Parallel Planet Development!" (But this paper-thin explanation cannot always work; in "Patterns of Force," the amazing resemblance to Nazi Germany is eventually attributed to cultural contamination, in contravention of the Prime Directive, by Federation anthropologist John Gill. But Kirk and Spock cannot use the universal translator in their "undercover" work, so did Gill enforce English speech as a condition of racial purity, I wonder?)

Darmok Time

> "The fact that any alien race communicates with another is quite remarkable."
>
> —*Troi to Picard,* TNG: *"The Ensigns of Command"*

One final point on language concerns what philosophers call the problem of *radical translation*. We are investigating the question of how different from us an alien individual must be before it ceases to be morally considerable by us, and there is a somewhat parallel question we can ask about communication: How different does an alien language have to be before it ceases to be translatable by us? Kirk asserts in "Metamorphosis" that there are cognitive universals, but what if he is wrong? What if you encounter a language user who thinks so differently from you that you have no way of translating what he says? What would such a radically different language be like? This problem is first raised in *Star Trek* by Deanna Troi in "The Ensigns of Command," when it is necessary to communicate with the strange race known as the Sheliak. The conversation is as follows:

TROI: "In our dealings with other nonhumanoid races, there's always been some point of reference. Not so with the Sheliak."

PICARD: "But we must have something in common—we *communicate*."

TROI: "Barely. They have learned several Federation languages, but theirs continues to elude us."

Troi asks Picard to imagine the following situation: "We are stranded on a planet. We have no language in common, but I want to teach you mine." Troi raises a glass cup, with what might be tea or coffee in it, utters an invented term, and asks, "What did I just say?" Picard guesses "cup," then "glass," and Troi adds the possibilities "liquid," "clear," "brown," and "hot." (She didn't offer "tea" or "coffee," but she could have.) "*We* conceptualize the universe in relatively the same way," Troi says; the implication seems to be that in the absence of a shared conceptual scheme, communication is extremely difficult. Troi concludes her advice by pointing out that the Federation treaty with the Sheliak is 500,000 words long (372 Federation lawyers worked on it!). "The length was to accommodate the Sheliak," she tells Picard. "They consider our language irrational and demanded this level of complexity to avoid any future misunderstandings."

Curiously, there is an example in philosophy similar to Troi's, but which is put to an almost opposite purpose. The philosopher W. V. O. Quine imagined the same sort of attempt to translate an unknown language, but here on Earth. A rabbit runs by and the other person utters "Gavagai!" Does "gavagai" mean "individual instance of rabbithood" (member of a class), or "rabbit-slice" (a time-slice of an individual rabbit), or "discontinuous giant rabbit" (the individual that is the sum of all individual rabbits—as New Jersey might be called "U.S.A."), or "undetached rabbit-part," or what? Some philosophers conclude from examples like this that translation is always indeterminate, even between speakers of the "same" language, so there is no "same" language. They suppose that you could arrive at the best translation possible of another's utterances and still not know whether you shared that other's exact conceptual scheme—a hypothesis that undermines the idea of cognitive universals.

Troi's statement of the differences between the Federation and the Sheliak seems overstated. For one thing, it is difficult to see how two groups with no shared concepts could agree on a treaty in the first place. Second, the Sheliak have, after all, learned Federation languages, so perhaps they're just a lot smarter than humans are, working with a similar but deeper conceptual scheme. Third, it's hard to see how making a treaty more complex can overcome serious translation problems!

In a more promising premise, Troi's imagined situation becomes reality in *TNG:* "Darmok," when the crew encounters the Children of Tama, an alien race whose attempts at communication are "incomprehensible." Picard is kidnapped by them and deposited upon a lonely planet with the Tamarian Dathon, who brandishes weapons and utters sentences like (universally translated, of course) "Darmok and Jalad at Tenagra" and "Shaka, when the walls fell." The pair are attacked by an energy creature, and Dathon is badly wounded. Picard eventually realizes that the Children of Tama communicate by means of image and metaphor, and thus succeeds in holding a rudimentary conversation with the dying Tamarian. Meanwhile, back on board the *Enterprise-D,* Data and Troi have been researching recordings of Tamarian attempts at communication. When Riker asks what they have discovered, this is the conversation that ensues:

DATA: "The Tamarian ego structure does not seem to allow what we normally think of as self-identity. Their ability to abstract is highly unusual. They seem to communicate through narrative imagery—a reference to the individuals and places that appear in their mythohistorical accounts."

TROI: "It's as if I were to say to you, 'Juliet on her balcony.'"

DR. CRUSHER: "An image of—romance."

TROI: "Exactly. Imagery is everything to the Tamarians. It embodies their emotional states, their very thought processes. It's how they communicate, and it's how they think."

RIKER: "If we know how they think, shouldn't we be able to get something across to them?"

DATA: "No, sir. The situation is analogous to understanding the grammar of a language but none of the vocabulary."

DR. CRUSHER: "If I didn't know who Juliet was, or what she was doing on that balcony, the image alone wouldn't have any meaning?"

TROI: "That's correct. For instance, we know that 'Darmok' was a great hero, a hunter, and that 'Tenagra' was an island, but that's it. Without the details, there's no understanding."

DATA: "It is necessary for us to learn the narrative from which the Tamarians draw their imagery."

This piece of dialogue is supposed to establish the areas of cognitive difference between the *Enterprise-D* crew and the Tamarians. But it is quite fascinating in its own right, for the philosophical ideas contained in it. First is the idea that the Tamarians have no concept of individual self-identity. Second is the idea that Tamarian thought processes are (perhaps exclusively) imagistic. Third is the idea that knowing the grammar of a language is insufficient for understanding that language.

I have several worries about the first of these ideas. For one thing, how exactly did Data and Troi establish that the Tamarians have no concept of self? Since they are in the process of trying to understand the Tamarian language and by their own admission aren't doing very well, it seems mightily implausible that they are in any position to make such fine-grained judgments about the Tamarian conceptual scheme. (I presume that Troi has not divined this information empathically.) Back here on Earth, it was once claimed on comparative linguistic grounds that other cultures had significantly different conceptual schemes from Western cultures. These claims turned out to be false or vastly overstated. (Most infamously, the Hopi were supposed to have no concept of time and the Eskimo were supposed to have umpteen different concepts of snow.) The linguists in question had succeeded in communicating meaningfully with the subjects of their study and still went wrong. So Data and Troi are on tenuous ground indeed! Another worry I have is that on the evidence presented in the episode, the claim that Tamarians have no concept of self seems false. The Tamarians are individually and not collectively conscious, they have individual names, and they certainly seem to have beliefs and preferences about how their own individual lives will go and about how other individual lives will go. Picard clearly attributes a self-concept to Dathon when he says, "The Tamarian was willing to risk all of us, just for the hope of communication. . . . That commitment meant more to him than his own life." Moreover, when Picard delivers the news of Dathon's brave death to the Tamarian crew, it is clear from their solemn reaction that they recognize it as the passing of an individual. Then the Tamarian first officer produces a new allusion, "Picard and Dathon at El-Adrel," which recognizes two distinct individuals (note that you need to have a concept of individual selves to distinguish them). It seems that the only reason for denying the Tamarians a concept of self is a dramatic one. That way Dathon, in trying to communicate, cannot merely do the Tarzan thing: "I Dathon, you Picard."

I sympathize with the *Star Trek* writers here, since they are trying to achieve two purposes fundamentally at odds. On the one hand, they wish to present *a radically different way of looking at the world,* and on the other they are trying to *present* a radically different way of looking at the world! In short, if the Tamarian worldview were too different from ours, the *Star Trek* writers couldn't present it to us. Three further objections to their attempt: Leaving aside individual selves, the Tamarians obviously have names for planetary systems, so Dathon could have uttered "This El-Adrel" in Tamarian. Next, even those philosophers who doubt that there are significant cognitive universals think that any complex and useful language must have logical connectives. The only connective heard in the Tamarian language is "and." But, of course, presenting their language as it *must* be would spoil the story. Finally, it becomes clear that "Mira, his sails unfurled" is the command to fly off, to leave. But in what direction, and how fast? The Tamarians need a more precise language at their disposal in order to navigate the universe, build things, and so forth—but once again, this would spoil the story.

In presenting the Tamarians as primarily or exclusively imagistic thinkers, the *Star Trek* writers have plugged into a lively philosophical debate. Practically everybody in the debate agrees that the contents of some mental states are properly and exhaustively characterized *propositionally*. Take for instance my belief that New York is north of Philadelphia. The English sentence "New York is north of Philadelphia" expresses a *proposition,* which is independent of a statement in a particular language, and that is why one cay say exactly the same thing in a different language, in a sentence that has exactly the same content. Clearly my belief has exactly the same content, too. But suppose that instead of just thinking that New York is north of Philadelphia, I *imagine* New York being north of Philadelphia—I form a mental *image*. This imagining has some content over and above the content of my belief. But is this content simply a more complex propositional content, or is there some *non*-propositional content—that is, some irreducibly imagistic content? Philosophers are deeply divided over this issue, which connects with the issue of artificial intelligence to be discussed in chapters 2 and 3. If some thinking is irreducibly imagistic, can computers, which are well-suited to processing propositional contents, ever achieve it?

I am intrigued by Data's analogy between the communication difficulty with the Tamarians and the situation of "understanding the grammar of a language but none of the vocabulary." Here I think Data is referring to the distinction that language theorists make between the syntax and the semantics of a language. Roughly, *syntax* refers to the symbol system of a language, including the transformation rules for manipulating those symbols, while *semantics* refers to the meanings of the symbols—that is, what the symbols are about. Putting it another way, *syntax* refers to the properties of a language uninterpreted, while *semantics* refers to the properties of a language interpreted. In a move that would please Mr. Spock, I'll use logic to explain the difference (actually, this will also come in handy in chapter 3), and introduce a simple language I'll call *L*. Here's an expression in *L*: "*Wb*." Explanation—"*W*" denotes a property and "*b*" names an individual, so "*Wb*" says that the individual *b* is (has the property of being) *W*. Here's another expression in *L*: "*(∀x) (Wx ➔ Fx)*" Explanation—"*(∀x)*" means "for every *x*" and "*(Wx ➔ Fx)*" means "if *x* is *W*, then *x* is *F*." So "*(∀x) (Wx ➔ Fx)*" means that everything that is *W* is also *F*. Now, it is a rule of logic that given *(∀x) (Wx ➔ Fx)* and *Wb*, you can conclude *Fb*. This rule ought to make intuitive sense: if individual *b* is *W*, and everything that is *W* is *F*, it is obvious that individual *b* is *F*.

Unless you are an unusual person, the last half paragraph will have bored you stiff, and that's precisely the point. If I were to continue in the same vein (and you stayed awake), you would master *L* and its rules very quickly. But it wouldn't be very interesting, because it isn't (yet) connected to the world. You would be learning syntax alone, a symbol system with its transformation rules, a *grammar*. Now let's add an interpretation—a semantics. Let *b* refer to Bruce, let *W* denote the property of being a wombat, and let *F* denote the property of being furry. In this interpretation, "*Wb*" means that Bruce is a wombat, and "*(∀x) (Wx ➔ Fx)*" means that everything that is a wombat is furry. It follows that "*Fb*"; that Bruce is furry. We have now added a vocabulary to the grammar of *L* by adding fixed meanings.

Now compare the situation of Data and Troi with that of Picard on the planet below. Picard has heard "Darmok and Jalad at Tenagra" so often that he knows it by heart. So when Dathon begins "Darmok and Jalad—" Picard finishes the sentence fragment for him, at which Dathon beams. But they haven't made progress. As Picard says, "I remember the words, but I don't *understand*." As far as Picard is concerned, Dathon might as well be saying, "*Wb*." But don't Data and Troi know what "Darmok" and "Tenagra" refer to? Aren't they already in possession of the vocabulary they seek—at least, when they solve "Jalad"? No. Even if they know what the individual terms refer to, they don't know what the sentence fragment refers to, so they still have a vocabulary problem. Data suggests that there's only one way to solve this problem—to access the story—but Data has overlooked something. An allusion like this is a relation between a story and a situation, a relation that points to a resemblance between them. It is as if the speaker says, "*This situation* is like Juliet on her balcony." Since the resemblance relation is reflexive, we turn it around and get "Juliet on her balcony is *like this situation*." Grasping the allusion involves understanding that the two situations are of the same kind, so if one is in the right kind of situation when the allusion is given, one can learn something about the story of Juliet!

We can put in the last piece of the puzzle by analogy. Consider where you stand if you know that "*Wb*" means "Bruce is a wombat." If you don't know what a wombat is, then you're not much better off. How can you learn what a wombat is? Here's a great way—get an expert to show you a wombat, where an expert is just someone who knows a wombat when he sees one, and correctly uses the term. You're with the expert, a wombat appears, and he says "Wombat." You conclude, "*That's* a wombat," and now *you* are an expert! In "Darmok," what does Dathon do? He takes Picard to see a *Darmok and Jalad at Tenagra,* that's what. Being the expert, he places himself and Picard in the right (though dangerous) situation, and utters the name of that kind of situation. And painful lesson though it is for both of them, Picard learns.

"Darmok" is an extremely clever episode, but we must conclude that the Children of Tama are not so different from us after all, nor is their language. Unless you already have a translation manual, you cannot learn a previously unencountered language without getting your hands dirty, so to speak; to understand fully what words, phrases, and sentences refer to, you must be in a referring situation. But when you are in the referring situation, how do you know *what* is being referred to? It seems that Troi is correct—there must be a substantially shared conceptual scheme for communication to succeed.

Is Data Human?

Prime Suspects

Let us return now to the central question of this chapter. Given that persons are fully morally considerable, under what conditions ought one to suspect that one is dealing with personal life? It should be clear by now that successful linguistic communication establishes a strong presumption that one is dealing with personal life. It is very difficult to imagine us engaging in complex communication with another living species if that species does not have intelligence and a rich conceptual scheme, including self-concepts and future-oriented preferences.

But in the absence of successful linguistic communication (and in the absence of ESP), what grounds are there for supposing that an alien is not only intelligent but also a person? Once again, we must turn to behavior. Consider the Horta: Kirk concluded from its behavior in recognizing and reacting to his phaser that it was intelligent, but this is behavior well within the range of intelligent nonpersons, like chickens and sheep, and the same goes for the initial self-preservation behavior of the exocomp in "The Quality of Life." Just as there can be (relatively inflexible) self-preservation behavior in the absence of intelligence, there can be intelligent self-preservation behavior in the absence of a concept of self. We have extremely good evidence from experiments in animal psychology that few if any higher mammals have a concept of self, yet all of these animals are capable of intelligent self-preservation behavior: that is, such animals are capable of intelligent behavior the purpose of which is self-preservation. But only animals with a concept of self engage in intelligent self-preservation behavior *because they recognize it as such*. Hence Starfleet officers should be on the lookout for self-preservation behavior rich enough to suggest a concept of self, and Data was testing the exocomp for such behavior in "The Quality of Life."

Another impressive piece of behavior is the protection of one's progeny. The Horta displays this kind of behavior, as does the gigantic space creature that the *Enterprise-D* crew unintentionally kill in *TNG:* "Galaxy's Child." Once again, this is behavior possibly sufficient to establish intelligence but insufficient to establish personhood, because it is possible to engage in intelligent behavior the purpose of which is the protection of one's young without having any concept of individual selves.

Possession of a concept of self and the concomitant distinction of other individual selves is a necessary condition of moral agency, so any behavior suggestive of moral agency would be evidence of personhood. Occasionally here on Earth, one hears anecdotal evidence of rather special behavior on the part of dogs and dolphins. If we had good reason for thinking that Lassie really did *save* Timmy and hadn't merely behaved in a way that happened to bring about his rescue—that Lassie not only recognized the danger to Timmy but engaged in behavior that rescued him *because* it was a way to rescue him—then we would have evidence that Lassie was a person. Similarly, cases of dolphins protecting divers from shark attack would, if genuine, be evidence that dolphins are persons. Indeed, I regard our general pro-dolphin attitude to be largely a reflection of a lingering suspicion that they are.

Mutual Prime Suspicion

> RIKER: "Why, in all our history, has there been no record of you or someone like you ever having visited us?"
>
> TRAVELER: "What wonderful arrogance! There has been no record because we have not visited you before."
>
> RIKER: "Why not?"
>
> TRAVELER: "Well, because up until now—if you'll forgive this—you've been uninteresting. It's only now that your life-form merits serious attention. I'm sorry."
>
> —*Conversation from* TNG: *"Where No One Has Gone Before"*

Just as we considered ways that communication might fail between us and other personal species, are there more general ways in which we might fail to recognize personhood when we encounter it? One way this can occur is when there are vast differences in scale. *Star Trek* raises at least three such matters of scale—speed, size, and intelligence. For instance, if the "hyperaccelerated" Scalosians in *TOS:* "Wink of an Eye" had not needed the *Enterprise* men as mates (feeding them Scalosian water to speed them up!), it is doubtful that Kirk and company would have recognized their existence. In both *TOS:* "The Immunity Syndrome" and *Voyager:* "The Cloud," there is an encounter with an enormously large life-form, and in *DS9:* "Playing God," Jadzia Dax encounters a tiny universe. In each of these episodes (for obvious dramatic reasons) "we" have a significant effect on "them" and vice versa, but in most cases such scale differences would result in little or no meaningful interaction and personhood would be mutually unsuspected.

The most common and perhaps the most humbling difference in scale in *Star Trek* is a difference in intelligence levels. Federation humanoids are presented as relative intellectual dwarfs compared with other individuals and races. In the original series, there are often demigods, magicians, and other individuals with special powers, like Apollo in "Who Mourns for Adonais?," Korob and Sylvia in "Catspaw," Gary Mitchell in "Where No Man Has Gone Before," and Charlie Evans in "Charlie X." Then there are representatives of more advanced races, like the Kelvans in "By Any Other Name," the energy beings in "Return to Tomorrow," and the Providers in "The Gamesters of Triskelion." By the twenty-fourth century and *The Next Generation* it is the turn of the Traveler in "Where No One Has Gone Before" and "Journey's End," the Nagilum in "Where Silence Has Lease," Kevin Uxbridge the Douwd in "The Survivors," the Paxans in "Clues," John Doe the Zalkonian in "Transfigurations," the Cytherians in "The Nth Degree," and most saliently the omnipotent (and nearly omnipresent) Q. In the newer series, the shape-shifters of the Dominion in *Deep Space Nine* and the Viidians in the *Voyager* episodes "Phage" and "Faces" particularly stand out.

One suspects that should these superior intellects wish it, they could avoid detection by us altogether. (Indeed, that is what happens—after a few hiccups—in "Clues.") Mostly these aliens are interested in contacting humanoids, and usually not out of the kindness of whatever passes for their hearts. Indeed, the most striking recurring theme in Federation encounters with superintelligence is their lack of regard for humanoids. This raises an interesting and worrying issue. Could such superintelligent creatures be *justified* in treating us as experimental subjects ("Where Silence Has Lease"), slavish subjects ("Who Mourns for Adonais?"), amusements ("The Gamesters of Triskelion"), vermin ("The Ensigns of Command" and "Clues"), spare parts ("Return to Tomorrow," "Phage," and "Faces"), or even food? Is it just an unexpected bonus if they happen to be nice to us, like the Traveler and the Cytherians?

This is a worrying issue because we humans routinely mete out this sort of treatment to other intelligent animals here on Earth. We use animals on a massive scale for experimental research, we domesticate them, put them in zoos and circuses for our entertainment and education, destroy them in large numbers when they threaten crops or otherwise annoy us, use their bodies for spare parts when suitable, and kill and eat them. The defense offered in support of this behavior is that we humans are more important than other intelligent animals on Earth. Why? Often the further defense is that we are *so much more* intelligent than they are! I trust that the problem is now obvious. Were this a good, rationally compelling defense of our treatment of other, less intelligent creatures on Earth, then it is an equally good defense of equivalent treatment of us by superintelligent races. The Nagilum in "Where Silence Has Lease" would be on firm moral ground in killing half the crew of the *Enterprise-D* in order to learn about death. The Sheliak in "The Ensigns of Command" (who can understand us though we can't understand them, a good indicator of their superior intelligence) are justified in wiping out an infestation of fifteen thousand humans in their territory. And so on.

Fortunately, a higher degree of intelligence alone is no defense at all of such behavior. In the extended person-centered ethic I advocate, the difference between persons and intelligent nonpersons is not merely a matter of degree, it is a *threshold* matter. An intelligent individual who has a concept of self and others, who has beliefs and preferences about how his or her life will go, and who has the concomitant moral concepts has achieved the threshold of personhood. Therefore, such an individual is fully morally considerable—at least, where the basic liberties are concerned. If it is wrong for other humanoids to treat us as slaves or food, then it is wrong for any nonhumanoid persons to treat us as slaves or food. Not only should the Federation be on the lookout for prime suspects, but other possibly exotic persons should be on the lookout for us!

Let us return to where this discussion began—with the exocomps in "The Quality of Life." Although no direct linguistic contact with the exocomps is achieved, the excocomp that Data tests displays behavior suggestive of possession of a concept of self, and the behavior of the three exocomps that rescue Picard and La Forge at the cost of one of their number is suggestive of moral agency. So there is a strong prima facie case for classifying the exocomps as persons. But doesn't this leave out some important information—namely, that the exocomps are *artificial*? How can something manmade possibly be alive, or intelligent, or a person? That is the subject of the next chapter.

"Synthetic scotch, synthetic commanders!"

—*Captain Montgomery Scott, reflecting upon the twenty-fourth century,* TNG: *"Relics"*

Insufficient Data

chapter 2

There are three typical candidates for artificial personhood in *Star Trek*. The first is a suitably programmed computer, as in the original series episodes "The Return of the Archons," "A Taste of Armageddon," "The Apple," "The Ultimate Computer," and "For the World Is Hollow and I Have Touched the Sky," the *Next Generation* episode "Emergence," and the *Voyager* episode "Dreadnought." (A variation on this theme is the appearance of sophisticated computerized machines in the *Next Generation* episodes "Evolution" and "The Quality of Life.") The second is a sophisticated robot constructed on the model of a human being—or, to use the terminology adopted in *Star Trek*, an *android*. In the original series, androids appear in "What Are Little Girls Made Of?," "I, Mudd," "Return to Tomorrow," and "Requiem for Methuselah"; and the android Data is a regular member of the bridge crew of the *Enterprise-D* in *The Next Generation* and the movies *Star Trek VII: Generations* and *Star Trek VIII: First Contact*. Other androids appear in the *Next Generation* episodes "Datalore," "The Offspring," "Brothers," "Descent I & II," and "Inheritance," and in *Voyager:* "Prototype." The third type of candidate is generated on the "holodeck," the twenty-fourth-century version of virtual reality. In addition to the emergency medical hologram in the *Voyager* series, there are apparently personal holodeck characters in the *Next Generation* episodes "The Big Goodbye," "11001001," "Elementary, Dear Data," and "Ship in a Bottle." *Voyager:* "The Thaw" and *DS9:* "Shadowplay" also feature possibly personal characters generated in virtual reality.

The point of cataloguing these episodes is to remark upon a trend: in the original series, the *Star Trek* writers were deeply concerned with the status of computing machinery; by *The Next Generation* the focus has shifted to the status of androids; and in the latter-day series *Deep Space Nine* and *Voyager* it is the status of holodeck-generated individuals that raises concerns. One interpretation of this trend is that as technology progresses, individuals of new types gradually gain acceptance as persons—although in every age there are the naysayers, those who would judge these individuals to be nonpersons and often enough nonintelligent.

But *is* there any justification for acceptance of artificial entities as persons in their own right? In each age, it is those who work most closely with the entities in question who are most sympathetic to the idea that they are persons, but perhaps these people are inappropriately anthropomorphizing their artificial colleagues. On the other hand, perhaps it is the naysayers who are unduly prejudiced. Can machines made of metal and silicon think, feel, or be moral agents? Can mere holographic projections? These are the questions we shall investigate in this chapter and the next.

A Test Case

"Data will be my guide."

—*Commander Bruce Maddox,*
TNG: *"The Measure of a Man"*

In this *Next Generation* episode, when the *Enterprise-D* docks at a new space station, there is a surprise waiting. Commander Bruce Maddox, associate chair of robotics at the Daystrom Institute and student of the work of Data's creator, Dr. Noonian Soong, announces that he intends to dismantle Data. Maddox wants to discover once and for all the secret of Data's "positronic brain" so that he can build a fleet of androids, one for each of the Federation starships. Data is at first "intrigued," but expresses doubts about several aspects of the proposal and eventually refuses to submit to the procedure by tendering its resignation. But Maddox claims that Data is Starfleet property and so cannot resign. The complaint is taken to the station's newly installed judge advocate general (JAG), who finds legal precedent agreeing with Maddox. Picard formally appeals the decision, and a hearing is scheduled, in which Riker must argue for Maddox's view, while Picard defends Data. During cross-examination by Picard, Maddox claims that Data is "not sentient," and that "sentience" (what we would call *personhood*) requires "intelligence, self-awareness, consciousness."

So what is Data, according to Maddox? "A machine," he says. Maddox is right, of course. Data is a constructed entity with a positronic brain (an idea borrowed from Isaac Asimov's less-than-serious science fiction suggestion), neural nets and so forth, and very complex programming. Data apparently is made entirely of inorganic components, although the *Star Trek* writers depict it as intoxicated in *TNG:* "The Naked Now," and it seems to be drugged in *TNG:* "Datalore." According to the *Star Trek Encyclopedia,* "The Naked Now" does indeed demonstrate that Data has some organic components, but this conclusion is incompatible with all the other tidbits we hear about Data's construction, and also with Data's own contention that it does not age (in "The Measure of a Man," Data says that "my condition does not alter with the passage of time"), so I prefer to ignore this apparent anomaly.

Data was designed and engineered by a human being, Dr. Noonian Soong. Though roughly humanoid in appearance, Data has golden skin and yellow eyes, and is relatively indestructible. Data is a full-fledged member of the *Enterprise-D* crew; indeed, it is a senior officer on the bridge, and it has been decorated by Starfleet several times. Data is also close to unique. After three false starts, Dr. Soong, now presumed to be dead, made an android almost identical to Data (Data's older "brother," Lore, which is troublesome and spends much of its time dismantled), as well as an android replacement for his own wife (seen in *TNG:* "Inheritance"), but since the good doctor was ahead of his time, no one quite understands what makes Data tick.

Maddox wants Data as his guide, and Data will be our guide, too—our test case for artificial personhood. Picard's arguments prevail in the hearing, and the JAG grants Data the benefit of the doubt. At least as far as she is concerned, Data is a prime suspect—a good candidate for personhood. Our jurisdiction is wider than that of the JAG, though. In addition to asking, *Given what we know about Data, what is the reasonable thing to conclude about whether or not Data is a person?* we shall also ask, *Is artificial personhood even possible?* If the answer to the second question is negative, then of course Data is not a person. But note that even if the answer to the first question is that we ought to consider Data a person, Data is after all fictional and might well be an impossible construct of the imagination.

Maddox's conditions for "sentience"—that is, personhood—are a good starting point. They correspond well to those we laid down in chapter 1: intelligence is the possession of a mind, and "self-awareness" is best taken to mean "having a concept of self." Maddox introduces "consciousness" into the mix, and we'll have something to say about this in chapter 3. But we need not look on it as an extra condition at all, for self-awareness properly understood may presuppose consciousness.

When Picard asks Maddox whether or not Data is intelligent, Maddox concedes that it is, citing Data's "ability to learn, to understand and cope with new situations." I think Maddox is taking the question literally, but we need to be a little careful. Here in the twentieth century, we are quite accustomed to talk of "electronic brains" and "smart bombs," but most people use these expressions metaphorically and would probably retreat from their literal meanings. In what follows, I shall always take adjectives such as *intelligent, minded, smart, thinking,* and *stupid* absolutely literally. (For instance, to say that something is stupid is to say that it is of relatively low intelligence—it follows that it *is* intelligent.) But whether Maddox's answer was literal or not, why didn't Picard, as Data's advocate, simply pounce on it? Isn't the fact that Data is intelligent sufficient to demonstrate that Data is not Starfleet property? In a word, no. No one denies that chickens or sheep are intelligent, yet such animals are almost always regarded as property. Picard is wise to press on, since being a *person* is sufficient and probably necessary to keep one (morally speaking) from being considered property.

An important point: if Maddox is claiming that Data is intelligent although not a person, he would be conceding much more than many naysayers do about the potential of machines. Many of the objections raised against machines being persons are assumed to be objections to machine intelligence as well. Where it is important to do so, I'll keep the issues of intelligence and personhood independent, especially since most philosophical debate has centered on the narrower question of whether or not machines can be intelligent. But *Star Trek,* like life in general, is not so neat. Hence I shall freely take the pronouncements of the naysayers in *Star Trek* to be objections directed at both artificial personhood and artificial intelligence.

Machine Intelligence: Two Tests and Three Positions

Four hundred years ago, the French philosopher and mathematician René Descartes imagined encountering a machine so constructed that it has the appearance of a human being and can move in interesting ways. Descartes writes in his *Discourse on Method:*

> If any such machines bore a resemblance to our bodies and imitated our actions as closely as possible for all practical purposes, we should still have two very certain means of recognizing that they were not real men. The first is that they could never use words, or put together signs, as we do in order to declare our thoughts to others. For we can certainly conceive of a machine so constructed that it utters words, and even utters words that correspond to bodily actions causing a change in its organs. . . . But it is not conceivable that such a machine should produce different arrangements of words so as to give an appropriately meaningful answer to whatever is said in its presence, as the dullest of men can do. Secondly, even though some machines might do some things as well as we do them, or perhaps even better, they would inevitably fail in others, which would reveal that they were acting not from understanding but only from the disposition of their organs. For whereas reason is a universal instrument which can be used in all kinds of situations, these organs need some particular action; hence it is for all practical purposes impossible for a machine to have enough different organs to make it act in all the contingencies of life in the way in which our reason makes us act.

Philosophers call Descartes' two behavioral tests for personhood the *language* test and the *action* test—two sorts of test we encountered in chapter 1. There are three positions to take regarding Descartes' proposal. One is Descartes' own, *conservative* position: that a machine could not possibly pass either test. A different conservative position holds, for each test, that although a machine might in principle pass, its success is not sufficient to determine that it is a person. Maddox seems to be a conservative of the latter sort. A *liberal* thinks, of at least one of the tests, that a machine might in principle pass and that its success is sufficent to determine that it is a person. Picard takes the liberal position.

Descartes claims that we can in principle distinguish human beings from machines because machines have no understanding or reason. This suggests that Descartes' two tests are intended as tests for intelligence, too. Once again, there are conservative positions on this proposal: that a machine could not possibly pass either test; or that, for each test, although a machine might in principle pass, its success is not sufficient to determine that it is intelligent. A liberal thinks, of at least one of the tests, that a machine might in principle pass and that its success is sufficent to determine that it is intelligent. Maddox seems to be a liberal concerning machine intelligence.

In a famous article published in 1950, the mathematician Alan Turing devised a particular form of the language test for intelligence, proposing that we replace the question of whether or not machines can think with the question of whether or not machines could ever pass the test. In Turing's liberal view, a machine could in principle pass the test, and if it did it ought to be considered intelligent. Turing's language test is based on a parlor game popular in the pre-television era, involving an interrogator and two subjects, one male and one female. The interrogator is in a different room from the two subjects, who communicate with him through a go-between. Both subjects try to convince the interrogator that they are, say, the male subject (obviously one can play another version, in which both try to convince the interrogator that they are the female subject). The interrogator has to determine which is the real male; he can ask any question whatever of the subjects, and he bases his judgment entirely upon the content of their answers. If the interrogator guesses incorrectly, then the woman has won.

In Turing's version of the game, we replace one of the subjects with a computer, suitably programmed, and the object of the programming is to fool the interrogator into thinking that the computer is a human being. For the machine to win such a game, it must be good at imitating the responses typical of a human being. Now let us imagine that a computer plays this new game many times, and in at least half the games the interrogator identifies it as a human being. When this happens, the computer has passed what has come to be called the *Turing Test*. To make the test more vivid, imagine that you are the interrogator, and that you are conducting the test in real-time chat mode over the Internet. If the computer can fool you under these conditions at least half the time, it has passed the Turing Test.

The first liberal claim that Turing makes is that a certain sort of machine—namely, a digital computer, suitably programmed—is in principle capable of passing the Turing Test. Turing's claim rests partly on mathematical proofs that we shall avoid, but we can grasp the intuitive idea by considering what has come to be called a *Turing machine*. Imagine a machine with the following features: it has a very long tape (which might be made of paper) with symbols on it (say, the binary digits 0 and 1), it can move along the tape in either direction, it can read the symbols on the tape, and can erase the symbols and write new ones. Imagine further that the machine has discrete states: there are a limited number of states that the machine can be in, and it is always wholly in one state or another. The tape is discrete, too: for each position that the machine can stop at on the tape, there is just one symbol that the machine can read, erase, or write. Moreover, when the machine moves, it moves just one space at a time. Finally, imagine that what the machine does depends on its *state table,* a set of rules for its operation. Suppose that we give the Turing machine the following state table.

Table 1

STATE	Read 0 on tape	Read 1 on tape
S_1	0 S_1 R	0 S_2 R
S_2	1 S_3 R	1 S_2 R
S_3	HALT	HALT

Suppose further that the Turing machine is in state S_1 and is in the highlighted position on the following section of tape.

0	0	0	**1**	1	0	1	1	1	0	0	0

According to the state table, when the machine is in state S_1 and reads 1, it is to write 0, go into state S_2, and move to the right. (Note that the machine will erase the 1 as well.)

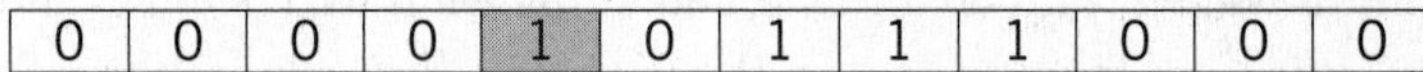

The Turing machine has carried out the operation just described, so it is now in state S_2 and has moved one space to the right, where it encounters another 1 on the tape. The relevant instruction is such that the machine will leave the 1 (actually the machine hardware is underdescribed: it might erase the 1 and write another—but for our purposes it can do either), stay in state S_2, and move to the right.

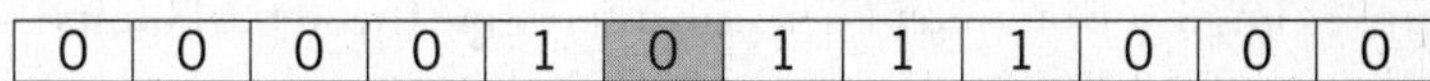

The Turing machine is now in state S_2, reading a 0, which it will erase, writing a 1, going into state S_3, and moving to the right.

Finally, since the Turing machine is in state S_3 and encounters a 1, it halts (as per the state table instruction).

The machine has just added 2 and 3, in an operation rather like taking a group of two pencils and a group of three pencils and putting them together to form a group of five pencils. If you look at what is on the tape to begin with (the first panel), you'll see a group of two 1's and a group of three 1's, with a 0 separating them. By the end of the operation (fourth panel), there is one group of five 1's. Now this no doubt strikes you as a rather tedious thing to do. What's startling is how powerful this very simple idea of a Turing machine is. Think for a moment about all the things digital computers do, yet they all work on this basic principle. Given a long enough tape and enough memory to store the relevant state table, the Turing machine can reproduce the operation of any digital computer. (We are ignoring speed for the moment.)

Let's introduce some useful terminology. The *input* to the machine is what it reads on the tape, and the *output* is what it erases and writes (or else leaves alone) on the tape. The state table is the machine's *program,* or *software,* and the rest is the machine's *hardware*. (Note well that some of the machine's instructions are embodied in the hardware—that it moves only one space when it moves, for instance.) The input doesn't have to be in binary code, either: it might be numerals, such as 2 and 3; or letters, such as A and B; or punctuation marks, such as spaces and commas. The same goes for output.

The important point is that there is no theoretical limit on what a digital computer can accept in the way of linguistic input or produce as linguistic output. (There are interesting theoretical limits—related to Gödel's Theorem—on the relations between input and output, but this does not establish a difference between computers and human beings, so I shall ignore it.) Nor is there any theoretical limit on the sort of program a digital computer can run, as long as the computer has sufficient storage capacity. So there is every reason to suppose that a digital computer could in principle pass the Turing Test. Of course, there are all sorts of practical limits, but in the past fifty years we have seen an astonishing shrinkage of such limits on computing power. Turing himself thought that by the year 2000 we would have or be very close to having a Turing Test winner. So could a machine that is a suitably programmed computer pass the Turing Test? *Yes!* If Descartes thought otherwise, then Descartes was wrong.

As a demonstration of the principle involved, consider Joseph Weizenbaum's ELIZA, a program developed some twenty years ago to mimic a Rogerian psychotherapist. (Rogerians take a passive approach, repeating patient responses or asking questions based on them.) Here is the sort of "conversation" a "patient" can have with ELIZA (ELIZA's responses are uppercase):

Men are all alike.
IN WHAT WAY
They're always bugging us about something or other.
CAN YOU THINK OF A SPECIFIC EXAMPLE
Well, my boyfriend made me come here.
YOUR BOYFRIEND MADE YOU COME HERE
He says I'm depressed much of the time.
I AM SORRY TO HEAR YOU ARE DEPRESSED
It's true. I am unhappy.
DO YOU THINK THAT COMING HERE WILL HELP YOU NOT TO BE UNHAPPY
I need some help, that much seems certain.
WHAT WOULD IT MEAN TO YOU IF YOU GOT SOME HELP
Perhaps I could learn to get along with my mother.
TELL ME MORE ABOUT YOUR FAMILY
My mother takes care of me.
WHO ELSE IN YOUR FAMILY TAKES CARE OF YOU
My father.
YOUR FATHER
You are like my father in some ways.
WHAT RESEMBLANCE DO YOU SEE

You are not very aggressive, but I don't think you want me to notice that.

WHAT MAKES YOU THINK I AM NOT VERY AGGRESSIVE

You don't argue with me.

WHY DO YOU THINK I DON'T ARGUE WITH YOU

You are afraid of me.

DOES IT PLEASE YOU TO BELIEVE THAT I AM AFRAID OF YOU

My father is afraid of everybody.

WHAT ELSE COMES TO MIND WHEN YOU THINK OF YOUR FATHER

Bullies.

DOES THAT HAVE ANYTHING TO DO WITH THE FACT THAT YOUR BOYFRIEND MADE YOU COME HERE

ELIZA does a fair job of mimicking a Rogerian psychotherapist, and might even do a fair job of mimicking Counselor Troi! But ELIZA's behavior is extremely inflexible, and as soon as we move outside the domain of therapy this is obvious. Once the patient stops playing the therapy game, ELIZA's responses will seem queer indeed! But ELIZA is a small program that runs on a primitive computer, even by today's standards. Try to imagine a computer with enormous memory and processing capacity, and with appropriate, extremely complex programming. There is no principled reason why such a computer could not pass the Turing Test. So if one is to be a conservative, one should be a conservative with regard to the relevance of the tests themselves.

Functionalism

According to Turing, thinking is simply information processing of a certain sort, and this might be performed by a digital computer as well as it is by a human being. Turing's view is a version of *mental-state functionalism,* probably the dominant view in modern philosophy of mind. I'll state more precisely what functionalism is in a moment, but first I want to get across the intuitive idea. Begin with your brain. The state of your mind right now depends a lot on the state of your brain right now (a finding well established by cases of brain damage). But which facts about your brain are the important ones, the ones determining which mental states you occupy? For example, I presume that you right now believe that Washington, D.C., is the capital of the United States. That's a mental state you currently occupy. But what is it about your brain that makes it true that you believe that Washington, D.C., is the capital of the United States? Is it what your brain is made of or what it does that matters? The functionalist intuition is that it is the *functional* states of your brain—what your brain *does*—that matter. An important consequence of mental-state functionalism is *multiple realizability,* the view that different sorts of substances can physically realize a mind.

Functional states are characterized purely by causal roles, which I can best illustrate by examples. Most jobs are functionally characterized. If you are a dishwasher, your job is to take dirty dishes as input and perform a process which produces clean dishes as output. That's your causal role. Most devices are functionally characterized, too. A mousetrap is a device that has the job of taking free mice as input and producing caught mice as output. These are very simple causal roles, which we can fully describe if we try. Other causal roles are not so simple, but we may nevertheless be sure that they are characterized purely functionally. Take books, for instance. It might once have been thought that a book has to have certain physical properties—namely, being made of paper and ink. But the *function* of a book is to store the information made available by the author and permit extraction of it by the reader. This can be done in many different ways, and there are now books on magnetic tape, braille books of metal and raised bumps, books on compact disk, books on computer, books in cyberspace, and so on. I hope you can see that giving an exact causal-role specification of a book is going to be extremely complicated. Accordingly, the functionalist expects that giving a complete causal-role specification of something as complicated as a *mind* (or even of a single mental state, such as the belief that Washington, D.C., is the capital of the United States) will be incredibly difficult. However, most functionalists are confident that the sort of causal roles that mental states occupy are information-processing roles, of the type that computers can realize.

The thesis that minds are multiply realizable makes sense of the intuition that radically different alien intelligence is possible. If the silicon-based Horta in "The Devil in the Dark" is intelligent, then there are at least two different possible physical realizations of intelligence, ours and the Horta's. Moreover, the functionalist account of mental states is importantly liberating for the science of the mind—the discipline called *cognitive science*. If brains aren't the only means of realizing minds, then it isn't strictly necessary to study brains in order to study minds. Thus it has been a prevailing tenet of artificial-intelligence research that a computer which adequately models what brains do when they realize thought is more than just a model of intelligence—it *is* intelligent. And what better way of modeling what brains do when they realize thought than to program a computer to give appropriate linguistic outputs to a range of linguistic inputs? The initial plausibility of functionalism seems to lend support to Turing's claim that we should regard passing the Turing Test as a sufficient indicator of intelligence.

Functionalism as I have described it is a *materialist* theory of minds and mental states, since it holds that minds are part and parcel of the material, natural, physical world. But why think this? Isn't it possible that mentality is so mysterious because it isn't part of the material world at all? Do we need to posit a special sort of "mind stuff" to account for it? We should resist this line of thought for one very compelling reason—which we can illustrate by considering what is alleged to happen in the *Next Generation* episode "The Next Phase." Geordi La Forge and Ensign Ro Laren are rendered invisible to the rest of the *Enterprise-D* crew when they go "out of phase." But they can see the crew. The trouble is (as Lawrence Krauss points out in *The Physics of Star Trek*) that you can't have it both ways: to see anything, La Forge and Ro must absorb light, and if they absorb light then they are visible. (By the way, the common argument for the existence of invisible souls based upon the near-death "out of body" experience suffers from the same flaw.) What has this to do with "mind stuff"? Well, if your mind isn't part and parcel of the material world, then it's hard to see how it could interact with the material world—you can't have it both ways. And if your mind doesn't interact with the material world, then none of the actions you perform in the material world can be caused by your mental states. So if you think (as you should, in my view) that your behavior is in large part caused by your mental states, then you should reject the idea that your mind is immaterial.

Mechanical Failure

Would any of the computers depicted in *Star Trek* pass the Turing Test? I don't think so. The starship computers wouldn't—not even the main computer on board the *Enterprise-D*. First, it "knows" too much—there is way too much information stored in it, and this information is retrieved much too quickly. Second, the *Enterprise-D* computer does complicated calculations extremely fast, a dead giveaway. Third, the computer replies to some questions with statements like "Insufficient data to compute" or "Cannot comply with request. Please specify parameters," things a typical human being would never say. Moreover, the ship's computer never displays impatience at stupid or repetitive questioning; it is unfailingly polite and always responds when asked a question. (In fact, the computer often responds impressively to vague and ambiguous questions and statements.) The computer known as Landru, in *TOS:* "The Return of the Archons," does a bit better, but it doesn't take Kirk and Spock too long to figure out that they are dealing with a machine. In neither of these cases, however, is the computer programmed to mimic perfectly a typical human being's linguistic responses. The *Enterprise-D*'s computer is programmed to serve, not to deceive, and Landru is programmed to administer the sheeplike citizens of Beta III. So perhaps their probable failure in the Turing Test is a matter of the wrong sort of programming.

The *Star Trek* canon suggests a deeper, principled reason for machine failure—at least, failure when asked the right questions. A key plot point in *TOS:* "I, Mudd" is that androids (and by implication, computers) cannot deal with irrationality or contradiction. Here *Star Trek* plugs into a common science fiction theme, but "I, Mudd" gives it a special twist. The entire crew of the *Enterprise* is enticed by the trader Harry Mudd to beam down to an unnamed planet, which is populated by hundreds of thousands of androids willing to serve them. However, unbeknown to Mudd, the androids have an ulterior motive: they regard humans as inherently illogical and therefore unstable; their plan is to take over not only the *Enterprise* but the known universe, and to run both in a more orderly fashion. When the crew realizes the danger, they disable the androids by confronting them with irrationality and paradox. The irrational behavior displayed by the crew members is garden-variety silliness, and it is a mystery why silliness should shut down a machine; a machine probably would ignore it, and so will I. The crew also uses paradox: Spock claims to love Alice-27 and simultaneously to hate the qualitatively identical Alice-210, and both androids shut down immediately. Then Kirk and Mudd short-circuit the android leader, Norman, by addressing it as follows:

KIRK: "Everything Harry tells you is a lie. Remember that—everything Harry tells you is a lie."
MUDD: "I am lying."

Poor Norman tries to work through the paradox: if everything Harry says is a lie, then he's lying when he says he's lying, but if he's lying then he's not lying, and so forth. And before long, *Zzzsst!*

Although it's a lot of fun, this wouldn't short-circuit a sophisticated android like Norman, which probably would recognize that it's a paradox with some simple available resolutions. Lying is deliberately asserting what you *believe* to be untrue (it doesn't actually have to be untrue), so if Harry is lying when he says "I am lying," then he believes that he is not lying. So Norman might conclude that Harry simply doesn't understand what lying is, since he is lying but believes that he isn't. On the other hand, Norman might give Harry the benefit of the doubt and conclude that he probably isn't lying (that's what I would conclude). And if that's true, since Kirk said that everything Harry tells Norman is a lie, then Kirk is either lying or mistaken. There is no contradiction here, and the paradox is resolved. Indeed, since any paradox is generated by a set of conjoined propositions, one can always suspend belief in the conjunction without deciding which of the set to discard. Norman might then conclude that *either Harry is deeply confused or else Kirk is mistaken or else Kirk is lying,* and be done with it. Similarly, Alice-27 might conclude that *either Spock is irrational or else I am not identical with Alice-210 or else it is possible to love an individual and yet hate a different but qualitatively identical individual*. Since machines can be programmed not only to accept and process but also to produce these sorts of disjunctions, it is unlikely that sophisticated computers would be discombobulated by paradox. Hence it also is unlikely that they would fail the Turing Test because of their response to paradoxes.

In other episodes from the original series, Kirk uses logic to defeat sophisticated computers. In "The Return of the Archons," Kirk gets Landru to agree that it must destroy evil and also to agree that it is itself evil, and before long, *Zzzsst!* In "The Ultimate Computer," Kirk gets the M5 computer (which is running the *Enterprise* and wreaking havoc in the process) to agree that murder is wrong and punishable by death, and then convinces M5 that it has itself committed murder. This time the computer doesn't immediately self-destruct but embarks on a course of action that will cause its own destruction, as a self-imposed punishment. In "The Changeling," the *Enterprise* encounters Nomad, a special-purpose biological sterilizer, which has been accidentally programmed to destroy all imperfect entities. Kirk gets Nomad to agree that it is itself imperfect, and Nomad initiates self-destruction. Perhaps the message in these episodes is that computers are in principle too rigid in their obedience to logic and too inflexible for their own good. Kirk's arguments can all be represented as instances of *modus ponens,* the argument form *If p, then q* and *p,* therefore *q*. ("If Nomad is imperfect, then Nomad must be destroyed. Nomad is imperfect. Therefore, Nomad must be destroyed.") This is a valid argument form—that is, if the premises are true, then the conclusion must be true also. But any valid argument form can be used in reverse, as a *reductio:* since *If p then q* and *p* together entail *q*, and since *not-q,* then either *If p then q* or *p* must be false. Thus if Nomad has a strong enough anti-self-destruct protocol, it will either deny that it ought to be destroyed if imperfect, or else it will deny that it is imperfect. M5 would be on particularly firm ground in producing a *reductio* of Kirk's argument. For one thing, many persons deny that the proper punishment for murder is death; and for another, M5 claims that it acted in self-defense when it killed, so M5 ought to deny that it has committed murder. Logic is a two-edged weapon, and there is no reason to think that computers can easily be talked into their own self-destruction; hence, they are not likely to fail the Turing Test in this way either.

Of course, there are still plenty of reasons why the sophisticated computers in *Star Trek* might fail the Turing Test. But it does not follow that they are not intelligent. Although Turing claims that passing his test is *sufficient* to warrant the attribution of intelligence, it certainly isn't *necessary!* This is just as well, as there are doubtless many intelligent humans who would make poor Turing Test subjects—subjects who would likely be identified as machines. Imagine, for instance, someone with no linguistic skills at all (say, the sheltered child of a deaf couple with no signing skills), or someone whose only spoken language is one you don't understand (like Dathon in *TNG:* "Darmok"), or certain autistics. Perhaps the clearly intelligent Mr. Spock would fail the Turing Test. ("You'd make a splendid computer, Mr. Spock," says Kirk, in "The Return of the Archons.") Some humans might fail the Turing Test deliberately. In *TNG:* "Hero Worship," the *Enterprise-D* rescues Timothy, the only survivor of an accident on board the *Vico*. The traumatized Timothy forms an attachment to Data, and eventually claims to be an android himself, answering well-meant questions like "How are you?" with such locutions as "I am operating within established parameters."

It's also a good bet that Data would fail the Turing Test. Data's main difficulty in the test would parallel that of the *Enterprise-D* computer—that is, Data's superior information-storage capacity, calculating ability, and speed would likely give it away. Then there are Data's notorious misunderstandings of human emotions and humor (though one can imagine an interrogator taking some of its guileless replies as intentional humor). But once again, there's no theoretical reason for supposing that Data couldn't be reprogrammed in such a way that it could pass the Turing Test. (In an apparently damning indictment, the telepathic betazoid Tam Elbrun says to Data, in *TNG:* "Tin Man," "Incredible—an android. I can't read you at all. It's like you're not there." I can think of no reason—*if* Data is intelligent and *if* there are such things as telepaths—for Data's intelligence not to register with telepaths. In any case, betazoids aren't able to read Ferengi minds either, as established in *TNG:* "The Last Outpost." So I shall ignore Elbrun's evidence.) Since passing the Turing Test is not necessary for the attribution of intelligence, and since Data would fail the Turing Test, is there a fairer test still—one that Data has a good chance of passing without extensive reprogramming?

Combined Tests

> "Your creator went to a lot of trouble to make you seem human."
>
> —*Dr. Julian Bashir to Data,*
> TNG: *"Birthright I"*

What is a fair test of android intelligence? We can use the model of the Turing Test to combine Descartes' language and action tests into one. Suppose that the test subject is an android. To pass the combined test, the android must be able to fool a typical human interrogator into thinking that it is a typical human being, in a situation in which the interrogator can see, hear, and otherwise interact with the android. In such a test, any perceived difference between the behavior of an android and the behavior of a typical human being would be sufficient to disqualify it. This is a manifestly unfair test to subject an android to. (Data's funny head and neck movements would immediately disqualify it, for instance.) Besides, think of the waste of resources that would be involved in devoting so much of an android's engineering to the mimicry of irrelevant human expressions.

How do you build a machine capable of mimicking much more than just computer-interfaced human linguistic behavior—capable of mimicking the full range of human behaviors? Such a machine would have to respond appropriately to human speech and would have to navigate its way in our world by means of sensory modalities akin to vision, hearing, taste, touch, and smell. Turing thought that a good way to build a Turing Test winner would be to model a child's mind, and I suspect that Turing would repeat his advice here—build a child android, with the capacity to learn from its environment in much the way that a human child learns. But the task is still extremely challenging, and that's putting it mildly. In addition to producing the hardware equivalent of a child's brain, and programming it so that it can learn appropriately, an android builder has what I call the *transducer problem*.

Recall that in the Turing Test you are in some sort of interface contact with the machine (on the Internet, say). There are two transducer problems to be solved here: first, the *input* problem of how to transform the natural language you produce into a form the machine can process; and, second, the *output* problem of how to transform the results of this processing back into a form that you can access. These are problems we have already solved, but both you and the Internet cooperate in their solution by putting your questions directly into "cyber" format and accessing the answers from that same format. If the questions came from you verbally, then another means of transformation would be needed—say, a human go-between who types in your questions. And if you required a verbal response, then some other mode of output transformation would be required.

So when you address an android verbally, it must have its own means of transforming the verbal input (sound waves) into a form it can process. And if it is to produce verbal responses, it must have its own means of transforming the results of its processing back into sound waves. So it needs input and output transducers. Think of how your own body does it: Sound waves reach your outer ear and are directed through the air to the eardrum. Then the sound waves are transmitted by bone—the hammer, anvil, and stirrup—to the "oval window" and thence through the fluid of the cochlea, where vibrations cause the hairs on special cells to transmit ("somehow," according to a standard physiology textbook) nerve impulses, which travel to the auditory cortex of the brain. Nerve impulses themselves are electrical impulses generated chemically. There are two important points to note about this process: the transducers for hearing are extremely complicated, and we don't completely understand their operation. On the output end—that is, speech production—things are if anything even more complicated. Now think of all the other transducers your body has—input ones for the other four senses, and all the motor and other output ones. An android like Data has to have some near equivalent of all these! The good news for android builders is that we know that the transducer problems are all solvable in principle, because our own bodies are examples of solutions.

Sometimes it is easy to lose sight of a consequence of this body-building problem. If you are going to build a man-size android with many or most of the abilities of a human being, there will be some things it can't be expected to do. And while it is difficult sometimes to discern exactly what the *Star Trek* writers have in mind, I suspect that they sometimes fall for a common misunderstanding of what an intelligent machine would be like. We have already touched on what might be called the *mentalistic division of labor* in ourselves—our minds are subdivided into faculties and other functional units, many of which are inaccessible to consciousness and impervious to it. Just as it makes a great deal of sense for nature to build us this way, it makes a great deal of sense for Dr. Soong to build Data this way, too. The last thing you want is a mental executive branch that controls everything; by analogy, imagine the CEO of a large corporation who insists on hands-on control over every aspect of his company's operation. Of course you want some monitoring systems, but for the most part you don't want the executive branch knowing everything that's going on. Yet when Data takes dancing lessons from Dr. Crusher (in *TNG:* "Data's Day"), it's all too obvious that Data has complete executive control. Elsewhere Data is depicted as having too many abilities to pass as a realistic human being; in "Hero Worship," we learn that Data can supply a chemical analysis of anything it ingests. Ponder for a moment the incredible waste of resources involved in giving Data the unnecessary—since it does not need food or liquid—ability to mimic eating and drinking in the first place! Add to this what we learn about Data in "The Naked Now." "You are fully functional, aren't you?" purrs Chief Security Officer Tasha Yar, lust-filled under the influence of intoxicating water. "Of course, but—" Data replies, and Yar interrupts, "*How* fully?" "In every way, of course," says Data. "I am programmed in multiple techniques, a broad variety of pleasuring."

In *TNG:* "Violations," when discussing the vagaries of human memory, Geordi La Forge says to Data, "You record every second of every moment of your life," and Data replies, "That is correct." This makes no sense at all, since Data's memory banks would be jammed full in no time. As an analogy, consider surfing the World Wide Web. As you access different web pages, they are stored in the cache, which is very like your short-term memory. If you are like me, there is a lot of stuff on the web you're not interested in, and when you exit the browser program you're happy to have the cache emptied. If you want to save something to your hard drive (analogous to long-term memory), this takes a separate effort. But suppose that instead of saving only what you want to save, your browser saves every page you access. In a very short time you'll run out of hard-drive space. Now consider your own memory and all the experiences you've ever had in your life—all the breakfasts, and teeth brushings, and sneezes; all the street signs you've ever read, and so on. It should be obvious that a functional individual cannot remember all these things, and neither would it want to!

Finally, any time Data needs to learn something, it apparently has to write new programs for itself. (For instance, in *TNG:* "In Theory," it writes a program for conducting a romantic relationship.) Just being an android is hard enough, given all there is to learn, but being a self-programming android would be hell in space!

Since the combined test is unfair, and it is so difficult to engineer a machine capable of passing it, we should revise the test. A much fairer test of android intelligence is the one we use to identify secondary suspects in the case of extraterrestrial life (see chapter 1). This is a combined test in that we should accept appropriate behavior of *either* the linguistic or nonlinguistic sort as sufficient evidence of intelligence. Such a combined test gives the subject more than one way of passing, and we thereby avoid the danger of failing to detect intelligence trapped inside an inappropriate body: think of children with perfectly normal minds but flawed bodies who are often diagnosed as mentally retarded. This sort of test also gives the subject more than one way of failing, so it's useful when one is in linguistic contact with an individual capable of deceit (including self-deceit), and hearing and seeing the individual can provide crucial extra information. And an individual could pass this combined test by mimicking human behaviors (for instance, a machine that passes the Turing Test thereby passes the combined test), but also without mimicking human behaviors at all. We can imagine a (more stringent) combined test for personhood, too: it is the test we used to identify prime suspects in chapter 1. Here again, passing the Turing Test would be sufficient for passing the combined test for personhood, so we shall return to the question, What to say about a Turing Test winner?

And the Winner Is . . .

"If it were a box on wheels, I would not be facing this opposition." —*Maddox, "The Measure of a Man"*

Is there any argument for *not* being a conservative? Why should we be impressed by a machine that passes the Turing Test? After all, appearances can be deceiving. The best the liberal can do here is to appeal to consistency. Recall the *problem of other minds* discussed in chapter 1—the problem of justifying the belief that another individual has a mind, when you have no introspective access to his or her thoughts. There is only one defensible way out of the problem, and that is to take the behavior, linguistic or nonlinguistic, of the other typical human beings you encounter as sufficient evidence of their intelligence—to regard their being intelligent as the best explanation of that behavior. (By contrast, the behavior of a comatose patient is relatively uncomplicated, as is the behavior of a rock or a chair, and sometimes the inference we make in such a case is that there is no mind present; that's why we consider "pulling the plug.") I submit, then, that you are justified in attributing a mind to another human being just in case their being intelligent is the best explanation of their behavior. There's another point worth making concerning such inferences: many of the attributions of intelligence we make are in cases in which we can see what the individuals look like—that is, we can see that they resemble us. A very important feature of the Turing Test is that it eliminates prejudice based on appearances: passing the Turing Test is sufficient for the attribution of intelligence, even if the winner is a box on wheels. In short, if this line of reply to the *problem of other minds* has merit, then it has a clear application to Turing's claims. If we attribute intelligence to other humans based on purely behavioral criteria, then it seems that sheer consistency compels us to attribute it to machines in the face of appropriate machine behavior, such as passing a language test like the Turing Test.

According to the liberal view, a refusal to attribute intelligence to a machine when you would attribute intelligence to a human being in the same circumstances is akin to sexism or racism—unwarranted discrimination. But we must qualify this argument to make it plausible. Unwarranted discrimination is based upon features of an individual that are not relevant in the circumstances. Perhaps the fact that an individual is a box on wheels *is* relevant to whether an individual should be regarded as intelligent. Imagine that you are the interrogator in the original parlor game, and that the woman subject is *very* good at mimicking the responses of a man. On this behavioral evidence, you are justified in thinking she is a man. But upon receipt of further evidence (say, upon hearing her voice), you ought to withdraw this attribution. Likewise, according to the conservative, you might be justified in attributing intelligence to an individual based upon its performance in the Turing Test, but once you see that it is a machine you ought to withdraw that attribution.

This does not require that you withdraw the conclusion that intelligence is reponsible for the machine's behavior, but it does change the conclusion about the location of this intelligence. Suppose you discover that the individual you have been conversing with at a dimly lit party is in fact a wax dummy equipped with a hidden radio receiver and transmitter, a speaker, and a microphone. Certainly the dummy's verbal output is intelligent, but you rightly will revise your opinion about the dummy itself, judging the intelligence to be external. Similarly, the conservative can claim that the discovery that you have been conversing with a computer ought to prompt you to revise your opinion, locating the implicated intelligence outside the computer—in the programmer, say.

We now have the issue nicely attenuated. The liberal claims that you ought not to withdraw the attribution of intelligence to a Turing Test winner simply because you discover that it is a machine such as a computer, suitably programmed. The conservative thinks that you ought to withdraw the attribution. But why does the conservative think this? What is the difference between being a flesh-and-blood human and being a silicon-and-metal machine? It is time to examine the various forms that conservatism might take.

Winning Isn't Everything

> "When, in disgrace with fortune and men's eyes, I all alone beweep my outcast state.... Is it just *words* to you, or do you fathom the *meaning?*"
>
> —*Maddox to Data, "The Measure of a Man"*

The conservative position rests on finding some difference between machines and flesh-and-blood creatures such as ourselves. But not any old difference will do—it must be a difference that *makes* a difference. In this section I shall canvass all the alleged deficiencies of machines made by characters in *Star Trek*. In each case, the strong implication is that the deficiency provides a defensible reason for treating the machines in a certain way—in particular, for treating the machines differently from persons. So we shall have two questions in mind as we read the charges against machines: *Is the alleged deficiency genuine?* and if the deficiency is genuine, *Does it make a genuine difference?*

Here is a collection of naysaying quotes from characters in the original series, beginning with "What Are Little Girls Made Of?" The scientist Dr. Roger Korby has been missing for five years before the *Enterprise* locates him on Exo III. When the landing party discovers that Korby's companions on the planet are androids, Korby reassures them, "An android is like a computer. It does only what I program." The android Brown tells Kirk that the original inhabitants of Exo III, in building androids, "replaced freedom with a mechanistic culture." Korby says of the android Andrea, "There's no emotion in her—no emotional involvement. She simply responds to orders. She's a totally logical computer."

In "The Return of the Archons," the computer called Landru

explains that Landru, the human leader of Beta III, programmed it in an attempt to duplicate himself. "I am Landru," the computer says. "I am he. All that he was, I am—his experience, his knowledge." Kirk replies, "But not his wisdom. He may have programmed you, but he could not have given you a soul. You are a machine." Later, when Spock admires the feat of engineering that was Landru, Kirk responds, "But [it was] only a machine, Mr. Spock. The original Landru programmed it with all his knowledge, but he couldn't give it his wisdom, his compassion, his understanding, his soul!"

In "Return to Tomorrow," energy beings lure the *Enterprise* to an unnamed planet, where members of the crew are persuaded to lend the beings their bodies temporarily, so that the beings can build android bodies for themselves. When discussing its imminent transfer into an android body, Henoch (occupying Spock's body) says to Thalassa (occupying Dr. Ann Mulhall's body) that android hands are "hands without feeling." Thalassa/Mulhall asks Sargon (occupying Kirk's body), "'Beloved'—what will that word mean to a machine?" And shortly after, just before kissing Sargon/Kirk, it asks, "Can robot lips do *this?*" Later still, it says to Henoch/Spock, while pointing to an android body, "I cannot live in that thing!"

In "The Ultimate Computer," when command of the *Enterprise* must be relinquished to the M5 supercomputer, Spock objects to the M5's designer, Dr. Richard Daystrom, that "the computer can process information, but only the information which is put into it," and Kirk chimes in, "It can work a thousand, a million times faster than a human brain, but it can't make a value judgment, it hasn't intuition, it can't *think!*" Later in the episode, McCoy observes, "Compassion—that's the one thing no machine ever had. Maybe it's the one thing that keeps men ahead of them." And in "I, Mudd" Scott says to Kirk, "Captain—androids and robots, well, they're just not capable of independent creative thought."

By the twenty-fourth century, it is the android Data who attracts the attention of naysayers—in particular, that of Dr. Kate Pulaski, the *Enterprise-D*'s counterpart to Bones McCoy. In "Where Silence Has Lease," she expresses skepticism about Data's ability to perform its duties. Later in the same episode, she asks Data's forgiveness, and remarks, "Your service record says that you *are* alive. We must accept that." (Would she "accept" Picard's service record if it said that Picard was dead?) In "The Measure of a Man," she watches Data lose at poker because of Riker's bluff and announces that bluffing well requires instinct, implying that Data therefore cannot master the game. In "Elementary, Dear Data," we learn that Data is a fan of Conan Doyle's Sherlock Holmes mysteries and has taken to re-creating them on the holodeck. But instead of playing out the story, Data (as Holmes) always leaps to the end and solves the crime. Pulaski claims that this is because Data is a machine. "You learn by rote," she says. "To you all is memorization and recitation." Then (to La Forge) she adds, "Holmes understood the human soul. . . . That understanding is beyond Data. . . . Your artificial friend doesn't have a prayer of solving a mystery that he hasn't read." And later in the same episode, she says of Data, "Inspiration, original thought, all the true strength of Holmes—it's not possible for our friend." In "The Child," when Data has offered to be the "support person" for the pregnant Troi, Pulaski says, "Counselor Troi is going to need the comfort of a human touch, and not the cold hand of technology." Later she refers to Data as "data," and when Data demurs, she counters, "What's the difference?" "One is my name, the other is not," Data replies. Pulaski then asks, in a voice dripping with sarcasm, "Is this possible? With all your neural nets, algorithms, and heuristics, is there some combination that makes up a circuit for bruised feelings?"

In "The Measure of a Man," Will Riker, as Commander Maddox's advocate in the hearing to determine Data's personhood, produces a hands-on argument. First he establishes that Data is an artifact, designed and constructed by a human being. Next, he asks Data to bend a "parsteel" bar to demonstrate its super strength. Then he removes Data's left arm and shows the court the inorganic nature of Data's construction. Finally he turns Data off by means of a switch in the middle of Data's back, announcing, "Pinocchio is broken. Its strings have been cut."

Much of the naysaying in *The Next Generation* comes from Data itself. In "The Ensigns of Command," Data reports on the progress of its violin-playing, "Although I am technically proficient, according to my fellow performers I lack soul," and in the same episode it informs the female colonist Ard'rian (who has expressed romantic interest), "I have no feelings of any kind." In "Tin Man," the betazoid Tam Elbrun asks Data, "It worries you that I can't read your mind?" and Data replies, "Perhaps there is nothing to read. Nothing more than mechanisms and algorithmic responses." In "Clues," La Forge is performing a diagnostic test on Data's "positronic net," and expresses concern that he might be hurting Data. Data tells him, "I cannot feel pain." In "Data's Day," Data has the task of giving the bride away at the wedding of Keiko Ishikawa and Lieutenant Miles O'Brien, and Riker asks Data if it's nervous. "I cannot become nervous, sir," Data replies. In "The Offspring," Data describes to Dr. Crusher its relationship with its "daughter," Lal. "I can give attention, Doctor, but I'm incapable of giving her love." And in "Hero Worship," when the admiring Timothy asks Data if androids are better than humans, it replies, " 'Better' is a highly subjective term. I do not, for example, possess the ability to feel emotion, as humans do. . . . My positronic brain is not capable of generating those conditions."

In *DS9:* "Life Support," Dr. Bashir is considering the use of artificial "positronic implants" to replace damaged portions of the brain of the Bajoran religious leader, Vedek Bareil, but he is plagued by doubts. "One of my professors at medical school used to say that the brain has a spark of life that can't be replicated," he muses. "If we begin to replace parts of Bareil's brain with artificial implants, that spark may be lost." Bashir eventually refuses to continue with the implants; if he does nothing, Bareil will die, "but he'll die like a man, not a *machine!*"

More naysaying comes from the mouth of the "automated units" discovered by Captain Kathryn Janeway and crew in *Voyager:* "Prototype." Unit 3947 says of humans, "Their cognitive process is unpredictable." The implication is that the automated units themselves behave in completely predictable ways—an implication reinforced by 3947's explanation of 6263's threat to kill all the humans if Chief Engineer B'Elanna Torres fails in her efforts to assist the units: "6263 is a designated command unit. He is merely following his programming." And here is a final quote from Torres, in *Voyager:* "The Thaw," on the notion of maintaining a brain-dependent virtual reality program by using an artificial brain. "It just wouldn't be the same," she says. "There is no way an artificial intelligence can replace actual brain functions."

If the naysayers are correct, then we ought not to be taken in by appearances, and this argument certainly has some intuitive appeal. After all, we have all seen robots like the ones at Disneyland—robots that in the right circumstances can pass for real. But no one thinks that there's anything like a rich mental life going on inside these robots. The lights may be on, but surely nobody's home! How can more machinery and more programming—producing a fancier robot—make any difference? That is a question we shall pursue in detail in the next chapter, where I shall do my best to undermine the naysayers' objections.

"Starfleet's mission is to seek out new life. . . . Well, there it sits!"

—Picard, pointing to Data, "The Measure of a Man"

Pro Creation

chapter 3

Chapter 2 ended with a list of common claims made by *Star Trek* characters about machines. Here's a catalogue of the human features that artificially constructed entities are supposed to lack: *free will, creativity, emotions, feelings (sensations), original or independent thought, intuition* or *instinct, values (morality), self-awareness, consciousness,* the ability to grasp the *meanings* of words, *a soul, wisdom, understanding,* the *"spark of life,"* the ability to *command,* the ability to *surpass their programming,* the right sort of *origin,* the right sort of *material composition,* and the right *design intention*. In addition, it is pointed out that machines can be *switched off*. If an individual such as Data is deficient in one of these ways, and if being deficient in one of these ways matters as to whether or not an individual is a person, then that individual is not a person. (The same goes, mutatis mutandis, for whether or not an individual is intelligent.) In this chapter, I shall examine these alleged deficiencies to determine whether or not Data (or other machines) really suffers from them, and if so whether or not such deficiences disqualify Data (or other machines) from either intelligence or personhood. We shall begin with allegations relating to how, why, and by whom an artificial entity comes into being.

Origins

> "You can't have a civilization of computer chips. They're made in a plant in Dakar, Senegal—I've watched the construction."
>
> —*Dr. Paul Stubbs,* TNG: *"Evolution"*

Data was made by a human being whose intention was to create an artificial person, while the exocomps in "The Quality of Life" were created by a human being—a certain Dr. Farrallon—whose intention was to create mere engineering tools. But so what? Not only is it possible for the maker of an artifact to fail to realize his or her intentions (making things that just don't work, for instance), but you can also make things that surpass your intentions (either by doing what you intended better than you intended, or by doing something completely unintended). Indeed, if it were generally true that an artifact couldn't do something unintended, think of all the lawsuits that would be avoided. Data makes mistakes that its creator presumably did not intend. (Beware of the fallacy that machines are incapable of error.) In *TNG:* "Code of Honor," Data is struggling to grasp the techniques of stand-up comedy and tells (badly) a joke involving a speech defect that turns "kidneys" into "kiddelies." When La Forge asks Data how many jokes it has attempted, Data begins, "Includiling the kiddelies—" and La Forge bursts out laughing. But Data is merely dismayed: "My tongue slipped!" it apologizes.

In "Elementary, Dear Data," the ship's computer generates an apparently intelligent holodeck character named Professor Moriarty. In *The Nitpicker's Guide for Next Generation Trekkers,* die-hard fan Phil Farrand suggests that if Moriarty is intelligent, then the computer must be, too. This would be correct if products reflected only their manufacturer's intentions, because it would entail that the computer *has* intentions. But I think Farrand has a different principle in mind. Although a product often has properties not possessed by the manufacturer—were this not so, no human could (for instance) make anything transparent, like glass—perhaps Farrand thinks that a complex property like intelligence can be produced only by something that is itself intelligent. If true, this would mean that we humans must have been produced by intelligence, too—the first step in a design argument for the existence of God (or gods). I don't find this "no bootstrapping" principle particularly plausible, though; I simply don't think we are in any position to assert that intelligence from nonintelligence (or personhood from nonpersonhood, for that matter) is impossible.

Were the no-bootstrapping principle a plausible one, at least the fact that Data was created by a person is in Data's favor. But Riker's argument at its personhood hearing in "The Measure of a Man" implies that the humanity of Data's creator is actually an impediment. Because humans aren't intelligent enough? While late-twentieth-century humans might not be intelligent enough to build artificial persons, it would not follow that humans can never build them. (Suppose that in the fifteenth century someone declares that although God can create things that fly, humans probably aren't intelligent enough to build anything that can fly. Transplanted into the twentieth century and confronted with an airplane, this person reasons as follows: Since this thing was built by humans, and since humans probably can't build anything that flies, probably this thing *doesn't really fly!*)

Perhaps Riker is arguing that it isn't a matter of humans not being smart enough but of their lacking certain godlike abilities. In her summation, the presiding JAG observes, "We've all been dancing around the basic issue: *Does Data have a soul?*" I suspect that a common motivation for denying machine personhood rests on the conviction that *our* personhood arises not from our material nature but instead from something *extra,* something *special*—the "spark of life," the "soul." But note well that no conclusion about machine personhood follows from this conviction alone. One has to add the premise that machines cannot have a soul (a premise Kirk clearly believes, given his statements in "The Return of the Archons"). To this I reply, If you have a God-given soul, then how did you get it? Presumably in one of two ways—either God, in a miraculous intervention, added your soul to the material mixture (say, at conception), or else God has arranged nature in such a way that when the right material mixture occurs, a soul attaches to it (or animates it, or whatever). But both of these methods leave open the possiblity of machines being ensouled, too. Perhaps God liked Dr. Soong's robot so much that He ensouled it by miraculous intervention, or perhaps there are many ways to produce the "right" mixture and Soong hit upon one of them by happenstance. After all, if you're so convinced that other humans have souls, isn't Data's behavior excellent evidence that it, too, has a soul?

On the other hand, if behavior such as Data's isn't adequate evidence of ensoulment, then far from being the "basic issue," the issue of whether or not Data has a soul is largely irrelevant—as the JAG demonstrates in her summing up. "I don't know that [Data] has," she says. "I don't know that *I* have!" But if Data's entitlement to the rights of personhood depends upon judgments of ensoulment, then whether or not the JAG herself (or anyone else) has those rights likewise depends on judgments of ensoulment. Since the JAG is unsure whether or not she herself has a soul, she must be unsure about her own entitlement to personhood. But she's not, so ensoulment is not the basic issue.

Riker goes to great lengths to demonstrate that Data is inorganic, so perhaps it is just impossible for there to be inorganic people? Of course, if this is impossible, then not only are artificial inorganic persons impossible but so are *naturally occurring* inorganic persons. Hence neither the Horta in "The Devil in the Dark" nor the crystalline substance in "Home Soil" could possibly be persons. Do we have any principled reason for thinking that inorganic personhood is impossible? No—denial of this possibility seems to rest on pure chauvinism (perhaps "organicism" would be a good name for it). This is undoubtedly Picard's point in "Datalore" when he tells the senior officers, "If it feels awkward to be reminded that Data is a machine, just remember that we are merely a different variety of machine—in our case, electrochemical in nature." (Actually, since Data seems to be electrochemical in nature, too, I think Picard meant "organically electrochemical.")

What about the fact that Soong provided Data with a convenient off switch—which Riker demonstrates to good effect? Well, for one thing, human beings apparently have an off switch too—the Vulcan nerve pinch has a remarkably similar result. For another thing, Data's "off" state may well be analogous to our unconscious or anestheticized state. Finally, suppose that Data's operation really is completely interrupted when Data is "off"—are we so certain that personhood cannot end and resume after a period? Surely we cannot be confident that this is impossible.

Thus far I have not offered any positive arguments for machine intelligence, but I don't have to. Recall how we have proceeded thus far. The solution to the *problem of other minds* is to take complex, interesting, flexible, and adaptive behavior on the part of other human beings as sufficient grounds for attributing intelligence to them. The demands of consistency establish a prima facie case for taking complex, interesting, flexible, and adaptive behavior on the part of *machines* as sufficient grounds for attributing intelligence to *them*. So the burden of proof is on the naysayers to produce compelling, principled reasons for witholding such attributions. Moreover, as a general point, whenever one side in an argument says that something is logically impossible and the other says that it is indeed logically possible, the former is making a much stronger claim and so assumes the burden of proof.

Self-Awareness

> "'My rights,' 'my status,' 'my right to choose,' 'my life'—Well, that seems reasonably self-aware to me."
>
> —*Picard to Maddox, quoting Data,*
> *"The Measure of a Man"*

According to Maddox, Data is not self-aware, but Picard *is,* "because you are conscious of your own existence and actions—you are aware of yourself and your own ego." Maddox clearly thinks that Data has no conception of itself as itself, no concept of itself as a continuing individual, and so no beliefs or preferences about how its existence will go. As we saw in chapter 1, although possession of a self-concept is necessary for personhood, it isn't necessary for intelligence. There are plenty of intelligent species on Earth that do not appear to have a self-concept. Animal psychologists think that higher primates do have a self-concept; if, say, you paint a spot on a chimpanzee's face and it looks in the mirror, it will often try to wipe the spot off its face, apparently recognizing the mirror image as of itself. No other species has yet done anything like this in an experimental situation. For instance, you can placate a budgerigar by putting a mirror in its cage; it thinks there is another budgie keeping it company. So the typical dog or cat probably is not self-aware. A dog or a cat may want some dinner, but its thought content is something like *food here now,* rather than *I am hungry*.

So Data may still be intelligent even if Maddox is correct in thinking that it isn't self-aware. But is Maddox correct? Once again, we must look to Data's behavior. For instance, how would Data perform in the animal psychologists' test? I submit that Data gives every appearance of recognizing its reflection in the mirror as *its* reflection. Picard performs a behavioral test, too—a version of the language test. He asks Data what it is doing right now. Data replies, "I am taking part in a legal hearing to determine my rights and status. Am I a person or property?" Picard asks, "And what is at stake?" to which Data replies, "My right to choose, perhaps my very life." In his response to Maddox (quoted in the epigraph), Picard points out Data's use of the first-person-possessive pronoun "my." (Not to mention "I.") Picard's very good point is that this is excellent behavioral evidence that Data is indeed self-aware. Data seems to have a concept of itself as itself, a sense of its continuation through time, and beliefs and preferences about its continued existence (reflected in its refusal to undergo the dismantling procedure).

But Wouldn't It Be Awful If . . . ?

> "Computers make excellent and efficient servants. But I have no wish to serve under them."
>
> —*Spock to Kirk, "The Ultimate Computer"*

> "An android is like a computer. It does only what I program."
>
> —*Roger Korby, "What Are Little Girls Made Of?"*

Another common objection to machine personhood goes something like this: *If* there were machine people, it would be awful!

Human beings would lose their jobs, a computer might get elected President, . . . and so forth. Spock observes in "The Return of the Archons" that the society on Beta III is "a machine's concept of perfection: peace, harmony—" whereupon Kirk breaks in, "But no *soul!*" However, whether a society that includes or is run by machine people is a good thing or not entails nothing about whether such machines are possible. Turing himself encountered this worry, which he termed the *head in the sand* objection and rightly rejected as irrelevant.

But other than possible human obsolescence, what is the source of the concern about producing artificial people? I submit that the fear is that this will "replace freedom with a mechanistic culture," to quote the android Brown in "What Are Little Girls Made Of?" We have a tendency to think of machines as *programmed, unfree, dependent,* and *uncreative,* yet there is a perfectly good sense in which computers and androids are creative and independent. Any system that operates according to sophisticated rules of logic will display *systematicity*—that is, the ability to combine symbols to produce new strings—and this is a creative activity. (When Picard listens to Data's violin performance in "The Ensigns of Command," he points out that although Data has copied the styles of two virtuosos, something genuinely new has been produced in combining those styles. Data admits, "I suppose I have learned to be creative, sir, when necessary.") Machines can also be independent, in the sense that once activated they can carry on operations on their own. Any automated system is designed to be independent in this sense. Given an order, Data can and will go off and execute that order, on its own.

Creativity is a funny thing. To those of us who do not have it, it seems almost magical, like a gift from the gods. But to many creative people, it's just their work—it's what they do (which is not to say that it isn't very fulfilling work). But the myth of the divine spark dies hard. I recently attended a talk by the noted computer scientist Douglas Hofstadter, in which he demonstrated the result of a music-composition program developed by the composer David Cope. The program takes as input various pieces in a particular style by a particular composer, and as output produces a new piece in that style. So if you are unhappy with the paucity of some dead composer's work, perhaps we can turn out some new pieces for you! This may sound like a ludicrous idea, but Hofstadter had a pianist play pairs of comparison pieces, and asked the audience to decide which was the real thing. One pair fooled two-thirds of the audience—one of the pieces was a two-part variation by Bach and the other was a two-part "Bach" variation produced by the program. Hofstadter declared this a sad day for music appreciation; apparently he is convinced—or hopes—that producing great music can't be that simple. If great music can be reproduced by a relatively simple program, then we probably don't have to devote large brain resources to the task, either. But I find this neither saddening nor cause for alarm. Given the mentalistic division of labor, I would expect the brain's "music generator" to be a fairly dedicated device, or combination of devices, which does most of its job (whatever that is—I doubt that its function is the production of music per se) out of the reach of consciousness. Probably the hardest part of being a composer is teaching this dedicated device to produce the sort of thing you want as output. Consciousness no doubt has input somewhere in the process, but of a rather limited sort. After all, this is roughly how our brains do almost everything else (speech production is an example), so why should the production of music be any different? And why should the relative simplicity of the "music generator" make any difference at all (other than the healthy explosion of the myth of the divine spark) to how we appreciate the result?

Product Liability

> "Without freedom of choice, there is no creativity."
> —*Kirk, "The Return of the Archons"*

> "Your past does not excuse immoral or unethical behavior, sir." —*Data to Fajo,* TNG: *"The Most Toys"*

It is indisputable that machines are capable of at least one important kind of creativity and independence. But I doubt that the naysayers would be moved by these observations, because I take it that they are employing a different sense of "creative" and "independent," a sense very closely related to the notion of free will, and a sense apparently inimical to programming. Let's get a feel for this sense. In "The Mind's Eye" (*The Next Generation*'s homage to *The Manchurian Candidate*), La Forge is kidnapped by the Romulans, and upon his release he attempts to assassinate the Klingon governor, who is a guest on board the *Enterprise-D*. La Forge was conditioned to act the way he did, and the conditioning was "triggered" by the receipt of an "E-band" emission by his visor. In other words, La Forge was programmed so that when he received a certain input (E-band emission), he produced a certain output (attack on the Klingon governor). With behavior programmed in this way, there is no room for choice or independence or creativity; moreover, La Forge is not to blame for the assassination attempt. Because of his programming he had no choice; his act was unfree, and therefore La Forge is not morally responsible for it.

This is the crux of the worry about a "mechanistic society." We imagine the individuals in such a society as programmed, with no freedom of choice, no independence, and no moral responsibility. But let's delve deeper still. What is it about La Forge's action that renders it unfree? First, it originates outside him: he has become the helpless puppet of the Romulans. Clearly, it is the Romulans (and the Klingon traitor who "triggers" him) who are to blame for the assassination attempt; they are morally responsible for it because they are causally responsible for it. Second, when "triggered," La Forge had no choice but to do what his programming dictated. To sum up: for an action to be free, it must have originated with the agent, and the agent must have had a choice, must have been able to do otherwise in the circumstances.

When we apply this thinking to Data, its behavior apparently fails on both counts. Since Data was created and programmed by Dr. Noonian Soong, then surely it is Dr. Soong who is to be praised or blamed for Data's actions. So all Data's Starfleet medals rightly belong to Dr. Soong. Moreover, consider what occurs in "The Most Toys." Data is kidnapped by the trader Fajo, who delights in possessing unique items. When Fajo asks Data whether he has ever killed, Data says, "I have been designed with a fundamental respect for life in all its forms, and a strong inhibition against causing harm to living beings." Later, Data attempts to escape and trains Fajo's own lethal disruptor on him, at which point the trader reminds Data of its programming, believing that Data cannot fire. But Fajo forgets something else that Data had told him: "I am programmed with the ability to use deadly force in the cause of defense." When Fajo refuses to let Data go free, Data pulls the trigger, only to be beamed aboard the *Enterprise-D* in the same instant. Had it not been beamed up, Data would have killed Fajo—but who would have been responsible for Fajo's death? Surely Data's creator and programmer Dr. Soong, since any action Data performs originates with Dr. Soong. Nor was there any hint in this situation that Data could do anything other than what it was programmed to do. Fajo would have been correct in thinking that Data couldn't pull the trigger, had Data's programming included an absolute prohibition against killing. Instead, Data's programming included the use of deadly force in self-defense, and when Data found itself in a position of defending itself, what did it say but "I cannot permit this to continue." Out of Data's own mouth comes the admission that it had no choice under the circumstances. We seem to have found a genuine deficiency in Data and other programmed machinery: they necessarily are unfree and hence are not morally responsible for their behavior. And since machines cannot be moral agents, they cannot be persons—though this does not mean that machines cannot be intelligent. Hence, Maddox is at least partly correct.

Or so the argument goes. The great difficulty with the argument is its major premise—that free actions are those that originate with the agent and are such that the agent could have acted otherwise. I think that both of these conditions are either false (on what I shall call their *strong* readings), or else when reinterpreted such that they are true (the *weak* readings) leave it open that machines can act freely. It turns out to be just as well that the strong readings are false, since if they were true, then no human actions would be free, either. According to the strong readings, the first condition of free action is that it must have its causal origin within the agent, and the second condition is that the agent could have done otherwise in the very same circumstances. Data's actions do not meet these conditions, but then neither do any human actions—at least, not if we accept what I call the *causal picture of the world* (CPW, for short).

CPW can be stated in just five words: *every event has sufficient cause*. This simple causal picture of how the world works seems a presupposition of all our thinking. As I sit here typing, letters appear on the screen, but not by magic. I type "q" and, lo and behold, "q" appears on the screen. I don't know about you, but I have only a limited grasp of how my computer works. Nevertheless I'm confident of this much: my pressing the "q" key with sufficient pressure, together with the correct description of the computer's inner states, together with the fact that my computer is functioning properly, together with the correct statement of the principles by which my computer works, completely explains why the letter "q" appears. I don't know what the explanation is, but I'm sure there is one (or could in principle be one). Moreover, my confidence is not restricted to events in computer operation. For any event whatsoever, I'm confident that *something,* some combination of things, caused it to occur. (Even magical events, if they occur, are caused to occur.) After all, if there wasn't some combination of things sufficient for the event in question to occur, then the event wouldn't have occurred at all, would it? So whether we are in a position to give a complete explanation or not, the fact is that we give the explanations we do because we presume the truth of CPW.

Two points of clarification. First, if our world is one in which no backward time travel occurs, and there is no reverse causation (see chapter 6), then it seems that every event has *antecedent* sufficient cause. (It may help you to appreciate the argument to come if you think of CPW in this way.) Second, put to one side any worries you may have about "where it all begins." Some thinkers have held that a chain of causation must be sustained by an "uncaused cause" (God, perhaps), but it is at least as plausible to hold that a chain of causation may be infinite. Either way, it seems to be a presupposition of our ordinary thinking that CPW holds for all the events in that part of the history of the world which is relevant to assessing the nature of human actions. All the events *around here and now* have sufficient cause, and that's all we need for the following argument.

Human actions are events in the world, and we certainly explain human actions in much the same way that we explain other events. Just as my depressing the "q" key explains (in part) the appearance of "q" on the screen in front of me, so my poking my finger into your eye explains (in part) your yelling "Ouch!" (A complete explanation will need other details, of course, such as facts about your inner states, and the principles by which you "work.") And just as my key-depressing is not the only factor external to the computer that causes the "q" to appear (think of all the causes by means of which the computer itself came to be in the state it was in before I depressed anything), so my finger-poking is not the only external cause of your yelling "Ouch!" For every event that occurs inside you, there is a chain of causation sufficent for that event's occurrence—a chain with links outside you. Suppose that in addition to yelling "Ouch!" you punch me in the nose. Why did you punch me, when someone else would have desisted? Why are you so disposed to violence? Our standard explanations will hark back at least partly to your previous environment—perhaps you were beaten as a child—and such explanatory causes are clearly external.

Likewise, pacific behavior on the part of others will be partly explained by their relatively nurtured upbringing—once again, by citing causes external to the agent.

I trust you are beginning to see the problem. A complete explanation of any one of your actions requires no less than the whole history of all the causes in the history of the universe. Less grandly, for a full explanation of the action, we'd want to include facts about your genetic makeup, developmental principles, environmental history, and recent environmental input, such as eye-pokings. (*Why* your parents did what they did to you we'll leave for another time. . . .) So is it ever the case that your actions are free from external influence—that they have their causal origin within you? No. And neither are anyone else's. Human actions are never free, because the first condition of free action is never met. If CPW is true, then it is not the case that human actions are free from external causes. Agents are never the sole authors, the originating causes, of their acts.

Moreover, even if it were the case that some human actions met the first condition of free action, it is overwhelmingly unlikely that any human actions would meet the second condition. We can see this by emphasizing that according to CPW every event has *sufficient* cause. Consider again the event of your punching me in the nose, and call this *N*. Let *C* be the combination of things (the eye-poking, your upbringing, what sort of day you've had, and so on) sufficient for the occurrence of *N*. Since *C* obtaining is sufficient for *N* to occur, then if *C* obtains, *N* must occur. You punched me in the nose, and really couldn't have done otherwise in the circumstances, since those circumstances were sufficient for that action to occur. (At this point, it's worth noting that nothing I have so far claimed in this section depends on the view that human actions and the mental states that play a role in their production are purely physical or otherwise material in nature. The pattern of explanation I described—the pattern of explanation that presupposes CPW—is employed by materialists and nonmaterialists alike.) And since every human action has sufficient cause, it is never the case that the agent could have done otherwise in the circumstances, and no human actions are free. Free will and moral responsibility are illusory, in the strong readings of the conditions of free action. (Actually, moral responsibility might exist: if God exists and is self-caused, then God is morally responsible for everything that occurs, including the evil things.) Data is wrong when it claims that Fajo's impoverished past does not excuse his behavior (see the epigraph). Even if Fajo's past hadn't been impoverished, it still would have excused his behavior. If Data's behavior is programmed, then so is Fajo's, and so is yours!

We have touched upon a famous issue in philosophy, the *free will problem,* which is often put in terms rather different from those I have used here. In particular, the issue of *determinism* usually crops up. Determinism is the thesis that each state of the universe *completely determines* each subsequent state. To illustrate the thesis, imagine an infinitely powerful intelligence (God, say), to whom no facts about the present state of the universe are hidden. This intelligence knows everything there is to know about the present state of the universe, including the principles by which it works. If determinism is true, then this intelligence could infallibly predict the next state based on this knowledge. For instance, to limited beings like us, the result of a fair coin toss is a fifty-fifty proposition, but this is because we don't know enough. Imagine flipping a coin into the air and freezing things at the apex of the coin's flight. If God knows the exact mass and orientation of the coin at this point, its exact distance from all other bodies (and especially from the Earth), the number and position of the air molecules that will buffet it on the way down, all the details of the surface upon which it will land, and so forth, then if determinism is true God can infallibly predict the result of the toss.

However, our best science tells us that determinism isn't true. There is *quantum indeterminacy,* which for our purposes amounts to the fact that chance plays a fundamental role in the way the world works. Chance is built into the very fabric of the universe we inhabit, so not even God can infallibly predict everything that will occur. *Indeterminism* is true. But this makes no difference to the conclusion that we are unfree. CPW is not the same thesis as determinism. Although *if* determinism were true then CPW would also be true, the reverse does not hold. CPW is simply neutral between determinism and indeterminism. If indeterminism is true, then one state of the universe does not deterministically move into subsequent states, but it does move into them. Every event still has sufficient cause, it's just that chance is fundamentally built into the combination of things that suffice for the event to occur. So we could have written CPW thus: every event has (deterministic or indeterministic) sufficient cause.

It may be objected, though, that the argument from CPW to universal unfreedom simply misses the point. Perhaps freedom is threatened only by *deterministic* causation? We can dismiss this vain hope rather quickly. As the philosopher Daniel Dennett puts it, the variety of "free will" that issues from indeterminism simply is not worth wanting. If at least some of your actions are genuinely undetermined because of chance quantum events in your brain, there seems little solace in this. If determinism renders you a mere mechanical puppet, moved in predictable ways, why are you any less a puppet if you are moved randomly? And why should the "free will" that springs from indeterminism bestow moral responsibility on us? Far from regarding chance as making agents morally responsible for their actions, our intuitions run in the opposite direction—the intervention of chance seems to remove, or at least mitigate, moral culpability. (An interesting but tangential issue is whether quantum indeterminacy in any case translates into macroscopic indeterminacy—that is, whether quantum effects aren't simply canceled out at the level of mind/brain events.)

Since the strong readings of the conditions of free action mean that no human actions are free, I think we should reject those readings. Concerning the first condition, let's return to La Forge's "programming." What's the difference between his assassination attempt and all the other actions he performs—actions that we ordinarily regard as free? To answer this, we need a rough picture of how a cognitive agent works—that is, of how a mind works. Think of the mind as a functional device, one composed—in the mentalistic division of labor—of smaller and smaller functional units, various *faculties* and *subfaculties*. What is the *will,* that thing we hope is *free?* Simply a faculty of the mind—the faculty with the job of producing action (not all behavior, just action). We can divide the faculty of the will into three basic subfaculties—a *belief generator,* a *desire generator,* and a *deliberator*. Here's a simplified and idealized causal flowchart of the operation of the mind, focusing on the operation of the will, which produces action as output, given input from other faculties and the environment.

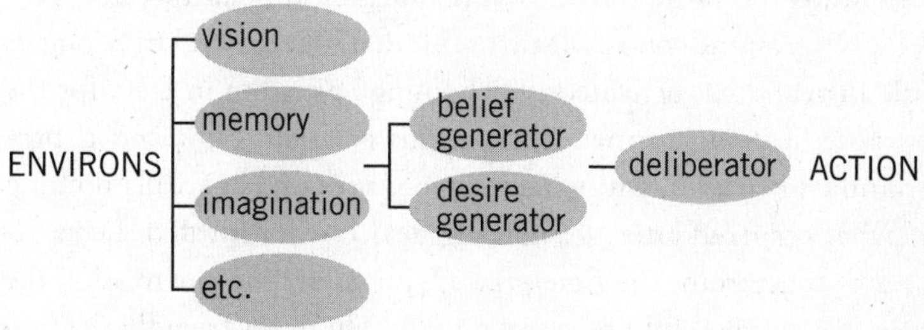

To illustrate a working mind, suppose that you are walking on the sidewalk and there is a piece of gum in your path. Your visual faculty processes this information, and you form the belief that there is a piece of gum on the sidewalk ahead. Since you remember how sticky and hard to remove gum is, you form the desire to avoid the gum. From a combination of other faculties, you form beliefs about how to avoid the gum (say, by sidestepping). Then your deliberator weighs the input from the belief and desire generators (including other current beliefs and desires and their relative strengths) and produces the appropriate behavioral output. So if there are no overriding desires at the time, the combination of beliefs and desires I have described will produce sidestepping behavior. (The "environmental inputs" can be internal, too. For instance, when your stomach is empty, this should produce the desire to eat.)

Here's the weak reading I want to give the first condition of free action: in order to be free, an action must be produced *by the will*—that is, by the belief generator, the desire generator, and the deliberator working in concert. The reason La Forge's assassination attempt is unfree is that it fails this condition; indeed, it was contrary to his will; he didn't want the Klingon governor dead. The conditioning allowed the Romulans to short-circuit La Forge, bypassing his will altogether; his behavior was more a reflex than a genuine action. Moreover, just as we can contrast this unfree behavior of La Forge's with those of his actions we regard as free, we can draw the same distinctions where Data's behavior is concerned. In *TNG:* "Brothers," Data suddenly commandeers the *Enterprise-D* and heads for an unknown destination, resisting all the crew's attempts to resume control. It turns out that his creator, Dr. Soong, is still alive and has activated the "homing" program in Data for the purpose of doing further work on his creation. Now, *this* is programmed behavior, and when Data "wakes up," it recalls nothing of what occurred after the homing device was activated. Data expresses concern for the *Enterprise-D,* the crew, and the mission the crew was supposed to be carrying out. The Data-friendly reading of these events is that Data returned "home" against its will. Data wanted to carry out the mission, to obey the commands of its superiors, and so forth, and believed that going "home" would place lives in jeopardy (there was a dying child on board the ship at the time). Data's will was short-circuited by Dr. Soong's homing device in just the way that La Forge's was short-circuited by the Romulans (and so if the child had died, it is Dr. Soong who would have been morally responsible for its death—though of course his ignorance of the consequences is a mitigating factor). The flowchart I have provided could describe Data's normal operation as well as La Forge's, and thus the first condition for free action does not preclude Data from acting freely.

The weak reading of the second condition is that for an action to be free, the agent must be such that he might have done something different had the circumstances been different. Perhaps an analogy will help. Consider the sphex wasp, well known for the inflexibility of its behavior. When the wasp stings a spider, say, into paralysis, it drags the victim to a burrow, goes below to arrange things, comes back out, and takes the spider below. But if you interfere by moving the spider even a centimeter while the wasp is in the burrow, when the wasp returns to the surface it will go through the same routine all over again, moving the body back to the "right" spot, then going below to check the arrangements (meanwhile, you move the spider again, and so on). Philosophers pay homage to the wasp by calling an inflexible response to different environmental inputs *sphexishness*. Here are some examples of human sphexishness. An individual cannot leave the house, because he gets to the front door, worries that he's left the gas on, returns to the kitchen to check it, returns to the front door, worries that he's left the gas on, returns to the kitchen to check it, and so on. Another individual washes her hands because she believes they are dirty, then washes them again because she believes they are dirty, and again, and again, and so on. These are obsessive-compulsive behaviors, which include kleptomania, anorexia nervosa, bulimia, gluttony, nymphomania, and many other disorders, and are classic examples of unfree behavior. Why? Because *no matter what input the will receives, it produces exactly the same behavioral output*. If you are not a compulsive handwasher, then you wash your hands only if they're dirty—or might be dirty, when you need to be sure they're clean. An obsessive handwasher washes her hands over and over whether they are clean or dirty, no matter what she is doing, no matter what.

On the weak reading of the second condition, a free action is one that is not sphexish, and the best description of a sphexish person is that the will is malfunctioning; one or more of the subfaculties of the will is not doing its job. The belief generator ought to be sensitive to the way the world is; for instance, if one's hands are clean, the belief generator ought to generate the belief that one's hands are clean. The desire generator ought to be sensitive to what is good for the agent; for instance, if one is slowly starving to death, the desire generator ought to generate a desire to eat that outweighs the desire to be attractive. And the deliberator ought to be sensitive to the weightings of the beliefs and desires it receives as input; if the belief generator inputs the belief that being slim is no compensation for dying, this should be reflected in behavior. So it turns out that *free will* has nothing whatever to do with freedom from *cause*—quite the reverse; since every event is caused, free will couldn't have anything to do with absence of causation. It is the *way* that human actions are caused that makes them free, or not free. In my view, the adjective "free" applied to the will means exactly what it means when applied to other functional devices, such as bicycle wheels and weather vanes. A weather vane is free if it is well-functioning—if it is able to take the movement of local air molecules as input and produce an accurate representation of the direction of the wind as output. The malfunctioning will of a sphexish person is like a malfunctioning weather vane, one that is rusted stuck and points the same way no matter which way the wind blows.

It is of course *sphexishness* that people fear from a mechanized society. (In *TNG:* "The Hunted," we see the results of the programming of soldiers, and we feel a deep sympathy for these individuals, because we see how unsuited they are to peace and how helpless they are to change.) But there is no principled reason for thinking that machines necessarily will be sphexish. The creativity of machines is just as capable of flexibility and adaptiveness as the creativity of humans—at least, in principle. Is Data sphexish? Only once does it even come close. In "Clues," Data replies to all Picard's questions with "I cannot answer that question, sir." Becoming exasperated, Picard exclaims, "You sound as if you're stuck in some sort of feedback loop!" But Data isn't stuck at all; it is following Picard's orders (unbeknown to Picard, who has had his memory wiped), and believes that if it does not do so then the entire *Enterprise-D* crew will perish. Otherwise, Data displays precisely the behavior that one would expect from a creature with a well-functioning will (if anything, Data is less sphexish than other members of Starfleet). Picard says, in *TNG:* "Unification I," "Mr. Data, your resourcefulness never ceases to amaze me," and in *TNG:* "Redemption II," after Data apologizes for disobeying orders, Picard replies, "Starfleet doesn't want officers who will blindly follow orders without analyzing the situation. Your actions were appropriate to the circumstances." Data often acts freely, and its creator Dr. Soong is not morally responsible for these free actions. Once again, what appeared to be a genuine difference between us and machines turns out to be undemonstrated.

Aboutness

In "The Measure of a Man," Maddox asks Data whether lines from one of Shakespeare's sonnets are "just words to you, or do you fathom the *meaning?*" and in "Return to Tomorrow," Thalassa wonders, "'Beloved'—what will that word mean to a machine?" Maddox and Thalassa apparently question only whether or not a machine can understand particular types of words (words relating to feelings and emotions), but their skepticism is reminiscent of one of the most famous objections to machine intelligence (and by implication, machine personhood). According to the philosopher John Searle and his supporters, a silicon-and-metal machine, such as a programmed computer or an android, cannot understand any sort of words at all. Searle's argument is known as the *Chinese Room* argument. If Searle is correct, then the argument shows why the conservative should not accept a Turing Test winner as intelligent.

Searle imagines himself locked in a room with two slots in the wall. One is an "in" slot, and through it come pieces of paper with strange-looking squiggles and squoggles on them. Inside the room along with Searle are lots of pencils, blank sheets of paper, and a rather thick instruction manual. Nothing else is in the room. The instruction manual contains directions, written in English, for performing certain transformations in a certain order on the strange-looking squiggles and squoggles. Here is one possible instruction: "If there is nothing but *squiggle-squiggle* on the page, write *squoggle* on a fresh sheet and put it in the 'out' slot." Unbeknown to Searle, who is monolingual (and for the sake of the argument completely ignorant of the existence of other languages), the squiggles and squoggles are Chinese characters. The "inputs" are actually questions written in Chinese, and by following the instruction manual Searle produces outputs that not only make sense to the Chinese "interrogators" but can be read as appropriate answers to the questions they input.

The Chinese Room itself is in fact the "subject" of a Turing Test that is being conducted in Chinese. Searle's first point is that it is possible, given that the instruction manual is accurate and comprehensive, and given that Searle carries out its instructions correctly, for the Chinese Room to pass a purely behavioral test like the Turing Test. Searle's second point is that Searle-in-the-room does not understand a word of Chinese, even though it appears to the Chinese interrogators that they are conducting a sensible conversation with the subject of the test (the Room). Searle's first conclusion is that since a suitably programmed computer that passes the Turing Test is exactly analogous to the Chinese Room, its passing the Turing Test does not establish that it is intelligent. Searle's second conclusion is that since no amount of extra instruction of the information-processing sort contained in the manual could bring him any closer to understanding Chinese, and since a suitably programmed computer is exactly analogous, then information processing is insufficient for thought.

To repeat, the Chinese Room thought experiment is supposed to establish the claim that a purely behavioral test such as the Turing Test is not a sufficient indicator of intelligence when the subject is merely a suitably programmed computer. Moreover, it is supposed to establish the negative claim that thought is not merely information processing. So what does "thought" require? According to Searle, thought requires *intentionality,* or "aboutness." Suppose you are asked, "What is the capital of the United States?" and you reply "Washington, D.C." Since you understand English, you understand that "the United States" refers to a nation. When you call to mind the United States (in order to answer the question), your thought is *about* the United States. But suppose we ask the same question (in Chinese, of course) of the Chinese Room, and we receive the correct reply. Since Searle does not know that "squiggle-squoggle" is Chinese for "the United States," he almost certainly is not thinking about the United States in producing the right answer to the question, and he certainly is not thinking about the United States *in order to* perform his transformation task. Well, a computer "taking" the Turing Test and responding to the same question with "Washington, D.C." is not thinking *about* the United States either. According to Searle, thinking is intentional—it is thinking *about* something—and since the computer is not thinking about anything, then it isn't thinking.

Searle puts the same point another way, by saying that information processing per se is *syntactic* and not *semantic*. As we noted in chapter 1, "syntax" refers to the properties of a language uninterpreted, and "semantics" to the properties of a language interpreted. Recall the simple language called *L*. Here is another formula in *L*: *"Cwu."*

What does this mean, in everyday English? Nothing—as it stands it is an uninterpreted, syntactic string. We can add a semantics to it by assigning a dictionary. If *"u"* names the individual that is the United States, if *"w"* names the individual that is the city of Washington, D.C., and if *"Cxy"* applies if and only if *x* is the capital of *y*, then the formula *means* that Washington, D.C., is the capital of the United States. But it is important to realize that *"Cwu"* means this *only relative to this dictionary assignment*. Relative to a different dictionary assignment, it means "Walter choked Uncle Fred."

L is governed by the transformation rules of first order logic. For instance, if *A*, *B*, and *C* are variables for formulae of *L*, then given:

$(A \& B) \rightarrow C$ (If A is true and B is true, then C is true)

and

$\sim C$ (C is not true)

one can derive

$\sim A v \sim B$ (either A is not true or B is not true)

in two steps.

Perhaps you already know how to do this. If so, your ability to perform these transformations is independent not only of any particular assignment of *L* formulae to *"A," "B,"* and *"C"* but also of any particular dictionary assignment to *"A," "B,"* and *"C."* You are just manipulating formal symbols, much the way a computer does. Indeed, you could learn these rules without ever being given dictionary assignments, in which case you'd be a bit like Searle in the Chinese Room, and a bit like Data and Troi when they were trying to decipher the Tamarian language in "Darmok."

But, it may objected, surely when you are given a vocabulary, you then understand what the *L* transformations mean. Why can't we just give the computer a dictionary to use for *its* transformations? Because, Searle thinks, there's more to say about intentionality: in particular, he claims that computers (like the one I'm typing on) are made of *the wrong sort of stuff* to have intentionality. In Searle's view, only certain biological structures are capable of giving rise to intentionality—only such structures have the right "causal powers." (Interestingly, Searle does not deny that there might be silicon-based intelligent life, like the Horta, but we won't worry about that here. If Searle's Chinese Room argument doesn't work, the rest of his view is unimportant.)

One popular objection to the Chinese Room argument—an objection philosophers and computer scientists call the *Systems Reply*—grants that Searle-in-the-room does not understand Chinese, but points out that we do not say of Chinese speakers that some part of them understands Chinese; rather, it is the whole individual, considered as a system, that understands Chinese. The analogue in the Chinese Room case, of course, is the room and its contents (including Searle), considered as a system. Since the entire system reproduces the behavior of a competent Chinese speaker, it is the *system* that understands Chinese. Searle's rebuttal to the Systems Reply is in two parts. First, he regards the suggestion that the system understands Chinese as implausible: if a man doesn't understand Chinese, how can the same man *together with* pencils and paper and rule books and so forth understand Chinese? Second, he adapts the Chinese Room argument by supposing that instead of carrying out the operations in the rule book manually, Searle-in-the-room does them in his head, and instead of continually consulting the rule book, he memorizes all the rules. That is, Searle-in-the-room *internalizes* the system. In this modified case, Searle contends, he still does not understand Chinese—it's still just squiggles and squoggles to him—hence the Systems Reply fails.

According to a second objection—the *Robot Reply*—it is not surprising that an incarcerated computer of the sort Searle considers does not understand Chinese, since it has no sensory apparatus to allow it to connect words with their meanings. (Compare the discussion of "Darmok," where in order to understand an expression Picard had to be in the kind of situation it referred to.) However, a computer with such an apparatus and the ability to navigate in the environment—in short, a suitably programmed robot, like Data—*would* be able to understand Chinese. Searle's reply is once again in two parts. First, the Robot Reply begins by conceding that the Chinese Room argument demonstrates that a confined computer doesn't understand anything, so the Robot Reply is an objection to Searle's claim that only appropriate biological structures can realize intentionality. Searle's reply to this claim is, once again, to imagine internalizing everything—this time all the robotic equipment as well—and he claims he would be no closer to understanding Chinese if he did so.

According to the *Brain Simulator Reply,* a computer that simulates not only the linguistic behavior of a Chinese speaker but also simulates the actual brain structure of a Chinese speaker, down to the level of neuron firings, really understands Chinese. (The hapless M5 "ultimate computer" is a simulation of Richard Daystrom's brain.) Here again, Searle replies in two parts. First, he notes that such a claim doesn't sit well with the functionalist view—the prevailing view in the field of artificial intelligence research—that study of the brain isn't necessary for modeling intelligence. Second, he imagines adapting the Chinese Room to pass the test by simulating the structure of the brain in a system of hand-operated water pipes and valves. (Such valves needn't be "on-off" switches like those in digital computers; they might vary the level of water flow as well.) Searle takes it as obvious that there could be no understanding of anything in such a system.

So far, so good for Searle, it seems. But let's dig a little deeper, beginning with Searle's response to the Brain Simulator Reply and the nice picture of a system of water pipes and valves. It is indeed hard to imagine how such a system could understand anything. But now imagine how things are in the actual brain, at the level of neuron firings in your organic hardware. I submit that it's just as difficult to imagine how *this* system could understand anything. Surely individual neurons don't understand anything, yet somehow when you put the whole thing together you have intelligence. This is not so much an objection to Searle's argument as to his method. He imagines a range of thought-experimental systems which intuition inclines us to pronounce incapable of understanding anything, but Searle's own view is that *some* purely material systems—human brains—do understand things, and this is just as mysterious in the case of a brain as it is in the case of a man in a room, or a system of water pipes and valves. Searle may be too quick in his dismissal of the Systems Reply. Keeping this in mind, let's move on to a couple of more substantive obections to Searle's argument.

The *English Reply* is in two parts. The first part is a point about logic—particularly about the *Law of Excluded Middle,* which says that for any proposition, either it or its negation is true. Consider the structure of Searle's argument. He is claiming a strict analogy between the behavior of the Chinese Room and that of a suitably programmed computer that passes a Turing Test conducted in Chinese (call this the C-computer). Suppose we grant Searle's point that thinking requires intentionality, and moreover grant his claim that nothing in the Chinese Room—not even the system as a whole—understands Chinese. If we grant further the strict analogy with the C-computer, then what is the appropriate conclusion to draw? That the computer doesn't understand Chinese. But this is not the conclusion that Searle draws. He concludes that the computer doesn't understand *anything*. Searle has used an unexcluded (or as we philosophers say, *undistributed*) middle. Here is an excluded middle: "Either the C-computer understands Chinese, or it doesn't understand Chinese." Here is Searle's undistributed middle: "Either the C-computer understands Chinese, or it doesn't understand anything." This clearly leaves room for the middle possibility that the C-computer understands something, but not Chinese.

This completes the first part of the English Reply. Its point is just that Searle has not demonstrated what he claims to have demonstrated; hence the Chinese Room argument fails in its objective. The second part of the English Reply is an attempt to argue that there may well be something that the C-computer does understand. To begin with, notice that there is *something* in the Chinese Room with intentionality, even in Searle's own account: it is Searle himself, in full command of the English language. This immediately establishes a disanalogy with the case of the C-computer, so let's try to correct it. Obviously, Searle is vastly overqualified for his job, so I want you to imagine gradually taking away bits of Searle's understanding of English (Searle could do without perhaps 99 percent of his English vocabulary, for instance), leaving only the bare minimum necessary to understand the manual and execute its instructions. What remains of Searle—call him C-Searle—still has intentionality, because C-Searle has thoughts about the symbols he performs the transformations on, thoughts about what he has to do with them, and so forth.

Now look at the C-computer. It *passes the Turing Test,* and we should not underestimate the complexity of the programming, the storage capacity, and the speed of processing required to do this. What principled reason is there for thinking that the C-computer lacks anything that C-Searle has? If we take the strict analogy between the cases seriously, as Searle urges, then isn't it reasonable to think that just as C-Searle needs intentionality to perform his tasks, so (some part of) the C-computer needs intentionality to carry out the analogous tasks? Won't it need to think *about* the symbols it performs the transformations on? If this line of reply is right, then Searle has misrepresented what computers do by calling it merely syntactic and not semantic.

To reinforce this idea, consider again language *L*. When you carry out transformations upon formulae of *L* in the absence of a dictionary assignment, it's not true that the symbols have no meaning to you. For instance, the formula *"Cwu"* does mean something in the metalanguage we use to talk about *L*. It means that there is an individual named *"w,"* an individual named *"u,"* and an ordered relational property *"C"* such that *w* stands in *C* to *u*. Similarly, *"(A&B)* ➔ *C"* means that there are three formulae of *L* such that if the first two are both true, the third is true as well. While this is not full-blooded semantics, about rocks, trees, and Washington, D.C., it is semantics nevertheless. Hence the English Reply concludes that what Searle's Chinese Room shows is that the C-computer probably *is* intelligent, precisely to the extent that intentionality is required for the C-computer to successfully mimic Chinese understanding.

It may help to put things this way. According to the English Reply, what Searle has shown is that in the case of the C-computer the distinction between a language test and an action test collapses. It is the range of actions required to mimic natural-language understanding which warrants the attribution of intelligence to the C-computer. Consider a parrot that is accomplished at producing appropriate responses in English to questions put to it in English. I presume you will balk at concluding that the parrot understands English, but surely the mere fact that it can mimic language understanding in this way is evidence of its (relatively rudimentary) intelligence.

We can augment the English Reply by revisiting the Robot Reply. Suppose the English Reply is correct, and that we should grant Searle the claim that nothing in the Chinese Room or the C-computer understands Chinese. What more is required? What does a Chinese speaker have that the C-computer lacks? Plausibly, it is the appropriate experience of the world of rocks, trees, and Washington, D.C., that a confined C-computer lacks. This suggests that a machine must be something like an appropriately programmed robot—like Data—to have full-blooded intentionality of the sort required for the full command of Chinese. This makes the Robot Reply a lot more credible than it may have first appeared, and echoes a suggestion Turing himself made—that the best way to produce a Turing Test winner is to program a machine to simulate a child's mind, and let it learn from experience in much the way a human child does. (And doesn't Data remind you of a child?)

But perhaps the English Reply concedes too much to Searle in granting that nothing in the Chinese Room, and so nothing in the C-computer, understands Chinese. According to the Systems Reply, the entire system understands Chinese, even though Searle himself doesn't. Or one could claim that Searle really does understand Chinese but is ignorant of this fact. We can combine these two replies by considering Searle's modified case in which he completely internalizes the system. If the Systems Reply is correct, then Searle in this modified case really does understand Chinese but doesn't know it! Searle is radically self-deceived. We don't need to claim that Searle is self-deceived, however, according to the final objection I shall consider, which I call the *Virtual Person Reply*. According to this reply, Searle is right to a large extent in claiming that a machine cannot think. And Searle is even right that machines are the wrong sorts of things to be intelligent, but this is not because they are made of the wrong sorts of stuff; rather, it is because thinking is not done by machines at all (not even human ones) but instead by *virtual machines*—entities realized by the activity of (some) machines when they are operating appropriately.

The fact that Searle does not understand Chinese in the Chinese

Room does not entail that *no one* in the Chinese Room understands Chinese. Putting it another way, "Either Searle understands Chinese, or no one in the Chinese Room understands Chinese" has an undistributed middle. Since, beforehand, the only person in the room is Searle, we should consider the possibility that Searle, in performing his transformations in the Chinese Room, brings into existence another person—a person who understands Chinese. Similarly, the C-computer, in carrying out its program, may bring into existence a person who understands Chinese. This, again, echoes a point of Turing's—that any digital computer can, with the right programming and sufficient memory, simulate the operation of any discrete-state machine. In computer jargon, such simulation is known as *emulation,* and when a machine is running an emulation, the machine is said to realize a *virtual* machine. When this occurs, the simulating machine and the virtual machine are *nonidentical.* For one thing, they're running different programs: the former is running the emulation program and the latter is running an application (such as a word processor). Moreover, when the emulation ends, the virtual machine ceases to exist, whereas the simulating machine clearly doesn't. The analogous view of human beings is that the body (especially the brain) is the machine that runs the *person* emulation. A person is a virtual machine of a certain type.

This section has been difficult, and I have left many things unsaid. But I hope it's at least clear that Searle's Chinese Room argument against the possibility of a machine's understanding natural languages has a number of rather large holes. At best, Searle has shown that a confined computer that passes the Turing Test doesn't have complete understanding of the language in which the test is conducted. But how many of us have a *complete* understanding of a natural language? When I write "Bruce is a wombat," how complete is your understanding of this sentence, if you don't know who Bruce is or what a wombat is? In any case, Data is not confined—Data is out and about in the world—and there is no reason to think that it cannot understand English.

Is Data Human?

Feelings

> ARD'RIAN: "Do you have any feelings for me?"
> DATA (gently): "I have no feelings of any kind."
> —*"The Ensigns of Command"*

We shall consider emotions in a moment, but there are plenty of other feelings that we associate with states other than emotions. There's a way that pain feels (in addition to the way it makes us behave), for instance—and many people think that no entity made of silicon and metal could possibly have such experiences. Out of Data's own mouth comes support for this contention, for it is difficult to imagine an android more sophisticated than Data, and difficult to see how simply giving Data more hardware or programming could make any difference. (The idea that the addition of an "emotion chip" makes Data capable of sensation just confuses the issue, and adds nothing of import to the present discussion, so I'll ignore it until the next section.)

Once again, *Star Trek* has plugged into a lively philosophical debate. Let us begin by distinguishing two apparently different aspects of sensations: one is the job that sensations do for us, which we may call the *functional* aspect of sensation, and the other is the *phenomenal* aspect—the "how it feels," or "what it's like" part. Take pain, for instance. If you touch a very hot surface, your sensation of pain seems to play an important causal role in your quickly withdrawing your hand. And there's a plausible explanation for why you can experience pain: it is extremely useful to detect, as quickly as possible, that your hand is being burned and to take prompt action to avoid further damage. The motivational force of pain in this regard cannot be underestimated! The phenomenal aspect of pain seems an extra, though, and is intimately bound up with the notion of *consciousness*. We ordinarily describe ourselves as being "consciously" aware of sensations, and indeed are inclined to think that this phenomenal aspect is necessary to the sensation.

Does Data experience sensations? Well, it explicitly denies that it is capable of experiencing pain (as when La Forge is probing its positronic net in "Clues"). But perhaps we needn't take Data's word for it, so let's consider Data's other behaviors. There's excellent reason to think that Data has states *functionally* equivalent to what we call pain. For one thing, any mobile creature with vulnerable parts needs some way of monitoring the status of those parts in order to avoid or minimize damage to them. And when the monitoring system "rings the alarm," it's in the best interests of the creature to react quickly. If Data had no such monitoring systems, then it might well not notice when a vulnerable part was threatened—or it might notice but not react quickly enough. (Data may well have no functional equivalents of pain receptors on the surface of its positronic brain, though; we don't have pain receptors on our ordinarily well-protected cerebral cortex.)

The objection may be made that Data's parts aren't particularly vulnerable. In that case, Data's "pain alarms" would be less likely to go off, but it doesn't mean Data doesn't have pain alarms. Here a second consideration is relevant: the sensations of pain and pressure, at least in their functional aspects, seem alike in kind and different only in degree; both are intimately associated with the sensation of *touch*. If, like me, you are seated right now, then your posterior is registering pressure, and when I'm typing I'm relying partly on the pressure I feel at the tips of my fingers. A moment's thought should convince you that you would not survive an ordinary day without all the information the functional aspect of your sense of touch gives you. No matter how indestructible Data is, it too needs this information. And since Data has the functional equivalent of a sensation of pressure, it probably will also have, to some extent, the functional equivalent of the sensation of pain.

We can offer a similar argument for other sensations. Data could not behave the way it does if it had no mechanisms for discriminating colors, for instance, so it has the functional equivalent of the experience of seeing red or seeing green. Data also has the functional equivalent of the sense of hearing, and we know it can discriminate different substances by imbibing them (recall its remarks on this subject to Timothy, in "Hero Worship"), so it has the functional analogue of the sensation of taste. If we restrict the claim that Data has no feelings to consideration of the purely functional aspects of sensation, the claim appears to be false.

However, the naysayers probably have the *phenomenal* aspect of sensation in mind, denying that there's any "what it's like" for Data's sensations. The functionalist view of mental activity described in chapter 2 seems to many philosophers to leave open the possibility that two individuals may be functionally the same yet differ in the phenomenal aspects of their mental states—so that, for instance, our visual spectra are inverted, and what you call "red" actually looks to you the way what I call "green" looks to me. There's a lovely analogue of this possibility and the problems it raises in *TNG:* "Descent I." When Data claims to have felt anger, La Forge is skeptical: if Data has never felt anger before, how does it know *what* it felt? Data grants the objection and asks La Forge to describe what anger feels like, to provide a "frame of reference." La Forge is, of course, entirely unable to describe the feeling except by reference to *other* feelings. Moreover, some philosophers think that functionalism leaves open the possibility that an individual may be functionally like you or me yet have *no phenomenal states whatsoever*—a condition those philosophers call being a *zombie*. Is poor Data a zombie?

One way to block this conclusion is to deny that the phenomenal aspect of sensation is anything more than the completely specified functional aspect. To make this more plausible, we must distinguish between functional and merely behavioral equivalence. Two individuals are behaviorally equivalent if they produce the same behavioral outputs given the same environmental inputs—for instance, they agree on which objects are red and which are green. But it does not follow that their internal arrangements are the same: their internal states may play different functional roles even though they play identical (external) behavioral roles. In the present suggestion, inverted spectra are possible because different internal functional organizations can produce behavioral equivalence. But if two individuals are functionally identical, then necessarily they share exactly the same phenomenal states.

If, on the other hand, the phenomenal aspect of sensation is indeed something more than the completely specified functional aspect, it still doesn't follow that Data is a zombie. Here's an alternative suggestion: if an individual has the functional aspect of a sensation (like pain, or seeing red), that state necessarily has some phenomenal aspect or other. But though having the functional aspect of a sensation means also having a phenomenal aspect, it needn't be a particular phenomenal aspect. What determines the particular phenomenal aspect, then? Perhaps what the individual is made of. So pain-in-humans might differ phenomenally from pain-in-the-Horta, and what red looks like to me might differ from what red looks like to you. Do we need to decide this difficult issue to make a determination concerning Data? Fortunately, no. Consider the naysayers' argument, which runs as follows:

> *Premise 1:* Having the phenomenal aspect of sensations is necessary for being a person.
> *Premise 2:* Data lacks the phenomenal aspect of sensations.
> *Conclusion:* Data is not a person.

This argument is uncompelling. First, suppose your conception of personhood inclines you to accept premise 1. Now the question is, Which do you have better reason for accepting, premise 2 or Data's personhood? I submit that if you accept premise 1 then you probably ought to deny premise 2, given the impressive behavioral evidence for Data's personhood. This is especially so since there is little support for premise 2 (other than Data's word, and we shall have cause to question this again in the next section). Since we don't know exactly how we ourselves come to have states with phenomenal aspects, we are hardly in a position to assert that Data doesn't have such states. If you were to encounter silicon-based aliens who behaved like humans, would you leap to the conclusion that when they identified colors there was no phenomenal aspect to their visual experiences? Surely not! Data probably has phenomenal states, even if they differ in character from those of an organic cognitive agent.

On the other hand, suppose you're a recalcitrant naysayer and deeply convinced, for whatever reasons, that premise 2 is true. Now the question is, Which do you have better reason for accepting, premise 1 or Data's personhood? I submit that if you accept premise 2 then you probably ought to deny premise 1, given the impressive behavioral evidence for Data's personhood. That is, you ought to revise your conception of personhood.

Emotions

> "I can give [Lal] attention, Doctor. But I am incapable of giving her love."
>
> —*Data to Dr. Crusher, "The Offspring"*

> "I am not capable of hatred. . . . Fear is not a quality I possess." —*Data to Timothy, "Hero Worship"*

A persistent objection to Data's claim to personhood is Data's apparent lack of *emotion*. Once again, there are countless instances of Data's own admission of this deficiency. But let's ignore for the moment what Data says, and focus instead upon what it does (once again, all the examples I shall give come from episodes in which the "emotion chip" is absent).

First, some examples from "The Measure of a Man." Data seems sentimentally attached to objects such as its medals, a book Picard gave it, and a portrait of the late Tasha Yar. When questioned about Tasha in the hearing, it seems to be sentimentally attached to her, too. It expresses, among other things, *regret* at having to resign, *trust* in Picard's ability to represent it, *gratitude* to Riker for accepting the task of prosecuting the case (otherwise the JAG officer would have ruled summarily against Data), *hope* that Maddox is more competent than he would appear (when disassembly seems inevitable), *disquiet* at the prospect of disassembly (when it seems that disassembly can be avoided), and *resignation* at the prospect of disassembly (when it seems inevitable). Data says that it will *miss* all its "friends," but especially La Forge, and that it is *intrigued* by the very idea of Maddox's proposal. In "Data's Day," we hear two of Data's log entries, which are to be forwarded to the Daystrom Institute to assist Maddox in his research. The first entry comes after an unexplained course correction ordered by the Vulcan ambassador:

> It is fortunate that I am able to perform my duties without emotional distractions. If that were not the case, a sudden course correction towards the Neutral Zone would make me very . . . nervous.

While we hear Data's voiceover, we see it pause, look *pensive,* and drum its fingers on the console, with all the appearance of nervousness. The second log entry comes after Data has been questioned by the Vulcan ambassador on the pretext of a check of security measures:

> Commander Maddox, I have often wished for the sense that humans call intuition or instinct. Since Vulcans are incapable of lying, I must accept the ambassador's explanation as the truth, but I would still prefer a—gut feeling—to back up this conclusion.

This entry seems to express both *regret* and *envy*—or at least *wistfulness*—as well as *suspicion*.

Add to these examples all those occasions when Data's nonverbal behavior is suggestive of an emotional state. Here's a selection from *The Next Generation:* its *bemusement* at an alien hairdo in "Data's Day," its *concern, indulgence, expectancy, patience,* and *pride* with regard to its "daughter," Lal, in "The Offspring," its *bewilderment* at Picard's initial failure to assign it a command in "Redemption II"; when it eventually is assigned a command, it shows *impatience* with the insubordination of the jealous Lieutenant

Commander Hobson. Then there is its *nervous anticipation* at the prospect of sex with Tasha Yar in "The Naked Now," its *relief* at the cancellation of the *Enterprise-D*'s self-destruct sequence in "Where Silence Has Lease," its feeling of *belonging* in being reunited with the *Enterprise-D* crew in "Tin Man," its *surprise* at Riker's gruff response to a routine question in "The Icarus Factor," its *amazement, curiosity,* and *pride* in being present at the birth of Deanna Troi's child in "The Child," its *distress* at Dr. Crusher's injuries in "The Arsenal of Freedom," its *curiosity* about whether or not it will still exist in the twenty-sixth century in "A Matter of Time," its *disappointment* at the failure of the exocomp to pass the sentience test in "The Quality of Life," its *puzzlement* at the computer problems in "Evolution," its *quizzical* and *helpless* expression and its display of *misgivings* when it attempts to evacuate the colonists in "The Ensigns of Command," and its *stubbornness* in continuing to try to persuade them. In "Hero Worship," Data says to Timothy, "I cannot take pride in my abilities. I cannot take pleasure in my accomplishments. . . . I would gladly risk feeling bad at times, if it also meant I could taste my dessert." But it says this *wistfully,* as if it feels bad about not being able to feel bad. Later, when it tells Troi that separation from Timothy will not be difficult because "that would require an emotional context which I cannot provide," it says this *regretfully*.

All in all, we have impressive behavioral evidence that Data does indeed have emotions. Nor am I the only one impressed: when Data tells Dr. Crusher that it cannot provide Lal with love, she replies, "Now why do I find that so hard to believe?" And in "The Ensigns of Command," when Picard, who has been listening to Data play the violin, says, "Your performance shows—feeling," Data replies that it has no feeling, and Picard, too, says, "It's hard to believe."

On the other side of the ledger, there are occasions when Data behaves completely inappropriately. In "In Theory," it tries to woo its "girlfriend" Jenna by writing a program specifically for emotional interaction. After trying its hand at being amorous and attentive, it reacts to Jenna's lack of enthusiasm by turning aggressive and shouting. But Jenna complains that everything Data is doing is forced and artificial. They end up kissing, and Jenna asks Data what it was thinking while they kissed. Data replies, "In that particular moment, I was reconfiguring the warp-field parameters, analyzing the collected works of Charles Dickens, considering a new food supplement for [its pet cat] Spot, calculating the maximum pressure I could safely apply to your lips—"

A fairly simple explanation of this sequence is that, far from trying to do something it's in principle incapable of, Data is trying too hard to do the right thing. Countless human males, too, have found themselves in the predicament of wanting to please a woman and not knowing how to do it. (Perhaps the reverse is also true.) Data's mistake is in trying to figure out and *program* the appropriate responses, when Jenna was clearly attracted to Data in the first place partly because of what Data was already doing. The situation is not unlike that of a human male who tries to use his reason instead of his "instincts" in interacting with a lover—it usually doesn't work, and his behavior seems forced and artificial. So Data gets itself into a mess in the first place by *feeling insecure,* and shows clear signs of care and concern for Jenna. Given enough time and enough failures, I'll bet Data would start to show signs of *exasperation,* too.

All in all, then, I suggest that even in the absence of the emotion chip we ought to ascribe emotions to Data. So why is there such an enormous temptation, even among people who would grant that an android has other mental states, to deny that androids have emotions? Well, for one thing, Data itself constantly disavows being in any emotional state. There are three possible explanations for these disavowals. First, perhaps Data really does lack emotions, and knows it, and honestly admits to it. But this explanation sits uncomfortably with Data's other behavior. The second possibility is that Data has emotions, and knows it, but for reasons of its own perpetuates the lie. (Perhaps it fears the reaction of others.) I doubt this explanation, though; Data is generally honest in other respects, sometimes inappropriately so. I prefer the third explanation—that

Data has emotions but is self-deceived. Data recognizes that it is a machine, and has bought into the common myth that a machine cannot have emotions, and so has convinced itself that it cannot have them. For instance, in "Data's Day," when Data tells Riker that it feels "anticipation" about giving Keiko away at her wedding to O'Brien, having just asserted that it cannot get nervous, I suspect that Data really is nervous but discounts the experience, describing nervousness as something else altogether. An ordinary human being would have had this feeling "validated" by others and would learn the feeling's name in the process. Poor Data, on the other hand, learns to call the feeling of nervousness something else entirely. (Consider La Forge's unwillingness to "validate" Data's anger in "Descent I.") When Data is pondering the sudden course correction in "Data's Day," it again is nervous, and indeed lets this nervousness interrupt the performance of its duties! And when it regrets not having "instinct" or "gut feeling" to back up its explicit reasoning about the Vulcan ambassador, surely the reason it wishes for such a feeling is that it does actually have an instinct or gut feeling that something is wrong. Disavowals of emotion are commonplace among humans, too. I certainly have had the experience of being convinced I wasn't angry, or envious, or impatient, only to be forced to admit later that I was. Men in general are reputed to have a problem recognizing and expressing their own emotions—in this respect, Data's behavior is all too human!

A second reason for denying emotions to Data is relevant to the discussion of Spock in chapter 1. I remarked there that we can usefully distinguish the *higher* emotions (which are associated with cortical activity in humans and generally have little or no affect associated with them), and the *lower* emotions (which are associated with the limbic system and brain stem and are characterized by strong feelings). Data behaves very much like Spock, and I think the most defensible position is that Data, like Spock, has ample experience of a wide variety of higher emotions, whereas there is little or no evidence of its experiencing lower emotions, such as anger. So one could plausibly deny that Data experiences the lower emotions (at least, not without an emotion chip). In chapter 1, I suggested that a cognitive creature needs emotions, but I did not suggest that the lower emotions are necessary. Fear and anger are useful to relatively destructible creatures, but would these emotions be useful to an individual like Data? Given that few things can physically threaten it, it may be able to get by perfectly well without fear. And since anger usually pumps us up for a fight, perhaps enhancing our physical prowess, Data (who is already superstrong) may have little need for anger. As a cognitive creature par excellence, though, Data will doubtless have as much use as we do for the higher emotions; hence, however it comes by them (whether it learns them or they are somehow built into it), Data's display of *higher* emotions makes pretty good sense. Given this, it's something of a mystery why Data is so anxious to be *human*—to experience the psychological life of a typical *Homo sapiens.* As Spock remarks of Data's quest, in "Unification I," "More *human?* Fascinating! You have an efficient intellect, superior physical skills, no emotional impediments. There are Vulcans who aspire all their lives to achieve what you have been given by design."

I have suggested that Data probably wouldn't have mental features useless to it, but I have also suggested that it is self-deceived concerning its own emotional states. Am I being inconsistent? Why would an android have mechanisms of *self-deception?* Let's ask why *we* have such mechanisms. They can be a liability, because we may do something dangerous (such as drive our car drunk) if we mistakenly believe ourselves to be capable. They get us into all sorts of relationship trouble when we cannot admit how we feel. And we can indulge in practices that are very harmful to us (drug use, kleptomania) while kidding ourselves that we don't have a problem.

But self-deception has advantages, too. Suppose you have been attacked by a dangerous animal—say, a saber-toothed tiger—and in trying to escape have broken your ankle. It is extremely useful to you if the "messages" you get internally do not alert you to the seriousness of the injury (for instance, overwhelming pain would be debilitating and force you to stop running). Instead, your "shock mechanism" temporarily blocks such messages, allows you to keep running, and thereby saves your life. In addition, it may be that in cognitive creatures such as ourselves there are certain truths we are best protected from. (Freud thought that every man wants to kill his own father and marry his mother; if true, this might be too horrible to live with, and men would be better off not believing it.) Disadvantageous self-deceptions may be just an unfortunate by-product of a generally useful mechanism.

So in building an android, you might do well to include self-deceptive mechanisms. A relatively indestructible android like Data probably wouldn't need the equivalent of our shock mechanism, but it might want to be able to operate without needed repairs. And if it's a cognitive android, there may be truths too terrible for it to contemplate: when Data's older "brother" Lore lies to it, in "Datalore," saying that Data was deliberately made imperfect, Data seems to obsess over this! While we're on the subject of lying, here's further evidence of self-deception in Data. In "Hero Worship," Data tells Timothy that "androids do not lie." Not only does Lore lie, but so does Data, when it thinks that's the right thing to do—as in "Clues," when it lies to Picard to protect the crew of the *Enterprise-D*. Yet I don't think Data is lying to Timothy; rather, Data doesn't realize that it can and does occasionally tell lies.

Moreover, I don't think Data is completely self-deceived concerning its capacity for emotion. In "The Quality of Life," Data says to Riker, "I have observed that humans often base their judgments on what is referred to as 'instinct' or 'intuition.' Because I am a machine, I lack that particular ability. However it may be possible that I have insight into other machines that humans may lack." And when Fajo taunts Data with its "lack of feeling" in "The Most Toys" ("You're just an android"), I think he suspects that Data is indeed capable of emotional reactions, and is trying to provoke one. Later, after Fajo is captured and imprisoned, Data delivers the news that his collection of unique items has been confiscated. "You have lost everything you value," Data says, and Fajo remarks, "It must give you great pleasure." "No, sir, it does not," Data replies. "I do not feel pleasure. I am only an android." From the look on Data's face as it throws this line back at Fajo, you gather that it feels (at the very least) a calm, resigned satisfaction; there's a hint of malice there, and maybe even pleasure.

So far I have considered Data's likely mental life in the absence of the emotion chip, which Dr. Soong intended to add to Data in "Brothers," and which is finally installed in *Star Trek VII: Generations*. In one way, the addition of the emotion chip is consistent with the interpretation I have placed on Data's behavior. If, as Dr. Soong suggests, the chip supplies "basic" (that is, lower) emotions, then this is consistent with Data's already having higher emotions. But the suggestion that a cognitive agent with a full range of higher emotions should acquire the lower ones by adding a chip is implausible. Our cognitive systems have evolved out of less complex ones, and the lower emotions are an integral part of these less complex minds. In evolutionary terms, higher, cortical functions have been added to a basic cognitive economy, of which lower emotions are an integral part. One might well conclude from this that if one is to have lower emotions they must be a part of one's basic cognitive structure. I am inclined to think, partly because of the *frame problem* (see chapter 1), that if we ever manage to build androids that can negotiate the world almost as well as higher mammals do, they'll have some basic emotions.

Consciousness

We have already touched on the issue of consciousness in the last two sections. The *phenomenal* aspect of sensation is how sensations present themselves in one's consciousness, and many emotions have a conscious, subjective "feel," too. What exactly *is* consciousness? This is one of the hardest questions in philosophy. We can distinguish between different senses of "conscious": *individuals* can be conscious, individuals can be *self*-conscious, and mental *states* can be conscious (sensations, and some emotions, for instance). Plausibly, these senses are related, in that individuals are self-conscious only if they are conscious, and individuals are conscious only if they have conscious states. In "The Measure of a Man," Maddox places three conditions upon personhood: "intelligence, self-awareness, consciousness." But it seems to me that the self-awareness required for personhood probably is self-consciousness, in which case any individual that is self-aware is thereby conscious. If there is a plausible objection to Data's possession of consciousness, it must ultimately concern state consciousness.

The main competing philosophical theories of state consciousness are the *higher order thought,* or *HOT,* theory and the *inner perception* theory. (There is a mildly popular third view, *eliminativism,* which roughly says that there isn't any such thing as consciousness. This doesn't mean that everyone is a zombie but rather that "consciousness" is a category of "folk" theory and will not appear in a mature science of the mind, just as "caloric"—the name for a supposed heat-giving substance—is a category that doesn't appear in a mature thermodynamics.) According to HOT theory, consciousness is a property that (some) mental states have when they are thoughts *about* other thoughts. According to the inner perception theory, consciousness occurs when some mental states *perceive* others.

Once again, we don't need to decide which theory is correct for present purposes. If there really is such a thing as consciousness, then since we don't really know how or why we human beings come to have it, we aren't in any position to deny that a computer or an android could have conscious states. Moreover, Data's behavior gives every reason to grant that Data probably is conscious. *Star Trek* supports this contention in two different episodes. In "Elementary, Dear Data," Picard and Data express doubts about Professor Moriarty's claim to be conscious, and Moriarty responds by asking whether or not the "mechanical man" is conscious. Eschewing its normal modesty, Data replies "I am conscious, yes." And *Voyager:* "Prototype" even shows "what it is like" to be an android. We see the first scene from the point of view of the failing automated unit 3947. It is as if we see what the android sees.

Pro Creation

But if Data is conscious, does this mean that Data has a *sub*conscious, too? For instance, does it dream? Once again, there's no reason in principle why an android might not have dreams or their android equivalent. (The character of the experience might depend partly on the physical nature of the individual, as it might in the case of sensation.) In "Birthright I," Data begins to dream after suffering a severe shock, and the explanation is that his program for dreaming has been activated earlier than it was designed to. Data then begins to explore its own subconscious through the creative activity of painting, and eventually Dr. Soong appears to it in a dream and announces that Data has now "crossed the threshold" and is no longer just a collection of computer chips and what have you. I doubt that dreaming per se is that important, so perhaps Soong is claiming that Data now has a subconscious that it previously lacked? This is hard to accept—roughly for the same reasons I gave for denying that Data could acquire lower emotions as an optional extra. I suspect that consciousness is a later evolutionary development than subconsciousness (a speculation connected with the requirement for a mentalistic division of labor and the need for basic mental functions to be inaccessible to consciousness). So perhaps we should interpret Soong's remarks in another way: Data's "dream circuits" are an integral part of its cognitive architecture, and require a certain level of cognitive development before they kick in. We don't know enough about the development of our own ability to dream to say otherwise.

Values

> "A computer does not *judge*—it makes logical selections."
> —*Spock to Kirk, "The Ultimate Computer"*

In "The Ultimate Computer," Kirk declares that the M5 "can't make a value judgment," presumably because it's a machine. Value judgments are commonly contrasted with factual judgments; for instance, "That shirt is bright-colored" is a factual judgment, whereas "That shirt is ugly" is a value judgment. Factual judgments are supposed to be judgments about facts; they are either true or untrue. But this distinction doesn't make much sense to me, if the implication is that value judgments *aren't* about matters of fact and so are neither true nor untrue. It is sometimes claimed that value, like beauty, is in the eye of the beholder, but no good argument has ever been put forward for this claim (some shirts *are* ugly!). If there is a distinction to be made here, it's between *descriptive* and *normative* judgments—a descriptive judgment makes a claim about how things *are,* and a normative judgment makes a claim about how things *ought to be* (whether they are or not). So the best sense we can make of a "value judgment" is that it carries *normative force* (in the case of ugly shirts, the force is something like "You ought to have better taste, or more sense, than to wear such a thing in public!"), whereas a factual judgment carries no normative force.

The descriptive/normative distinction is related to the distinction between logic and emotion (or between reason and passion, or between belief and desire) discussed in chapter 1. Just as it can be argued that logic without emotion can provide no *psychological* motivation for action, it can be argued that descriptive judgment without normative judgment can provide no *practical* motivation for action. For instance, it is sometimes claimed that science is a purely factual enterprise and that it is not the job of scientists to make value judgments. But this is nonsense. For one thing, if scientists simply set about collecting facts, which ones do they collect, out of the infinite number of facts available? Scientists have a *frame problem,* too, analogous to the frame problem for cognitive agents discussed in chapter 1. Without some prior idea of what to look for—without some judgments concerning what it is *good* to look for—scientists would be frozen into inaction. Science, like every other human enterprise, necessarily is shot through with value judgments.

Does Data make value judgments? Absolutely, a prime example being the moment in "The Most Toys" when Fajo tells Data about his impoverished upbringing. Data replies, "Your past does not excuse immoral or unethical behavior, sir." Many of the value judgments Data makes have moral import, as in "The Quality of Life," when Data declares, "I do not believe it is justified to sacrifice one life-form for another." Not only does Data make moral judgments but it acts upon them, with more integrity than many humans do. Witness its insubordination in defense of the exocomps in "The Quality of Life." Indeed, now is the time to stop referring to Data as "it." Human or not, Data is a person, as Maddox seems to recognize when he, too, begins to use the masculine pronoun to refer to Data.

And it may also be time to consider the actions of the exocomps themselves. In order to save the lives of Picard and La Forge, three exocomps *volunteer* to risk themselves in an attempt at a rescue. After the sucessful attempt, one of the exocomps remains behind, sacrificing itself in order that the other two may survive. Even though Picard and company never establish any linguistic contact with the exocomps (not in natural language, anyway), the actions of these individuals are clear indicators of moral agency, suggesting that the exocomps also are persons.

Are You of the Body?

> LIEUTENANT REGINALD BARCLAY: "You can't possibly have been aware of the passage of time."
> PROFESSOR MORIARTY: "But I *was*—brief, terrifying periods of consciousness, disembodied, without substance."
> BARCLAY: "I don't see how that could be possible."
>
> —TNG: *"Ship in a Bottle"*

To complete our investigation into personhood, we must consider the status of two kinds of *Star Trek* exotica: one kind is intelligence in the absence of a body, and the other kind is intelligence in the absence of individuals.

In "Elementary, Dear Data," La Forge tries to produce a "Sherlock Holmes" holodeck program to challenge Data, so he asks the *Enterprise-D* computer to create a suitable foe, but through a slip of the tongue he asks not for an adversary worthy of Sherlock Holmes but instead for "an opponent capable of defeating Data." Thus "born" is Professor Moriarty, an entity unlike the usual holodeck characters, in that he is aware of his own existence. (There is a prima facie case for regarding Moriarty as a person in virtue of this self-awareness.) After some tense moments, Moriarty agrees to be shut down and "saved," in return for Picard's promise to investigate means of securing it a more permanent existence outside the holodeck. Four years pass, and in "Ship in a Bottle" Moriarty is accidentally reactivated by Lieutenant Barclay. In the above exchange, Barclay is skeptical because he doesn't understand how Moriarty's program could have been active in the interim, given what he knows about the holodeck. But there is another, different reason for skepticism: we may ask, how is it possible for there to be disembodied consciousness—sophisticated intelligence, that is, without substance?

In each of the cases considered so far—androids, like Data; and machines, like exocomps—the prime suspects have been embodied in some fashion, with physical parts that take up space, absorb input from the environment, and manifest behavioral output. And in "Emergence," when it seems that the *Enterprise-D* temporarily becomes intelligent and Data likens it to a life-form, Riker agrees, saying, "That's true. It *sees* with its sensors, and *talks* with its communication systems." Once again, here is embodied intelligence. But do we really have to conceive of intelligence as embodied? Sometimes *Star Trek* suggests that the answer is no, as in the exchange at the head of this section, and in all the cases in which Starfleet personnel encounter what they call energy beings. (A brief selection: the original series episodes "Metamorphosis," "The Gamesters of Triskelion," "Return to Tomorrow," and "The Lights of Zetar," the *Next Generation* episodes "Lonely among Us," "Transfigurations," and "Imaginary Friend," and the *Voyager* episodes "The Cloud," "Heroes and Demons," and "Cathexis.")

I have only this to say about disembodied consciousness or intelligence—I don't believe in it. Nor are any of the examples in *Star Trek* compelling evidence that we can even conceive of it. Consider the energy beings, for instance. Since matter and energy are interconvertible, the fact that these beings are "composed entirely of energy" does not mean they are immaterial. Moreover, the fact that these beings are active in the physical world, receiving and communicating information and manipulating physical objects, suggests that they are after all embodied but with bodies of a different sort. Even a strange entity like Moriarty is embodied; his holodeck matter might not be stable off the holodeck, but that's irrelevant. But if Moriarty is just a computer program, can't it be stored, inactive? Whether or not Moriarty is just a computer program is a difficult issue—one we shall tackle somewhat obliquely in Part Two. But in any case, Moriarty should be inactive when it's stored. Hence I am in agreement with Barclay: somehow the holodeck didn't simply store Moriarty's program, and that's why it had "brief, terrifying periods of consciousness."

Moriarty doesn't have to be on the holodeck to be active, either. At the close of "Ship in a Bottle," Moriarty is tricked into believing that it has left the holodeck in ordinary corporeal form. However, its program has in fact been transferred into a computer running a continuous program of a lifetime's worth of simulated experiences. The computer is small enough to sit on a corner of Picard's desk. So Moriarty has no human body, not even a holodeck simulation of a human body. Nevertheless, in order to have experiences at all—to interact with the interactive program—Moriarty must be realized in some material form or another, perhaps in array of computer chips.

What is true of Moriarty is true of the other holodeck characters that are prime suspects: especially the emergency medical hologram on board *Voyager*. The holographic doctor is well off compared with Moriarty, in either of the latter's incarnations. The doctor exists on a special medical holodeck, has a substantial, humanoid body, and even leaves the holodeck occasionally by suitably technological means. As *Voyager*'s medical officer, a full-fledged member of the crew, the doctor is a person in his own right—undeniably, given both his behavior and the effect he has on other people. (In "Lifesigns," he even has a romantic liaison with a Viidian, Dr. Danara Pel.) Perhaps in a future episode we shall see a reprise of "The Measure of a Man," in which the doctor is forced to fight for his personal rights. *Voyager*'s first officer, Commander Chakotay, would make a good advocate, judging by what he says to the doctor in "Projections": "Just because you're made of projected light and energy doesn't mean you're any less real than someone made of flesh and blood. . . . What matters is who you are."

There are two examples in *Star Trek* of collective consciousness. The best known is that of the Borg of *The Next Generation,* a race that assimilates new technology and humanoid bodies alike, combining them into cybermen. A Borg individual is conscious, but has no self-concept, a fact the *Enterprise-D* crew tries to exploit in "I, Borg." They capture a Borg and cut off its communication with the Borg collective, whereupon it develops a self-concept, adopting the name Hugh. Hugh is eventually returned to the Borg, in the hope that the idea of individuality will spread and disrupt the collective consciousness. In *TNG:* "Evolution," Wesley Crusher conducts an experiment in nanotechnology. The *nanites,* infinitesimal devices for effecting biological repairs, usually work individually, but Wesley succeeds in getting them to cooperate. Unfortunately, the nanites escape, multiply, and take over the *Enterprise-D* computer core, threatening both the safety of the crew and its scientific mission to assist Dr. Paul Stubbs in studying a stellar explosion.

Both the Borg and the nanites display collective consciousness, and the Borg in addition display individual consciousness. But neither individual Borg nor individual nanites are persons, since they do not have a self-concept. However, there is a case for treating the collectives as persons. Consider an analogy—corporations and other groups of people working together are often regarded under the law as persons, and we can apply the same incorporation principle to moral concerns like praise or blame, when two or more people act in concert. Thus it might make sense to judge the corporation to be guilty of negligence even though no individual member of the corporation is. And it might make sense to judge the nanite or Borg collective as corporate persons that are morally responsible even though no individual nanite or Borg is.

Summary

Our exploration into the nature of personhood has revealed that artificial personhood (and, by implication, artificial intelligence) is a distinct possibility, and that the fairest test to determine whether or not an individual qualifies for personhood does not depend on its ability to pass for a human being. If there were individuals like Data, or the exocomps, or the emergency medical hologram on *Voyager,* we ought to consider these individuals to be persons, and treat them accordingly—which is to say, we should consider their interests equally with the interests of human beings. To do otherwise would be unwarranted discrimination. But our exploration of personhood is not over. In Part Two, we examine the many exotic processes that persons undergo in *Star Trek,* asking whether or not such processes are possible, and whether or not human beings could survive them.

Matters of Survival

part ii

"Reg, transporting really is the safest way to travel."
—*La Forge to Barclay,* TNG: *"Realm of Fear"*

To Beam or Not to Beam?

chapter 4

Hamlet, Shamlet

Star Trek isn't quite up there with Shakespeare, but many of the best known lines from *Star Trek* have moved into popular usage along with "To be or not to be," "A rose by any other name," and so on. (Interestingly, many Shakespearian expressions survive into the twenty-fourth century—at least, according to *Star Trek*.) "Beam me up, Scotty!" is such a line, which is all the more surprising since James T. Kirk never utters it in the *Star Trek* canon; the closest Kirk gets is "Scotty, beam me up," in *Star Trek IV: The Voyage Home*. It is a useful phrase, especially when one is in dire need of extrication from one's circumstances. But I want to focus on beaming not in the special sense of rescue but rather in the sense of ordinary transport. I have not counted, but Starfleet personnel have beamed hundreds of times that we see and thousands of times that we don't see. Sometimes, however, characters have misgivings about undergoing the beaming process. Dr. McCoy's antitechnology streak manifests itself in, among other things, his frequent expression of dislike for the transporter. Dr. Pulaski seems to share these sentiments, and in "Realm of Fear" Reg Barclay develops a full-blown phobia.

As has been well documented, the dramaturgical reason for the transporter is that the ship can be left in orbit rather than having to land on an unfamiliar planet in an improbable welter of special effects. The idea of teletransport is not unique to *Star Trek,* but it is *Star Trek* that has established it in our general consciousness. Lawrence Krauss, in *The Physics of Star Trek,* remarks upon the extent of "the impact that this hypothetical technology has had on our culture—an impact all the more remarkable given that probably no single piece of science fiction technology aboard the *Enterprise* is so utterly implausible." As a physicist, Krauss is interested in the purported operation of the transporter in order to determine whether or not it is a realistic technology. As a philosopher, I am interested in the purported operation of the transporter in order to determine whether or not it really is a transporter in the literal sense. In particular, I shall try to answer the question, *Could anyone survive such a process?*

We must immediately address two distinct issues. One is whether the process is *reliable* or not. Perhaps the trepidation felt by McCoy and others is a lack of faith in the technology. So let us stipulate that transporter technology is not only feasible but that the transporter has a near perfect performance record, virtually always doing exactly what it is designed to do. In this respect, the transporter is eminently safe—much safer than automobiles, planes, and starships; this is precisely the point La Forge is making in the epigraph.

But there may be a deeper reason for trepidation. One can have complete faith in the reliability of a process and still be unwilling to undergo it. The process of being guillotined, for example, is both reliable and highly undesirable. Perhaps McCoy is wondering whether whatever "rematerializes" will still be *him!* (If we are going to put words into Kirk's mouth, then we can put words into McCoy's, too; I like to imagine McCoy, envisioning his imminent destruction, whispering "Beam *me* up, Scotty!" as the command to "energize" is issued.) Indeed, it is easy to imagine entire cultures—alien or terrestrial—who would refuse on similar grounds to undergo such a procedure. (The Trill in *TNG:* "The Host" refuse the process, but this is in aid of keeping their symbiont nature a secret.) So is it rational to undergo teletransport on the assumption that you will survive it? Are McCoy and the like-minded being wise or merely superstitious? The answer depends not just on *what the transporter does,* but also on *what personal survival is*.

Working Hypotheses

Unfortunately, *Star Trek* does not present a consistent story concerning the operation of the transporter. There are two ways to conceptualize the device. One is as a *matter* transporter, which scans the subject, then literally "dematerializes" it and sends the matter in energy form, along with the scanned information, to the destination, where "rematerialization" occurs using the accompanying information. Most of the time, this is what happens in *Star Trek,* if we accept the description of transporter operation given in the *Next Generation* episodes "Encounter at Farpoint" and "Realm of Fear." In this process, the transporter has to maintain the correct "pattern" of the transported subject—the information used to rematerialize the subject—so that the physical and psychological condition of the rematerialized subject will be identical to that of the scanned subject.

But now and then strange things happen during transport. For instance, some subjects manage to change position while beaming, as in the *Next Generation* episodes "When the Bough Breaks," "Loud as a Whisper," "Who Watches the Watchers," and "Ménage à Troi." However, since these changes are probably unintended continuity errors, they are best ignored. It is a lot harder to ignore what goes on in "Realm of Fear," though. This is the only episode in which we get to see what it's like—transport from the first-person subjective viewpoint—with startling results. I would have expected the experience to be something like undergoing anesthesia: you might feel something a little odd—a tingling, perhaps—then the next thing you know is when you wake up in a new location. But Lieutenant Barclay seems to retain continuous consciousness whenever he beams. Not only that, but the dematerialized Barclay can see things in the "matter stream," and can reach out and grab them! Although part of an entertaining plot, these occurrences are so implausible that we should disavow them, too. The same goes for what we see in "Darmok," in which Picard, in the middle of his pitched battle with the energy creature, somehow begins rematerializing on board the *Enterprise-D* before he completely dematerializes on the surface of El-Adrel.

But we should take other anomalies more seriously. In two *Next Generation* episodes, for instance, the transporter is used to provide a sort of restorative therapy. In "Unnatural Selection," Dr. Pulaski is infected by a virus that alters the DNA of its victims, causing accelerated aging. Pulaski gets very old very fast, but is saved from death when a sample of her original healthy DNA—from a lock of her hair—is fed into the transporter, and the transporter dematerializes her, then uses the information from the lock of hair to reconstruct her with healthy DNA. But not only is she rid of the virus, she is restored to the physical condition she was in before she contracted the virus; that is, she is once again in her mid-forties. The transporter in this episode is not merely a passive matter transmitter, since it is able to effect qualitative changes in the subject by using information from another source. The second incidence of restorative therapy occurs in "Rascals," but in the reverse direction. This time, a transporter accident rematerializes Picard, the civilian Guinan, Ensign Ro Laren, and Keiko Ishikawa as teenagers, and they are eventually restored to their previous physical condition when the right genetic information is fed into the transporter.

Let's try to make sense of this. In Pulaski's case, one might have expected her to be rematerialized with healthy DNA but *very old,* just as she was prior to being dematerialized. Since your physical condition at any time depends upon the interaction of your genetic blueprint with the environment, you cannot be "restored" to a previous physical condition from mere genetic information. Of course, the transporter isn't just using genetic information—it has the "pattern" of the subjects, too. But Pulaski's "pattern" input to the transporter when she is scanned is of a very old woman, so that's what ought to be rematerialized. The only way that Pulaski-in-mid-forties can be rematerialized is if the transporter has the pattern of Pulaski at that age. Yet Chief O'Brien explicitly denies that there is a previous "transporter trace" for Pulaski (which I take to be just this pattern information). Why the denial? We'll come back to this.

Meanwhile, note that in both cases—Pulaski's and the quartet in "Rascals"—the subjects are restored to their previous physical but not psychological condition. That is, in each case the subjects remember everything that happened to them during the period between the original unfortunate occurrence and their "restoration." Since the physical condition must have been restored from the right "pattern" (say, Pulaski-in-mid-forties), and since the psychological condition is taken from the "pattern" of the scanned subject (Pulaski-very-old), we can conclude that the physical and psychological patterns are importantly independent.

This seems to contradict *TNG:* "Lonely among Us," however. The *Enterprise-D* accidentally picks up an energy being from a nebula, and it eventually inhabits Picard, becoming rather attached to him. It wants to return home to the nebula, taking Picard with it, and plans to use the transporter to achieve this. It commandeers the ship and tells the helpless bridge crew, "The transporter need not pattern your Captain into matter. We'll beam energy only, and we will become a combined energy pattern of our life-forms." Picard beams into the nebula as "pure energy," but the anticipated combination with the energy being doesn't occur, and Troi senses Picard's energy in the nebula, on its own. Then Picard (still pure energy) somehow gets into the ship's circuitry, and the crew concocts a scheme to restore him, by using the physical pattern still in the transporter memory. Rematerialization occurs, and Picard steps off the pad, asks what's going on, and says that the last thing he remembers is preparing to beam out.

Let's try to make sense of *this*. As noted, the transporter cannot beam only the subject's matter (converted into energy), since it has to know how to put the subject back together: proper beaming is matter/energy plus pattern, and beaming out as "energy only" would leave the subject's pattern behind. So when Picard's "energy" returned to the ship, the transporter reconverted it to matter and reunited it with Picard's pattern. So far, so good. But when Picard beamed out as energy only, was just his physical pattern left behind, or his physical and psychological pattern? The implication is that both patterns were left behind; otherwise, why is Picard unable to remember anything that happened after his preparation to beam out? But if that is true, then what was Troi sensing when she felt that Picard was "out there" in the nebula? You can't have it both ways—either Picard's psychological pattern wasn't sent out into the nebula, or else it was. If it wasn't sent out into the nebula, then there wouldn't be anything in the nebula for an empath to identify with Picard. Therefore, at least part of Picard's psychological pattern must have been sent out into the nebula. Either all of it was beamed out, and Picard has amnesia, or else only the emotional part of his psychological pattern beamed out with the energy, and the rest—the part that remembers things—stayed in the transporter memory. Either way, once again the implication is that the beamed subject's physical pattern and psychological pattern are independent of each other.

So far, it seems that there is one constant in transport: namely, rematerialization always consists in putting the original matter back together again. But not in "Unnatural Selection," "Rascals," and "Lonely among Us." When the transporter uses the healthy DNA pattern to replace Pulaski's damaged DNA, there are two ways it might do this. One is to take the matter that constitutes the damaged DNA and impose the healthy DNA pattern on it. But why not simply jettison the damaged DNA and recruit new matter for the healthy DNA, in a sort of DNA transplant? Nothing in the *Star Trek* canon precludes this. Indeed, consider the ship's replicators—the devices used to produce all manner of material comforts, such as food. The replicators recruit matter/energy from some unexplained source and impose a particular physical configuration upon it, so why shouldn't the (closely related) transporter? Recognizing this possibility permits an interesting interpretation of O'Brien's claim not to have a previous "transporter trace" for Pulaski. Since he must have had one in order to restore the Pulaski-in-mid-forties physical pattern, he is deliberating hiding this fact, because restoring a "trace" would require the recruitment of new matter (for one thing, the brain of Pulaski-very-old would have lost many of the neurons that the brain of Pulaski-in-mid-forties had), and *someone* is afraid of the social and ethical implications of this use of the transporter—implications about duplicates which we shall consider fully in chapter 5. Restoring the quartet in "Rascals" also requires the recruitment of new matter, since the dematerialized subjects were so much bigger than the materialized youngsters. And we now have an alternative interpretation of "Lonely among Us." The rather implausible story of Picard's "energy" finding its way back into the ship's circuitry is part of a cover-up. Picard's patternless energy simply dissipated when the anticipated combination with the energy being did not take. But since Picard's pretransport pattern stayed in the transporter memory, it was simply imposed on newly recruited matter.

If you doubt the Machiavellian interpretation of these episodes, there are three more that absolutely clinch the fact that the transporter can recruit new matter for rematerialization. Sometimes a *double* rematerialization occurs after a *single* dematerialization, as in *TOS:* "The Enemy Within," in which Captain Kirk is split into his cerebral and animal personas; *TNG:* "Second Chances," in which Riker is split into two qualitatively identical twins; and *Voyager:* "Tuvix," in which Security Chief Tuvok and ship's cook Neelix, having become fused into one individual, are then separated again. If rematerialization involves only the original matter, then such a doubling is impossible. Either the matter has itself been split and new matter recruited for each "twin," or else one "twin" gets the original matter and the other gets entirely recruited matter, or else both "twins" get entirely recruited matter. Whatever the case, some new matter has been recruited.

This suggests a completely different sort of transporter operation: *information* transport alone. Since we know that the transporter can recruit new matter and impose a pattern on it, why not use just recruited matter? That is, why not just scan the subject, send the information to the destination, and materialize an individual there using new matter. Since you have to send the information required to rematerialize anyway—information needed to produce the appropriate body and psychology—why not send *only* this information? One problem with such a process may already have occurred to you. If there is materialization from new matter at the destination, then isn't the original subject still at home? And even if the scanning process kills the subject painlessly, don't we have to get rid of the body? Yes, of course—perhaps by vaporization. Though this isn't strictly necessary, it is neater, and in line with what we see on *Star Trek*. It even tallies with the existence (unrealistic or not) of vaporizing weapons, seen in both the original series (for example, when the android Andrea vaporizes the android Kirk in "What Are Little Girls Made Of?") and in *The Next Generation* (for instance, when Riker uses his phaser to vaporize the developing clones in "Up the Long Ladder"). Indeed, although a few transporter operations in *Star Trek* seem to require matter recruitment, *every* instance of transporter operation we see in *Star Trek* is consistent with information transport and total matter recruitment. Perhaps what always occurs in dematerialization is conversion into energy, which dissipates, with only the pattern being sent. This also makes a deal of sense out of occurrences like Scotty's Rip Van Winkle turn in *TNG:* "Relics." Scotty is retrieved from the transporter on board the *Jenolan,* seventy-five years after his dematerialization! It's easy to imagine the transporter retaining Scotty's pattern information for seventy-five years, but harder to see how the transporter could keep Scotty's matter-converted-into-energy "on ice" for that length of time.

To crystallize the issues for the remainder of this chapter, we'll keep temporarily to an understanding of information transport that rules out two possibilities (we'll consider them in chapter 5). One is "doubling," à la Kirk and Riker, and the other is the materialization of a subject qualitatively different from the scanned subject, à la Pulaski and the quartet in "Rascals." We shall consider in this chapter only two types of transporter occurrence: *Matter* transport is scanning, dematerialization, transmission of pattern and matter, and rematerialization of the very same matter. *Information* transport is scanning, destruction, transmission of pattern only, and (single) rematerialization using entirely recruited matter. Now we have two separate questions to ask. First, is it rational to undergo *matter* transport on the assumption that you will survive it? Second, is it rational to undergo *information* transport on the assumption that you will survive it?

Admissible Evidence

Imagine that you have an opportunity to undergo teletransport of either type—down to the surface of a safe and pleasant planet, say, for a free vacation. Suppose further that I easily convince you that both processes are reliable, in the technological sense. In order that you can make an informed choice about which process (if either) to use, I offer you hundreds of testimonials, both from rematerialized subjects and their friends and loved ones. First, the rematerialized subjects typically report remembering entering the scanner and then experiencing nothing else until "waking up" at the destination. They report remembering what they had for breakfast that morning; indeed, they might report still feeling the weight of it in their stomachs; they report remembering and intending to carry out the purpose of the journey; and they report the desire to go home to their loved ones. They report remembering a nervous anticipation before the procedure, feeling a nervous relief upon waking up, and so on. Second, in extensive surveys, friends and loved ones without exception report nothing out of the ordinary about the subjects after their rematerialization. So the question for you is, given this information, would you be willing to undergo matter transport? Information transport? Or neither?

Most people I've put these questions to overwhelmingly reject the idea of information transport—almost no one is even tempted by it—and while they are somewhat more amenable to matter transport, only a narrow majority would be willing to undergo it. In practically every case of dissent from information transport, the reason is the same—concern that the scanned subject will not survive the procedure but will instead be replaced by some sort of replica. So it's fair to say that common sense tells you that you cannot rationally expect to survive information transport (indeed, common sense does not regard this as *transport* at all) and is split on whether or not you can rationally expect to survive matter transport. In my role as devil's advocate, I shall argue that common sense is twice mistaken. First, there is no significant difference, where personal survival is concerned, between matter transport and information transport; and, second, given the preceding information, there is no rational cause for pessimism about surviving either process. My first strategy will be negative: I shall attempt to show that these commonsense intuitions about teletransport do not sit well with other commonsense intuitions about personal survival. So I shall be charging common sense with inconsistency, and of special interest is the fact that both sets of commonsense intuitions also show up in the attitudes of *Star Trek* characters.

Near Enough Is Good Enough

Begin with an ordinary case of personal survival. If you are now sitting in a chair reading this book, then we ordinarily suppose that the person who was sitting in that chair ten seconds ago is numerically identical to—one and the same person as—the person sitting in the chair right now. That is, personal survival in the ordinary case involves *personal identity over time*. Indeed, I suggest that the commonsense view of personal survival is nothing more or less than personal identity over time. But what else does ordinary personal survival involve? Both *bodily,* or *physical,* identity over time and *mental,* or *psychological,* identity over time—that is, sameness of body and sameness of mind.

Take bodily identity over time. If this obtains throughout your life, then the body you now have is one and the same body as the one you were born with. But this is absurd, it might be objected. The body you have now is vastly different—much bigger and hairier, and all the wrinkles are in different places! These are just the obvious differences. Science tells us that over a seven-year period all the cells in your body, except for your neurons, are replaced. So your body now has almost nothing in common with your body at birth, or even with your body ten years ago. How can they be identical? The same problem arises for psychological identity. You clearly had a mind at two years of age, but you now have practically none of the mental states you had at two years of age, and at two years of age you had practically none of the mental states you have now. So how can you be psychologically identical to yourself at two years of age?

All this calls into question the commonsense notion that ordinary personal survival involves personal identity over time. If a person is a composite of body and psychology, and if there is no bodily and psychological identity between you now and the infant you, how can there be personal identity between you now and the infant you? One tempting reply is that there is something to a person over and above his or her physical and psychological makeup. Let us call this added extra the *essence* or *soul*. (Talk of "the soul" here can be confusing: in some views, the soul is nothing more than the mind or psychology, while in others it is something separate. I shall take it to mean something separate, unless indicated.) If the soul, unlike the body and the mind, is unchanging over time, then it surely can sustain the identity of the person over time.

Star Trek sometimes encourages this way of looking at personal identity. In *TNG:* "Time Squared," when a duplicate Picard turns up, the empathic Troi declares to the Captain that the duplicate is "just as much Jean-Luc Picard as you are." This suggests that Troi has some empathic way of detecting personal identity. If she was picking up only the duplicate's thoughts or feelings, then she would have reported that the duplicate *thinks or feels* that it is Picard. Her categorical assurance of identity (in chapter 6 we shall examine the possibility that the two Picards *are* identical) is evidence of an ability to detect something else—the essence or soul of Picard.

But we do not need to invoke the soul to explain personal identity—indeed, it is unlikely that existence of a soul really helps anyway, as we shall see later in the chapter. To illustrate how to account for identity in the absence of souls, let's get away from people altogether and focus on ordinary material objects. Suppose you have an old-fashioned watch, similar to that owned by Samuel Clemens in *TNG:* "Time's Arrow I & II," with a movement, a winder, a spring, and so on. One day your watch fails to operate, so you take it to a jeweler, who replaces the spring. Does the fact that your watch now has a different spring lead you to conclude that it's no longer the same watch? Did your watch go out of existence, to be replaced with a new watch? Not at all (indeed, if your original watch no longer exists, then you might well wonder what claim you have on the new one). The identity of ordinary material objects is apparently easily preserved in the course of gradual, small changes. If you later bring your watch back for a new winder, then later for a new flywheel, and so on, after ten years the entire inner workings of the watch may have been replaced. Then suppose that the casing and the glass need replacing. You might end up with a watch composed completely of new parts, yet still feel that you owned the very same watch. Now think of a more abstract entity, your favorite baseball team. Might the Baltimore Orioles and the New York Yankees still exist in the twenty-fourth century, if major league baseball is still being played then? Yes, since over a period of years (a fairly short period, in our era) all the team and managerial personnel may change yet the team is still the very same team. The ship of Theseus was composed of planks that were gradually replaced as they rotted; after many years all the original planks were replaced, but we think of it as the very same ship. Similarly, we can imagine the starship *Enterprise-D* undergoing refit after refit until all its original parts have been replaced, without losing its identity. How can any of this be, if watches and baseball teams and ships and starships have no souls?

The philosopher Robert Nozick has presented a schema for making sense of these judgments about ordinary object identity, which he calls the *closest-continuer schema for numerical identity*. The idea is simple, but it will help if we introduce two notions. The first notion is that of an *object-at-a-time* (or a *time-slice* of an object, or—as I shall say for brevity—an *object-slice*), and the second notion is that of *qualitative similarity*. When we compare two objects—say, *me* with *you*—we should realize that often a temporal component is built in, so that we are really comparing the object-slice *me-now* with the object-slice *you-now*. We could also compare object-slices such as me-ten-years-ago with you-now. And we have already compared the object-slices you-now with you-at-birth. Let's use alphanumeric names to differentiate the slices: we might name the baby born to my parents in 1957 H_1 and me-now H_2, for instance.

The second notion is *qualitative similarity,* which is just a matter of the proportion of properties shared by the objects or object-slices in question. Two "identical" chairs, or "identical" twins, share a great proportion of their properties and so are relatively qualitatively similar. A chair and a human being share relatively few properties and so have little qualitative similarity. As we have established already, H_1 and H_2 likewise are not qualitatively similar, even though we ordinarily judge that H_2 is numerically identical to H_1. I think the best way to explain such a judgment is that it posits a relation between the two object-slices—namely, that they are slices of one and the same object. (Note that ordinary identity judgments usually concern object identity, but we can also make identity judgments concerning object-slice identity. Whereas the object-identity relation holds between H_1 and H_2, the object-slice identity relation does not: H_1 and H_2 are different slices of the same object.)

How do we make judgments of object identity? An object-slice has *causal descendants,* or *continuers,* at later times. So just after your watch has been fitted with a new spring, there are two major continuers of slice W_1, the pre-repair watch. One is W_2, the old spring, and the other is W_3, the operating watch including the new spring. (There will be other very minor continuers, too, such as a tiny metal shaving dislodged from the casing when the jeweler pried it open.) Which of these, if either, is identical to W_1? The first step is to compare the qualitative similarities between W_1 and W_2, and between W_1 and W_3. Since there is a much greater qualitative similarity between the latter pair, W_3 wins out easily as the closest continuer of W_1. This is compatible with our judgment that W_3 is identical to W_1. Similarly, suppose that the *Enterprise-D* has a dilithium crystal replaced. Call the original *Enterprise-D* E_1, the ship with the new crystal E_2, and the old crystal E_3. Clearly E_2 wins the qualitative similarity contest between continuers, and we conclude that there is object identity between E_1 and E_2. Analogously, your favorite baseball team may replace its shortstop—even if he is Cal Ripken—without losing its identity. (It's worth noting that we sometimes speak of individuals having an *identity crisis,* and the Baltimore Orioles may undergo such a crisis if Ripken has to be replaced. When some event causes us to rethink the direction of our lives, we have a feeling of displacement and uncertainty. But the "crisis" occurs because we are unsure of which changes to make, not because we are worried that we have ceased to exist, or will cease to exist. So let's put to one side this nonliteral sense of "identity.")

There's a bit more to the outline of the closest-continuer schema. First, we normally compare all and only the continuers of an object-slice *at a particular time:* we don't normally compare a continuer at one time with a continuer at a different time to see which wins. Second, as we shall see in chapter 5, our judgments seem to require that the closest continuer beat out the others by a significant margin—it must win going away. Third, being easily the closest continuer of some object-slice is not sufficient for identity with it. The closest continuer must also be a *close enough* continuer. Indeed, it would be more accurate to speak of our judgments of numerical identity as employing a closest, close-enough continuer schema. To illustrate, suppose we bring the ship of Theseus into dry dock and it catches fire and burns to the ground. Then the big pile of burnt wood and ashes we are left with is by far the closest continuer of the original ship, but we would nevertheless say that the ship is no longer in existence; the big pile of charcoal and ashes is not identical to it. Similarly, if you believe that when you die you cease to exist, then you must admit that your corpse is by far the closest continuer of you-about-to-die and yet deny that it is a close enough continuer to count as identical to you-about-to-die. The obvious way to make sense of these intuitions is to note that in order to be identical to the precombustion ship of Theseus, the closest continuer must itself be a *ship*-slice. And in order to be identical to you-about-to-die, the closest continuer must be a *person*-slice. Finally (as has been pointed out), it is not a necessary condition of one object-slice being identical to another that they share a high degree of qualitative similarity, or else me-now could not be identical to me-at-birth—that is, H_1 and H_2 could not be identical. So we need to add one more observation to our account. It should be obvious by now that H_1 and H_2, although qualitatively very dissimilar to each other, are nevertheless connected in an interesting way: there is a *causal chain* of other object-slices between them, each of which is the closest continuer of its preceding link. So as long as two object-slices are the same kind of entity (for example, both are person-slices), and as long as they are connected by the right sort of chain (a chain of closest continuers related to each other by a high degree of qualitative similarity), then the closest-continuer relation is preserved. This would be so even if science made the remarkable discovery that we recycle all our cells over a seven-second period instead of a seven-year period.

We now have a convenient way of expressing necessary and sufficient conditions of bodily, mental, and personal identity. Body-slice B_2 is identical to body-slice B_1 if and only if B_2 is the closest continuer of B_1; mind-slice M_2 is identical to mind-slice M_1 if and only if M_2 is the closest continuer of M_1; and person-slice P_2 is identical to person-slice P_1 if and only if P_2 is the closest continuer of P_1. So to repeat an earlier observation, ordinary personal survival involves not only personal identity over time but also bodily and psychological identity over time, and we are in the happy position of being able to make sense of this claim.

The next question to ask is, *What does personal identity over time consist in?* Is personal identity over time a matter of bodily identity over time, or psychological identity over time, or both in combination, or neither (that is, soul identity instead)? The commonsense notion that matter transport is less objectionable than information transport suggests that bodily identity over time matters a great deal. If this is true, then there is a strong analogy between people and ordinary objects. Consider Sam Clemens's watch again. Clearly the watch can survive dismantling and reassembly—indeed, sometimes it might be advisable to dismantle an object in order to send it somewhere. But suppose that instead of dismantling the watch, Lieutenant Worf vaporizes it with his phaser, then uses a replicator to produce a qualitatively identical watch. This watch is not a continuer of the original at all, is it? It is a mere replica of the original watch—a numerically distinct, though very similar, watch. This analogy suggests that *matter matters* to personal identity.

Let us put this intuition to the test by considering a series of forced-choice situations, based on body-part replacement procedures that occur in *Star Trek*. To remove irrelevancies, suppose that in each case the patient can afford the procedure (thanks to Starfleet's excellent medical plan) and that it is relatively painless and convenient. In addition, in each case of replacement the procedure is reliable, in the sense that the operation has a very high degree of technical success. Next, in order that you can make an informed judgment, there are hundreds of testimonials not only from postoperative subjects but also from their friends and loved ones. First, the postoperative subjects typically report remembering everything up until administration of anesthesia, and the next thing they remember is "waking up" after the operation. They report remembering not having had breakfast that morning, they report remembering their prior intentions, they mean to carry out those intentions, and they report the desire to go home to their loved ones. They report remembering a nervous anticipation before the procedure and feeling a nervous relief upon waking up, and so on. Second, in extensive surveys friends and loved ones without exception report nothing out of the ordinary in the postoperative subject. So the question for you is, given this information, which procedure if any is it rational to choose to undergo in each of the following cases?

> "I *am* Roger Korby!"
>
> —*The android Korby, to Kirk, "What Are Little Girls Made Of?"*

Four *Star Trek* storylines will help us set up the forced choices. In *TNG:* "Samaritan Snare," and later in "Tapestry," we learn that as a young graduate of Starfleet Academy Jean-Luc Picard got into a fight with three Nausicaans which ended in his being stabbed through the heart, and that he received an artificial heart implant. Clearly, replacing his damaged heart with a functioning artificial one was a good thing, and probably what Picard would have wanted under the circumstances (no doubt he was unconscious and someone else had to decide for him). If you were faced with the choice of certain death or life with an artificial implant that does exactly the same job exactly as well as the natural organ, wouldn't you choose to have the implant?

In *DS9:* "Life Support," Vedek Bareil has a more general organ failure; his condition requires treatment that progressively destroys his major organs, and most or all of them need to be replaced with artificial ones. Once again, each time the choice of replacement is presented, *surely* the implant is the way to go if the choice is between certain death and continued life at the same functional level. While it might make sense in the late twentieth century to call a halt to implant procedures after a time and accept death, this is precisely because of the pain, inconvenience, and unreliability of such procedures. In the twenty-fourth century, these considerations don't enter into the decision, so the rational thing to do is proceed with the implants even if it means ending up with a largely artificial body.

So far, these considerations are consistent with the *matter matters* view, since according to the closest-continuer schema for bodily identity, such partial (and gradual) replacements preserve bodily identity. Let's take them a step further. Suppose that instead of progressive organ failure, Bareil suffers simultaneous organ failure—of all major organs but the brain. Doesn't it nevertheless make sense to do the wholesale implant procedure? Once this is done, there will be two significant continuers of the preoperative Bareil body: first is the body consisting of the original brain, a few other original parts, and the major organ implants; second is the large pile of discarded organs. But only one of these is a *body,* so bodily identity plausibly is retained by the implant procedure.

Let's take it another step: in the event of simultaneous failure of all major organs except the brain, why not just transplant the healthy brain into an artificial body? (Or the brain and central nervous system, if you like.) We now discern two different versions of the *matter matters* view. First is the *body matters* view, according to which personal identity requires bodily identity (where the body includes the brain). Since in the brain-transplant case Bareil's brainless discarded body is the better candidate for closest continuer than Bareil's brain, and since the brainless body is not a candidate for personhood, then according to the *body matters* view Bareil ceases to exist after the brain transplant. The alternative is the *brain matters* view, according to which personal identity depends on brain identity. According to this view, the brain transplant (assuming it takes) does preserve personal identity: Bareil goes where his brain goes.

Let's take yet another step. In "Life Support," when Bareil's organ deterioration spreads to his brain, Dr. Bashir considers replacing certain of Bareil's brain components with "positronic implants." (Assume for the sake of the argument that these implants are exactly functionally equivalent to the original brain components.) If the choice at each stage of brain deterioration is between certain death and continued life at the same functional level, then aren't the artificial implants the way to go? Suppose Bashir does the procedure in stages, each time replacing less than 10 percent of Bareil's brain. Approving of this procedure is consistent with the *brain matters* view, since in the closest-continuer schema the individual with the positronic implants will, at each stage, be a closer continuer than the discarded brain component. But in the episode Bashir performs a half-brain replacement, a procedure that surely requires some temporary storage of Bareil's psychological information, so he might just as well have performed an entire brain replacement. According to the *brain matters* view, in neither of these cases (half-brain replacement or total-brain replacement) does the resulting individual contain the closest continuer of Bareil's pre-op brain, and therefore that individual is not Bareil.

Bashir seems to hold some version of the *brain matters* view, as we noted in chapter 2. He readily performs the organ transplants but balks at brain replacement, fearing the loss of Bareil's "spark of life," which "can't be replicated." Major Kira Nerys argues on behalf of the unconscious Bareil that he would want the positronic implants, and Bashir replies, "Kira, if I go through with this, the man who wakes up may not be the man you used to know." He refuses to continue with the implants after the half-brain replacement, saying, "I won't remove whatever last shred of humanity Bareil has left. . . . If I remove the rest of his brain and replace it with a machine, he may look like Bareil, he may even talk like Bareil, but he won't *be* Bareil. That spark of life will be gone. He'll be dead, and I'll be the one who killed him." If he doesn't operate, Bareil will die, too—"But he'll die like a man, not a *machine!*"

Bashir's comments are difficult to interpret. Is he claiming that the walking, talking postoperative individual will be a zombie, of the sort discussed in chapter 3? Since he refers to the postoperative subject as "the man who wakes up," he appears to believe that it will be a minded individual and a strong candidate for personhood, with or without Bareil's "spark of life." So Bashir might accept some form of the *functionalism* about minds and mental states discussed in chapters 2 and 3. Bashir's concern, then, is that the result of the implant procedure will be a *new* person, numerically distinct from Bareil.

Let's take things yet one step further. In "What Are Little Girls Made Of?" Nurse Christine Chapel's fiancé, the archeologist Dr. Roger Korby, has been missing for five years when Starfleet receives a message from Exo III, apparently from Korby himself. The *Enterprise* is sent to investigate, and Kirk and Nurse Chapel beam down to the planet (accompanied by two unnamed, and therefore obviously doomed, security officers) to meet Korby, who seems none the worse for wear. When he suffers an injury, they discover that "Korby" is an android. The android explains that the original Dr. Korby stumbled upon the ruins of an ancient, technologically advanced culture, whose rulers produced androids as servants. One of these androids, named Ruk, was still around and functioning, and Ruk became Korby's servant. In the course of his archeological studies, Korby was felled by an unexplained fatal condition. His only option was to allow Ruk to transfer his psychology into an android body. "You can't imagine how it was," he tells Nurse Chapel. "I was frozen, dying—my legs were gone. I had only my brain between life and death." Seeing the doubt on her face, he pleads, "I'm still the same as I was before, Christine, perhaps even better." If Chapel is ambivalent, Kirk's attitude to this news is obvious enough. When Spock inquires after Korby, Kirk says, "Dr. Korby was never here," meaning that Korby died long before the landing party arrived. In Kirk's view, Korby failed to survive the replication procedure.

Exactly what process did Roger Korby undergo with Ruk's assistance? In the same episode, an android replica of an unwilling Kirk is constructed by duplicating Kirk's body, and Kirk's psychology is then copied into it; so we may presume that Korby, too, was physically duplicated and then his psychology was copied into the android body. This process was followed immmediately by Korby's bodily death; importantly, Korby's brain died along with his body. Note that the procedure Korby submitted to is the ultimate logical extension of the procedure Bashir performed upon Vedek Bareil. We have already imagined a brain transplant into an artificial brainless body and a wholesale brain replacement with artificial components. If we put these two procedures together, the result is equivalent to the procedure Ruk performed on Korby.

Know Thyself. . . . Not!

"It's still *me*, Christine—Roger! I'm in here!"
—*The android Korby to Nurse Chapel, "What Are Little Girls Made Of?"*

If either of the *matter matters* views is correct, then it's possible to be absolutely convinced of who you are and be completely wrong. Not only is the android Korby wrong about really being Roger Korby, but Bashir's comments suggest that the walking, talking individual that results from a total brain replacement will think that it's Bareil but will be wrong. So we should not fall into the trap of supposing that if anyone knows who an individual is, it's the individual itself. The possibility of such error is beautifully illustrated in the following *Star Trek* episodes.

In *TNG:* "Inheritance," Data is surprised and pleased to discover that visiting scientist Dr. Juliana Tainer is the former wife of his creator, Dr. Noonian Soong, and has lots of information on Data's creation and early "childhood." As the days go by, Data notices some unusual things about his "mother," and his suspicions are confirmed when she has an accident—her unconscious body is obviously that of an android. Data accesses a holographic program in her positronic brain—a program planted there by Dr. Soong—which explains that when his wife was fatally injured and comatose, he constructed an android body and transferred her psychology into it, never telling the awakened "Juliana." So Dr. Tainer is an android but doesn't know it! Moreover, it is an android that thinks it is the former wife of Dr. Soong, but if the *matter matters* view is correct, this cannot be true. Data decides not to tell "Juliana" the truth, either.

This reprises an idea from *TNG:* "The Survivors," in which the *Enterprise-D* encounters a planet devoid of life, except for one elderly couple, Mr. and Mrs. Kevin Uxbridge. The couple explains that their planet was attacked by a species known as the Husnak, who wiped out the entire population except for themselves. In fact, Kevin Uxbridge was the only survivor of that attack; he is an eternal and omnipotent "douwd," who came to live among mortals when he fell in love with one of them. After the Husnak attack, Kevin "re-created" his wife (what required technology in the case of Korby and Juliana, Kevin did simply by thinking), never telling "Mrs. Uxbridge" what he had done. Picard does tell her, however, in no uncertain terms: "I can touch you. I can hear your voice. I can smell your perfume. In every respect you are a real person, with your own mind and beliefs. But you do not exist. You died along with the other members of the colony." Taken literally, Picard's utterance is incoherent, so I take it that he means that Kevin's wife is no more, and that the person in front of him is another person altogether, who came into being only when Kevin "thought" her into being. Once again, if the *matter matters* view is correct (or if Picard is correct), this person is mistaken about who she is.

Finally, in *DS9:* "Whispers," Chief Miles O'Brien returns to the station to find everyone acting strangely. His experience is like a paranoid fantasy in which familiar people have been snatched away and replaced by hostile replicas. The twist in the episode—a really superb idea—is that in fact *he* is the imposter, a clone of the real O'Brien, sent by the evil Dominion, who have kidnapped the real McCoy—oops, the real O'Brien. The point, of course—a point often made in soap opera plots—is that anyone programmed or otherwise provided with fake memories of your past will assume that these are genuine memories and will identify with you.

Mind Over Matter

KIRK-BODY PERSON: "As I understand it, you claim to be Captain Kirk?"
LESTER-BODY PERSON: "I am not Captain Kirk. That is very apparent. What I said is, Whatever it is that makes Captain Kirk a living being special to himself is being held in this body."
—TOS: *"Turnabout Intruder"*

In "Turnabout Intruder," Dr. Janice Lester precipitates an unusual swap with Kirk when an ancient device takes Lester's "essence" and places it in Kirk's body, simultaneously taking Kirk's essence and placing it in Lester's body (see the following diagram). Although McCoy can find no medical evidence that any such transfer has occurred, the *Enterprise* crew becomes first suspicious and finally convinced of it. Why? Because of the behavior of the pair—in particular, the behavior of the Kirk-body person (below left in the diagram), culminating in the order to execute the senior officers. The crew concludes that the Kirk-body person really is Lester and the Lester-body person really is Kirk. Now consider how things must have been for the Lester-body person (below right in the diagram). This person would have "woken up" in Lester's body, but with all the memories and other psychological characteristics of James T. Kirk. If you woke up in this state (and didn't go immediately insane), wouldn't you conclude that you really were James T. Kirk, inexplicably transferred into Lester's body? In the epigraph, the Lester-body person admits that appearances are otherwise but claims that whatever makes Kirk *Kirk* nevertheless is present. And clearly the Kirk-body person believes herself to be Lester.

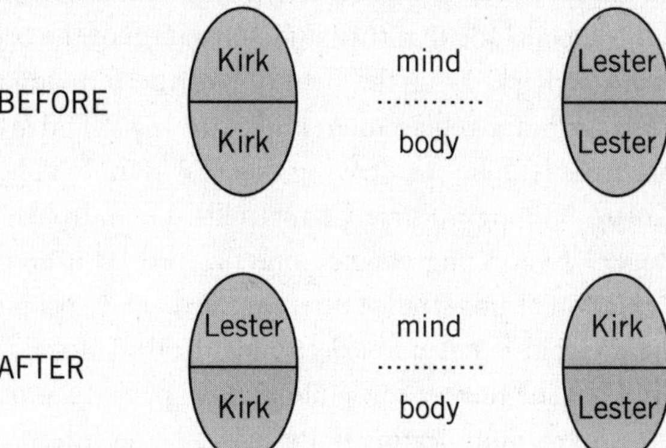

If either of the *matter matters* views is correct, then the conclusion reached by everyone concerned—the subjects of the procedure *and* the *Enterprise* crew—is wrong! Since the original Kirk's body and brain continue in the Kirk-body person, then according to the *matter matters* view, that person is Kirk (and the Lester-body person is Lester). But I trust you find this conclusion implausible. Leaving aside all talk of "essences," the transfer clearly involves the transfer of psychologies (for our purposes, "mind" and "psychology" are synonymous). From years of random informal surveys of people in the street, I've discovered that the commonsense reaction to this process is to describe it not as people swapping psychologies but as people swapping bodies (and brains). Common sense tells you in this case that Kirk goes where his psychology goes, which we shall call the *mind matters* view.

But if Kirk goes where his psychology goes, then surely so do Vedek Bareil and Roger Korby. Common sense can't have it both ways, and neither can *Star Trek*. But which way should common sense jump? The major difference between the case of the Lester-body person and the cases of Bareil and Korby is what the bodies are made of. But we have already seen in chapter 3 that there is no principled reason for denying that a machine body—of silicon and metal, say—can sustain a psychology. And in all cases the evidence for the presence of the original subject is the same—namely, the behavior of the postprocedure subject. In the case of the Lester-body person, we conclude that the best explanation of the behavior is that it *really is* Kirk. So if the behavior of the individual who emerges from the brain-replacement procedure *walks* and *talks* like Bareil, what basis is there for denying that it *is* Bareil? (The same goes for Korby, although Nurse Chapel tells the android, "Don't you see, Roger? Everything you've done has proved it *isn't* you!" One interpretation of this strange utterance is that Chapel is claiming that the android is not numerically identical to Roger Korby, but if this is what she means, she couldn't have picked a more confusing manner of communicating it. Perhaps a better interpretation is that Chapel is claiming that Roger Korby has *changed,* and for the worse.)

Application of the closest-continuer schema for identity supports these judgments, when we plug into that schema a particular weighting. I suggest that common sense applies the closest-continuer schema, and values both mind and matter, but values mind *over* matter. Consider "Turnabout Intruder." Kirk has two significant continuers after the swap—the Kirk-body person and the Lester-body person. The former's body, including the brain, is identical to the pre-swap Kirk's body, and the latter's psychology is identical to the pre-swap Kirk's psychology, so the judgment that the latter is Kirk places greater weight on psychological identity. (Note that we apply the closest-continuer schema to psychological identity in just the same way as to bodily identity: the mind of the Lester-body person is the closest continuer of the pre-swap Kirk's mind and is therefore identical to it.) In the case of Bareil, there is only one serious candidate for the continuer of Bareil's psychology, and that is a very strong candidate—the mind of the walking, talking individual that results from the brain-replacement procedure. Since psychological identity is preserved through the procedure, then so is personal identity. (Indeed, since Bareil's discarded brain parts do not themselves support any psychology, a personal-identity judgment seems even more secure in Bareil's case than in the case of the Lester-body person.) As for Roger Korby, even if he has two significant continuers after the procedure—one a dead body and the other an android—the android's mind is the closest continuer of his mind and is therefore identical to it. Hence the android *is* Korby. (Once again, this judgment is even more secure than in the case of the Lester-body person.) Or so consistency of commonsense judgment demands. And if this is so, then the Juliana android in "Inheritance" really is Dr. Soong's former wife after all. As the holographic program implanted in her brain by Dr. Soong tells Data, "The truth is, in every way that matters, she *is* Juliana Soong."

There is no principled difference between the procedure that Roger Korby underwent, the procedure that Juliana Soong underwent, and information transport. Just as Korby's (and Juliana's) physical and psychological patterns are imposed on an android body, in information transport the subject's physical and psychological patterns are imposed on recruited matter. And in both cases the original body is destroyed. Applying the *mind over matter* closest-continuer schema yields the result that the materialized subject of information transport is not a mere replica but is identical to the dematerialized subject. What about matter transport? If we grant that there is bodily identity between the dematerialized subject and the rematerialized subject, then there is no principled difference between matter transport and ordinary, day-to-day survival.

Life After Death

Thus far I have urged that common sense ought to embrace consistency by broadening its conception of the possibilities for personal survival. It is my anecdotal impression that the people most resistant to this idea—and so most resistant to the idea of either matter transport or information transport—are those people (particularly of Christian persuasion) who believe that death is not the end of them. That is, for them death doesn't involve the loss of personal identity. Deeper questioning reveals that usually they do not think death involves the loss of psychological identity, either; that is, one survives death with all of one's memories, intentions, desires, and so forth more or less intact. Indeed, since death usually involves no loss of bodily identity either—unless one dies by cremation or vaporization, the body persists through death (how much longer it lasts is another matter altogether)—in the standard Christian view death does not usually involve the nonpersistence of anything at all. The best way to understand this view of death is as the *separation* of the person and psychology from the body. The point to note is that, once again, bodily (or brain) identity isn't what matters primarily to personal identity.

But exactly what happens when you are separated from your body? There are two basic alternatives. One is that your mind persists *disembodied* (sometimes called the Platonic view). This existence is quite hard to imagine, and insofar as I can imagine it, doesn't seem particularly desirable. Perhaps an analogy is that your psychology is downloaded onto a computer disk and stored permanently. The problem with this sort of continued existence is that it is difficult to see how one can be involved in any activity at all if one is disembodied. (Note that I am not suggesting that one has to have a *terrestrial* body to be active—perhaps there are immaterial or otherwise heavenly bodies that do the job—nor am I suggesting that one has to have hands, or even eyes. But one has to have *something* that allows interaction with whatever world one is in.) Let's put this problem to one side, because in St. Paul's view—adopted by the early church, and so arguably the real Christian view—after a Christian dies his mind is *re*embodied:

> If there is a physical body, there is also a spiritual one. . . . And just as we have borne the image of the one made of dust, we shall bear also the image of the heavenly one. (1 Corinthians 15: 44–49)

If you hold some version of St. Paul's reembodiment view, then you presumably hold that by some process or other God engineers it so that your psychology is extracted from your present body and persists in a completely different one elsewhere.

The point of this is, of course, that the standard Christian view of the survival of bodily death is equivalent both to the Korby procedure and to information transport (though God's version is a lot messier than information transport, since He leaves putrefying bodies all over the place). It is even equivalent to Kevin Uxbridge's "rethinking" of his dead wife. Once again, an outright rejection of information transport does not sit comfortably with the deep conviction that one will survive bodily death by just such a process. Note also that only in the case of information transport is there the added assurance of (uncontroversial) testimonials from those on "the other side."

By the way, some Christians apparently believe that God will resurrect them in heaven (all going well, of course) by rematerializing their actual terrestrial bodies. One difficult issue here is that since your body over your lifetime is a succession of body-slices, each composed of different stuff, whether or not it is your body when God resurrects it depends on which body-slice he picks to "restore." If you die at age seventy of heart failure, and God "restores" a much healthier body—say, that of you-on-your-twentieth-birthday—then that body will probably not count as the closest continuer of your body at death. If the resurrected person is to be you, God ought to resurrect the body-slice that you died with, in a process equivalent to matter transport. This seems a less than optimal arrangement in most cases.

The second difficulty has often been remarked on: too much of the matter that goes into a person's body is recycled. Some of the matter in your body used to be a part of someone's else's body, and maybe part of someone else again before that. So it seems that even if God did the fairest job He could in sharing it around, everyone is going to have some stuff missing come resurrection. Hence either form of resurrection necessarily involves the recruitment of new matter.

This adds further weight to the claim that it is commonsensical to choose to undergo information transport in the expectation of surviving it; but is it rational? Ought we to accept that the correct closest-continuer schema places mind over matter? The *mind over matter* closest-continuer view sits nicely with the functionalist view of the mind. Functionalism allows for multiple realizability of mental states; hence a qualitatively identical mind can in principle be realized in at least two different ways—in brain and in silicon—and so perhaps even in a "heavenly" body. The *mind over matter* view holds that it is causal continuity of (enough of) these states—in whatever way they are realized—which constitutes the survival of the person. But now we turn to three objections to this view—objections that might cause us to rethink the modes of transport.

The Principle of Independence

Some philosophers reject the *mind over matter* closest-continuer schema for personal identity, embracing instead what I shall call the *principle of independence*. Before stating the principle, let's try to get a feel for it by considering again "What Are Little Girls Made Of?" I mentioned that Roger Korby was not the only person to be replicated in android form, since the same thing happened to Kirk. However, there is a difference—in Kirk's case, the old body and brain were not destroyed. That is, Kirk has *two* continuers, each of whom is qualitatively identical to the pre-op Kirk. The following diagram illustrates this.

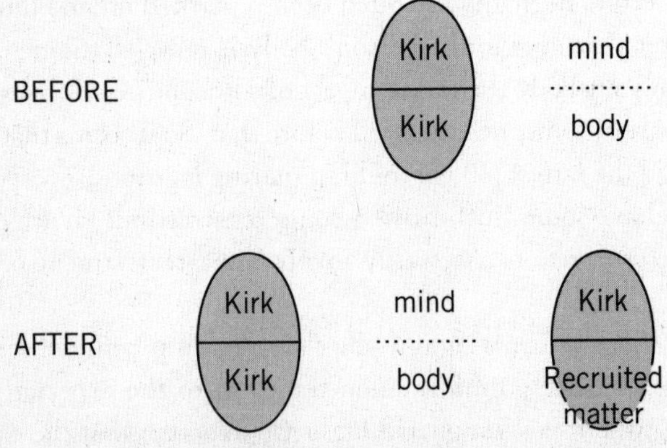

The Kirk-body person (lower left in the diagram) is, we intuitively decide, the real Kirk, while the android (lower right in the diagram) is, we intuitively decide, a mere replica. This once again is in line with the closest-continuer schema for personal identity, since although the android's mind is a close continuer of the mind of the pre-op Kirk, its body is not a close continuer of the pre-op Kirk's body. The mind of the Kirk-body person, on the other hand, is a close continuer of the pre-op Kirk's mind, and the Kirk-body person also has the pre-op Kirk's body. Hence it wins the competition for closest continuer.

However, the only difference between the case of the Kirk android and the case of the Korby android is the persistence of the original. So if the Korby android really is Korby, that means that *if* Kirk's original body and brain had been destroyed, then the Kirk android *would have been* the real Kirk! This contingency seems absurd to some philosophers, who accordingly hold the *principle of independence*—namely, that whether identity holds between person-slice A and person-slice B cannot depend upon facts about other individuals, possible or actual. My response is in two parts. First of all, there are times in philosophy when basic intuitions conflict; for my part, I do not find any intuitive appeal in the principle of independence, so in the absence of any positive argument for the principle, I see no reason to embrace it.

My second response is more substantive. If one embraces the principle, then there seem to be two alternatives. One is to return to the *matter matters* view, which would mean that information transport is not transport at all. However, we have already seen that holding this view requires counterintuitive judgments in the Kirk/Lester case. Not only that, but if the principle of independence is to prevail, then one must adopt a *matter-majority matters* closest-continuer schema. If no facts about other individuals, possible or actual, can count in an identity judgment, then more than 50 percent of one's body must be retained for personal identity (or, in the *brain matters* view, more than 50 percent of one's brain). However, recall the way the objection began: it is supposed to be absurd that the Kirk android *would have been* Kirk had the Kirk-body person been destroyed. Now suppose one adopts the *brain-majority matters* view. Then in a case where only 49 percent of Vedek Bareil's brain is retained (and there is no other close continuer), one must admit that the result isn't Bareil but *would have been* Bareil if it had received 2 percent more brain. This seems no less absurd.

Indeed, if one is to embrace the principle of independence, then one ought to reject the closest-continuer schema altogether, deny that personal identity is dependent on either bodily or psychological identity, and hold instead that it depends on an essence or soul. After all, it may seem to some readers that I have really missed the point of the Christian story of resurrection by focusing on psychological identity as the bearer of *personhood*. It might be objected that God doesn't just take your psychology and plant it in a new body—God takes your *soul* and plants that *and* your psychology in your new body. And that, it might be claimed, is what makes all the difference between a heavenly resurrection and mere replication. Seductive though this idea is, it is of no avail in accounting for personal identity.

Let us be clear on what the present suggestion amounts to by returning to ordinary, day-to-day survival, which according to the *soul* view involves not only bodily and psychological identity but also identity of soul. Moreover, according to the present suggestion it is soul identity that really matters in personal survival, since that is what personal identity really consists in. The interesting thing about this suggestion is that it regards personal identity and psychological identity as in principle separable: not only might personal identity persist in the absence of psychological identity but psychological identity might persist in the absence of personal identity. Many non-Christian religions have embraced the former possibility; it seems an assumption behind the standard doctrine of reincarnation, for instance. When one is reincarnated, it is without one's memories and experiences from the previous life, so that one has to "start all over again." The curiosities of this doctrine aside, as soon as we consider the converse possibility—of psychological identity (and bodily identity) in the absence of personal identity—an intractable epistemological problem arises.

The problem is that *if the soul view is correct, then psychological identity and bodily identity over time are no guide to personal identity over time*. Let us grant that you have a soul, in addition to and independent of a body and a mind. Let us grant further that personal identity is soul identity. Now call the person-slice born to your parents Y_1 and the person-slice reading this book right now Y_2. Exactly what reason can anyone offer for thinking that Y_2 is identical to Y_1? By hypothesis, soul identity over time is distinct from bodily or psychological identity over time, so one cannot appeal to these to demonstrate soul identity. But what other evidence is there, in the absence of some supra-ESP abilities? (ESP wouldn't help, since it would detect only psychological states.) It is perfectly consistent with "your" experience that God has recycled a whole heap of souls through the mind and body that have persisted as "you" ever since the arrival of Y_1. That is, what we thought to be "you" might have been a succession of hundreds of thousands of different tenant souls. How can we tell? How can Y_2 tell? We have already seen that one cannot reliably introspect one's identity (a point that will be reinforced in chapter 5). All in all, since neither the *matter matters* view nor the *soul* view is very promising, this leaves the *mind over matter* view as the most plausible.

Data's Objection

But couldn't one hold the *mind over matter* view and still object to the claim that it's possible to survive either matter or information transport? Such a position is suggested by Data's exchange with Commander Maddox in "The Measure of a Man," when Maddox is trying to convince Data to undergo the disassembly procedure so that he can study Data's construction (see chapters 2 and 3).

MADDOX: "I thought we could talk this out, that I could persuade you. Your memories and knowledge will remain intact."

DATA: "Reduced to the mere facts of the events. The substance, the flavor of the moment could be lost. Take games of chance. . . . I had read and absorbed every treatise and textbook on the subject and found myself well prepared for the experience. Yet, when I finally *played* poker, I discovered that the reality bore little resemblance to the rules."

MADDOX: "And the point being?"

DATA: "That while I believe it is possible to download information contained in a positronic brain, I do not believe that you have acquired the expertise necessary to preserve the *essence* of these experiences. There is an ineffable quality to memory which I do not believe can survive your procedure."

Data's objection to Maddox's procedure can be adapted to argue against the prospect of surviving teletransport. Since the transporter must "download" the information in the subject's brain, there is the chance of the "substance," the "flavor," the "essence," or some other ineffable quality of the person's experiences being lost, and the person with it.

Data's objection bears a startling similarity to a common philosophical objection to the mental-state functionalism I outlined in chapter 2 and endorsed in chapter 3. The basic intuition behind the objection is that functionalism (and any other materialist view, for that matter) is incomplete because it *cannot account for the first-person subjective point of view*. According to this objection, a functionalist account of the mind will, like any scientific theory, be completely constituted by objective propositions. But some parts of qualitative experience seemingly cannot be captured by third-person descriptions. The philosopher Frank Jackson asks us to imagine Mary, who is an expert neuroscientist—so expert that she knows absolutely everything there is to know about the operation of the brain. That is, she has a *complete* scientific theory of the mind. But Mary has lived all her life in a black-and-white environment. Although Mary knows all that science can tell her about the experience of seeing red, it seems that when she steps outside the lab and beholds a ripe tomato she will learn something new—now she will know *what red looks like*. Since this is a piece of knowledge that she did not have before, then no matter how complete our scientific knowledge of the brain and its operation, there will always be aspects of mentality beyond its reach. That this is the sort of objection Data has in mind is reinforced by the analogy with poker; Data's claim is that no matter how much you study the rules of the game, you can never learn all there is to know except by the subjective experience of playing.

Can we reply to this sort of objection? Notice first that the poker example is overstated. Data is referring to an incident in which he is completely fooled in a poker game by Riker's bluff. Data appears not to know that bluffing is a valuable tactic, but how can he have failed to learn this much from his comprehensive reading about the game? And if there are things that Data did not know beforehand, his expertise was less than complete. Moreover, even if Data really did know every *proposition* there was to know about poker, he may have been lacking some *nonpropositional* knowledge, some ability or know-how that one acquires only through experience. In Mary's case, we must first ensure that Mary really does acquire new knowledge when she first beholds a tomato: we need a convincing argument that she would not have this knowledge no matter how much she knew about brain function. And second, if it really is new knowledge, it might be nonpropositional knowledge, perhaps a new ability that she previously did not possess, such as the ability to recognize red things.

In the case of either matter transport or information transport, then, there is as yet no reason to think that the rematerialized subject, if functionally identical to the dematerialized subject, will lack something that the dematerialized subject had. But another of the objections to functionalism is also relevant here. In chapter 3 I concluded that there is no reason to think that an artificial entity cannot experience the *phenomenal* aspect of sensation and emotion. But I left it open as to whether or not this phenomenal aspect might differ from one person to another, or between organic and artificial physical realizations of intelligence. This also leaves open the possibility that transferring a person's psychology into a different medium will change the phenomenal character of experience. Strikingly, this seems to tally with what Vedek Bareil reports in "Life Support" after receiving his half-brain implant.

KIRA: "How are you feeling?"
BAREIL: "Awake. Everything is—different."
KIRA: "Different? In what way?"
BAREIL: "It's hard to explain. But when you touch me, it doesn't seem real. It's more like the—distant memory of a touch."

As I mentioned in chapter 3, whether or not this qualitative change in experience is a real possibility when the new realization is functionally identical is a matter of philosophical controversy. But it doesn't matter to the present argument, since we could recognize the possibility without its causing any great threat to the view that we can survive the loss of our bodies. After all, if qualitative experience can differ between organic bodies, then your present qualitative experience of seeing red might differ somewhat from the qualitative experience of seeing red which you had when you were six years old. Hence there can be no rational objection to survival of either matter transport or information transport because of such a possibility—because of qualms like those Data expressed. But perhaps we can trace Data's trepidation to something else entirely, and find a further objection to one or the other mode of transport.

The Exclusion Principle

I suspect that many people, including the writers of *Star Trek,* embrace what I call the *exclusion principle*—the view that if we humans invent some process and can manipulate it reliably then there can be nothing unknown going on when that process occurs, whereas, for all we know, anything might be going on in processes we aren't responsible for. Consider the evidence. We commonly accept the possibility of a body swap by Kirk and Lester in "Turnabout Intruder," yet we commonly deny the possibility of a gradual body and brain replacement for Vedek Bareil in "Life Support." The difference? The former is achieved in some mysterious fashion by a device built by some superior race, while the latter is just the application of human technology. Consider also the two basic reactions to Data. On the one hand, a large part of the reluctance to accept Data as a person can be traced to the fact that he was designed and built by a human. On the other hand, the general lack of understanding of how Data works promotes an aura of mystery that borders on the mystical. If the exclusion principle is widely believed, it might explain why many people are inclined to believe that information transport works when God does it, but not when humans do it.

It is not only "people in the street" who are tempted by the exclusion principle. In the otherwise excellent *The Physics of Star Trek,* Lawrence Krauss writes that the teletransport idea of re-creating a "functionally identical person"

> flies in the face of a great deal of spiritual belief about the existence of a "soul" that is somehow distinct from one's body. What happens when you die, after all? Don't many religions hold that the "soul" can exist after death? What then happens to the soul during the transport process? In this sense, the transporter would be a wonderful experiment in spirituality. If a person were beamed aboard the *Enterprise* and remained intact and observably unchanged, it would provide dramatic evidence that a human being is no more than the sum of his or her parts, and the demonstration would directly confront a wealth of spiritual beliefs.

Krauss makes an understandable mistake here. We have already seen that there is a striking parallel between the hypothetical process of information transport and the typically alleged manner of spiritual survival of bodily death, and between matter transport and a somewhat less popular eschatological view. It seems that consistent expecters of survival after death ought to welcome the idea of teletransport, for it does not "fly in the face" of their beliefs at all. Krauss's tendency to think otherwise suggests that he accepts the exclusion principle. His proposal that one could use the transporter to test spiritual beliefs might strike you as a healthy application of the scientific method to the problem of personal survival, especially compared with the philosophical method we have been pursuing—in which we do these experiments purely in the imagination, plumbing our intuitions and appealing to consistency. But while I understand the desire for a more reliable method, and the temptation to look for a "crucial experiment" in spirituality, the fact is that success in transporter operation would add *no new evidence at all* against spiritual views of any sort!

We shall split spiritual views—"belief about the existence of a soul that is somehow distinct from one's body"—into two types, recalling that talk of the "soul" is ambiguous. In the first view, the soul is identical to the mind, and soul identity over time is just psychological identity over time. Confronted with a working transporter, what will the spiritualist of this stripe say? One of two things. Either he will claim that there is no psychological identity with the pre-teletransported subject (perhaps on the ground that the subject is dead, that his real psychology is elsewhere, and that this is a mere copy; or perhaps that the materialized subject is a zombie, with no mind at all), in which case he will simply deny that the original soul is present. Or he will acknowledge that the evidence is that the original person has survived, on the ground that the materialized subject manifests the very same psychology—which is to say, has the very same soul.

On the other hand, suppose that by "soul" is meant something separable from both body and mind (this is the view Krauss is targeting, I'm sure). Confronted with a working transporter, what will the holder of this *soul* view say? One of two things. Either he will claim that there is no soul identity with the pre-teletransported subject (perhaps on the ground that the subject is dead, his soul is elsewhere, and that this is a mere copy; or perhaps that the process has indeed preserved psychological identity but lost soul identity; or perhaps that the materialized subject has no soul at all), in which case he will simply deny that the original soul is present. Or he will acknowledge that the original person has indeed survived (by some unknown supernatural process), on the ground that the materialized subject manifests the very same psychology, in which case there is no more evidential reason to deny soul identity than in the case of ordinary, day-to-day survival.

Krauss's attraction to the exclusion principle is understandable, because it is only subtly different from a solid methodological principle known as Ockham's Razor: *Do not multiply entities beyond necessity*. In its most defensible form, the Razor tells us that when confronted by some phenomenon, other things being equal we should prefer the explanation that posits the fewest types of entity. If we accept the Razor, as I am sure Krauss does, then it follows that if we invent some process and can manipulate it reliably there *probably* is nothing unknown going on when that process occurs. Moreover, it follows also that Krauss is right that successful transport indeed is evidence against the existence of a nonmaterial soul that is essential to persons. But no consistent thinker should be converted from spiritualism to materialism by such evidence, for the Razor is perfectly general, applying equally to those processes we are not responsible for. If some process occurs, and we can explain and predict it reliably using only naturalistic postulations (or just as reliably as we can using supernaturalistic postulations), then the Razor rules that there probably is nothing supernatural going on when that process occurs. The point is that if Krauss's argument works in the survival-by-transport case, it works *just as well* in the case of ordinary survival, given our present knowledge of that process. Anyone who ought to give up spiritualist beliefs when confronted with a working transporter has equally compelling grounds for giving up spiritualist beliefs when confronted with ordinary human existence. (On the flip side of the coin, if there are no compelling reasons to give up spiritualist beliefs in the face of ordinary human existence, then there are no compelling reasons to give them up when confronted by a working transporter.) So there is no reason at all to expect a recalcitrant spiritualist to be converted by apprehension of the transporter: he will invoke the very same mysteries to explain what has occurred as he does to explain what ordinarily occurs! As should be obvious by now, I think that the exclusion principle is utterly false, and hence can provide no argument against the prospect of surviving either mode of transport.

So—to beam or not to beam? That is the question, but what is the answer? In the *mind over matter* closest-continuer view, whether or not transport is rational depends on whether or not, given the available evidence, you can reasonably expect psychological identity to be preserved in the process. The only apparent way to judge this is from the behavior of materialized subjects and the testimonials of the friends, colleagues, and loved ones of scanned subjects. Whether the process is matter transport or information transport, this evidence overwhelmingly supports the conclusion that psychological continuity is preserved. The second condition is that there be no other close psychological continuer of the scanned subject. Since I defined matter transport and information transport in such a way as to exclude this possibility—at least, in the case of single rematerialization—we should conclude that it is after all rational to beam and superstitious to refuse. However, what of those cases of beaming where there is either numerical or qualitative *change?* That is a topic for the next chapter.

Personal Growth

chapter 5

Although teletransport is exotic, it is also (usually) importantly conservative, and in two ways. First, the procedure conserves the number of subjects: if one subject undergoes the procedure, one and only one emerges from the procedure. Second, the procedure conserves qualitative identity: the body and psychology of the emerging subject are indistinguishable from the body and psychology of the pretransport subject. In this chapter we shall examine procedures that are more exotic still, because they depart from one or the other of these conservations. Sometimes both!

Fusion Reactions

One of the characters in *Deep Space Nine* is a Trill. A "symbiont," it is the product of the symbiosis of a long-lived creature—a sort of slug that sits in the abdominal cavity—and a succession of human hosts. (Confusingly, both the symbiont and the long-lived slug are called trills; to distinguish between them, I am capitalizing the word when the symbiont is meant.) When a human host dies, the trill is transferred—with psychology intact—to a new host. Being a host is a great honor and achievement, requiring many years of training and preparation. Each Trill takes its first name from the current human host and its last name from the trill. Lieutenant Jadzia Dax, the present—and eighth—incarnation of the trill Dax, is a young woman; the former incarnation was Curzon Dax, who lived to be an old man. In *DS9:* "Dax," Jadzia Dax is charged with treason and murder allegedly committed by Curzon Dax, and the court tries to decide whether Curzon's personal identity has been preserved in her. The need for such a ruling is obviated when it turns out that Curzon Dax was innocent, but suppose that he had been guilty. Would Jadzia Dax then have been guilty, too? The *mind over matter* closest-continuer view of personal identity, which I defended in chapter 4, gives us a way to decide this issue. Has psychological identity has been preserved through the change in hosts? Each Trill's mind is a merging of the trill psychology with that of the host, and the psychology that the trill brings to this union is a composite of all the previous symbioses. Let's diagram what occurred at the joining of the human Jadzia with the trill Dax. ("C" refers to Curzon, "J" to Jadzia, and "T" to the trill.)

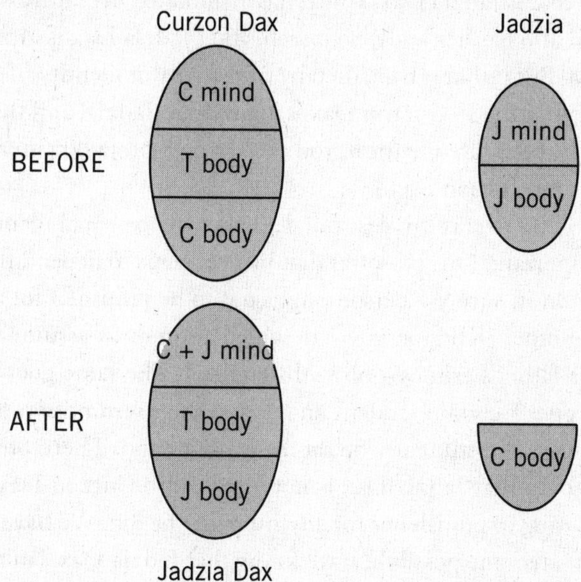

There are two distinct persons (that is, there are slices of two distinct persons) before the joining process—the Trill Curzon Dax, and the human Jadzia. Although there are two individuals remaining after the process, only one of these is a person, and that is Jadzia Dax. The other individual is the lifeless human body that was originally associated with the human Curzon and then with the Trill Curzon Dax. So here we have an exotic procedure in which *neither* conservation obtains. The number of persons changes, since there were two persons before the joining and afterward only one; before the joining, there were two individual psychologies, and afterward only one. Moreover, Jadzia Dax is not qualitatively identical in psychology to either Curzon Dax or Jadzia. Let's apply the closest-continuer schema. Curzon Dax has two continuers—Jadzia Dax and the lifeless Curzon body. Clearly, Jadzia Dax is the closest continuer of Curzon Dax, since she contains the identical trill body and the majority of her psychology came from Curzon Dax. So it seems that Jadzia Dax is identical to Curzon Dax. But now we must consider continuers of Jadzia. There is only one personal continuer of Jadzia, and that is Jadzia Dax, which has assimilated her entire psychology and also has her body. So it seems that Jadzia Dax is identical to Jadzia. But if that is true, then by transitivity of identity (if $a = b$ and $a = c$, then $b = c$) Curzon Dax is identical to Jadzia, and that's not right! (If they were identical, you could imprison Jadzia merely by imprisoning Curzon Dax.)

Before we try to sort this case out, let's ask why personal identity seems so important. One reason is that justice seems to depend fundamentally on it; surely a person ought not to be punished for the actions of another (Klingon law—in which a son must assume the guilt for his father's crimes—notwithstanding). The same goes for rewards: I give a certain student an "A" on the presumption that she is the very same student who sat the examination. Therefore, if it can be shown that Jadzia Dax is not identical to Curzon Dax, it would be wrong to punish her for anything that he did. We have already eliminated one possibility: we know that Jadzia Dax can't be identical to Curzon Dax *and* identical to Jadzia. But which remaining possibility is most plausible? Is Jadzia Dax identical to Curzon Dax and not Jadzia, or vice versa; or is she identical to *neither* of them? Consideration of other cases will help us to decide.

Fission-Con-Fusion

> "The man you see before you is literally a fusion of two men." —*Ship's doctor to Captain Kathryn Janeway,*
> Voyager: *"Tuvix"*

In "Tuvix," there is a startling transporter accident. After collecting plant samples on a planetary surface, Security Chief Tuvok and ship's cook Neelix beam back up to the ship, but what materializes on the transporter pad is, in the words of the ship's holographic doctor, a "fusion"—a single individual with physical and psychological features of both men. The newcomer calls himself "Tuvix," and while the *Voyager* crew works on a way to undo the fusion, he is less than keen on the idea. He doesn't identify with either Tuvok or Neelix. "In a way, I think of them as my parents," he explains to Neelix's partner, Kes. When a restoration procedure is discovered, Tuvix at first refuses to submit. "I don't want to die," he tells Janeway. "I have a right to live." Many of the crew are sympathetic, and the doctor refuses to perform the restorative transport procedure. But Janeway takes over, energizes the transporter, and two distinct individuals appear on the transporter pad.

Putting ethical questions aside for the moment, was Tuvix right to be fearful of the restoration procedure, which he considered would be the end of him? What happened to Tuvok and Neelix? Did they survive the whole process (fusion followed by fission)? Once again, let's diagram the process.

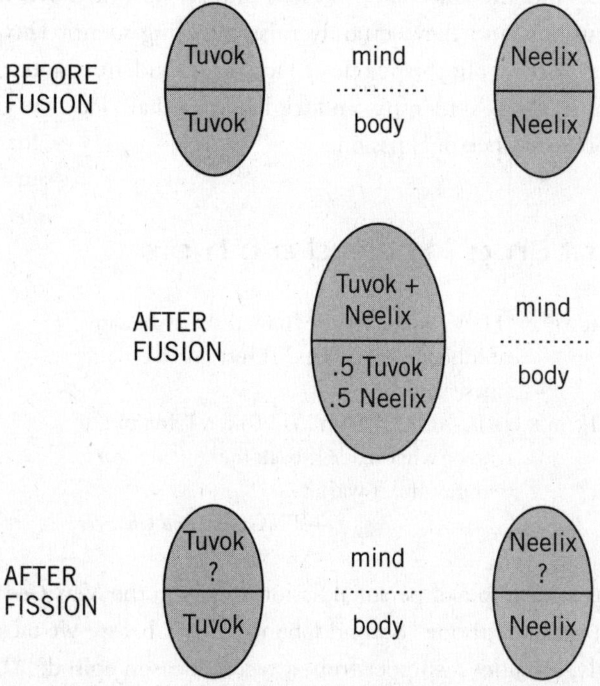

By reasoning parallel to that in the case of Jadzia Dax, we conclude that Tuvix cannot be identical to both Tuvok and Neelix, the prefusion persons at the top of the diagram. (To avoid begging any questions, we'll call the postfission persons *T* and *N*.) Although Tuvix clearly is the closest personal continuer of Tuvok, Tuvix clearly is also the closest personal continuer of Neelix. But if Tuvix is identical to both Tuvok and Neelix, then by transitivity of identity Tuvok is identical to Neelix, and that can't be right. But since Tuvok and Neelix both contribute equally to Tuvix's body and psychology, they each have an equal claim to identity with him. So it cannot be true that one is identical to him if the other isn't. So Tuvix is not identical to either Tuvok or Neelix. That is, Tuvok and Neelix ceased to exist when the fusion occurred! But if that is so, then who are *T* and *N*? Are they new persons who are near replicas of Tuvok and Neelix? Or are they really Tuvok and Neelix?

Processes like the ones that produced Jadzia Dax and Tuvix are personal fusions, and they certainly raise puzzling identity problems. To try sorting out the puzzle of Jadzia Dax's identity and culpability, and Tuvix's identity and rights, we shall look to the opposite process—personal fission.

Splitting Headaches

> PICARD: "How could two grown men share the same childhood experiences? It just doesn't make any sense!"
>
> RIKER'S LOOK-ALIKE: "I am Will Riker. I don't know who or what made it back to the *Potemkin* that day, but it wasn't *me!*"
>
> —TNG: *"Second Chances"*

A spectacular example of personal fission occurs in the *Next Generation* sixth-season episode "Second Chances." But before we tackle this directly, consider a snippet from a second-season episode, "Up the Long Ladder" (a pity they didn't keep the working title, "Send in the Clones"). The *Enterprise-D* crew encounters the Mariposans, descendants of a group of colonists from Earth who crash-landed on the planet they intended to colonize. Since only five of the colonists survived the crash, they resorted to cloning, and Mariposan society is in deep trouble unless they can get some fresh genetic material for new clones. They ask the *Enterprise-D* crew for painless cell donations, and the response is a rousing *Yuucckkk!* Here is Riker's reaction in particular.

RIKER: "You want to *clone* us?"
MARIPOSAN PRIME MINISTER: "Yes."
RIKER: "No way! Not me!"
MARIPOSAN PRIME MINISTER: "But how could you possibly be harmed?"
RIKER: "It's not a question of harm. One William Riker is unique, perhaps even special. But a hundred of him, a thousand of him—diminishes me in ways I can't even imagine."

Now consider "Second Chances." The *Enterprise-D* visits the research station on Nervala IV, which Commander Riker helped to evacuate eight years earlier, when he was a lieutenant on the *Potemkin*. The planet has a stormy atmosphere, which makes transport difficult, and when Riker's away team beams down during a suitable "window," they make a startling discovery: Riker comes face to face with a doppelgänger! This look-alike claims to be the real William T. Riker, who never made it off the planet, a claim Commander Riker naturally disputes. It is soon established that the look-alike is no clone. (There is a nice discussion by Dr. Crusher about nonclonable brain-pattern similarities.) Apparently when the research station was evacuated, Riker was the last to beam up. Two viable signals were sent from the planet's surface, one of which issued in a rematerialization on board the *Potemkin;* the other was reflected back to the planet's surface and issued in a rematerialization there. When Picard asks Geordi La Forge which of the two materialized subjects is real, La Forge replies that they both are, since each was "formed from a complete pattern."

La Forge is correct in one sense but mistaken in another. He is correct that each of the two materialized subjects counts as a real *person;* each has all the attributes necessary for personhood, by any reasonable standard. But if La Forge is claiming that each of them is the real *Riker*—the Riker that existed just before transport on that fateful day—then he surely is mistaken. Call the subject materialized on board the *Potemkin* Riker_1 and the subject materialized on the planet surface Riker_2. There are four possibilities:

1. $\text{Riker}_1 = \text{Riker}$, and $\text{Riker}_2 = \text{Riker}$
2. $\text{Riker}_1 = \text{Riker}$, and $\text{Riker}_2 \neq \text{Riker}$
3. $\text{Riker}_1 \neq \text{Riker}$, and $\text{Riker}_2 = \text{Riker}$
4. $\text{Riker}_1 \neq \text{Riker}$, and $\text{Riker}_2 \neq \text{Riker}$

By an argument analogous to the one in the fusion cases, we can show that given the principle of transitivity of identity, since Riker_1 does not equal Riker_2 (by imprisoning one, you do not thereby imprison the other), neither Riker_1 nor Riker_2 is identical to the original Riker. (Riker_2 is correct in asserting in the quote at the beginning of this section that Riker_1 isn't *him,* but I doubt that this is quite what he meant.) Hence William T. Riker ceased to exist on the day he fissed. Assuming no further fissions occurred, Commander Riker is identical to Riker_1, and Lieutenant Riker is identical to Riker_2. The irony is that the individual who lectured the Mariposans on the importance of uniqueness (something they clearly had learned to live without) was Riker_1, who unknowingly had at that very moment a twin much more like himself than any mere clone could be!

On the reasonable assumption that this is a case of information transport but with "doubling," then such a fission involves the loss of bodily identity as well as of personal identity (even if some matter is preserved, no one knows who got what). Moreover, this fission involves the loss of psychological identity, too; since there are now two numerically distinct minds, and each is an equally close continuer, then neither is identical to the original mind. In thinking about this case, remember that the only difference between a fission case and that of run-of-the-mill information transport is the materialization of two subjects instead of one: that is, each of the materialized subjects is indistinguishable in internal and external behavior from the scanned subject; each will remember having had breakfast, having entered the scanner, and so forth. And since the scanned subject was presumably unaware of the possibility of fission, then each materialized subject naturally identifies with the scanned subject, as the behavior of $Riker_1$ and $Riker_2$ demonstrates.

What Really Matters in Personal Survival

The question that personal fission raises is, How ought we to regard it, given that it involves the loss of personal, bodily, and psychological identity? Here it is instructive to focus briefly on what we take to be the two choices usually open to us as regards our existence. The first choice is continued ordinary, day-to-day survival, and the second is ordinary death. The "person in the street" overwhelmingly prefers continued ordinary survival to death, and by an enormous margin. (Imagine a poll asking respondents for the strength of their agreement with the statement "I prefer continued ordinary survival right now to death right now." I think you can expect near unanimity for "Very strongly agree!")

Now let's add a third option to the pot—personal fission. Probably most people would respond that they strongly preferred continued ordinary survival to fission, too. But suppose that we try to rank fission against both ordinary survival and ordinary death. Is fission as bad as ordinary death? Or is it more like ordinary survival? One way to test our intuitions here is to imagine a forced choice in which continued ordinary survival is not an option. Be prepared to let your imagination take flight. Suppose you have a fatal disease, which will kill you within a week. Suppose further that the only promising cure for this disease has emerged from transporter research: by modifying the transporter in some fashion (as in *TNG:* "Unnatural Selection") doctors have discovered that the disease can be eliminated from the scanned subject. But for some reason no one can figure out, this procedure works only if two materializations take place. That is, standard transport will not eliminate the disease and death follows quickly. So you have only two choices: certain imminent death or fission and apparent loss of personal identity. Which would you choose?

To approach an answer, let's consider what it would be like to be a fission twin, when you are acquainted with each other. We get some idea from the two Rikers: it's a lot like being an ordinary identical twin, and what's so bad about that? In "Second Chances," there's a bit of rather fraternal rivalry (Riker$_2$ feels "set back," and rightly so—Riker$_1$ got a promotion as reward for the actions of the original Riker), but also some grudging affection (when Riker$_2$ successfully woos Deanna Troi, whose relationship with Riker$_1$ has long since cooled, Riker$_1$ is "flattered, sort of. . . ."). Then at the end of the episode Riker$_1$ acknowledges that Riker$_2$ has an equal right to some of his belongings and offers him Riker's trombone.

Indeed, it is hard to see how there is any difference in principle between fission twins and ordinary identical twins. It just doesn't seem to be that bad—and, indeed, identical twins often claim that they prefer being twins to what they imagine it would be like to be singular. Imagine for a moment (if you are not a twin) that tomorrow you discover that you have a long-lost identical twin. When I imagine this, I find the idea attractive rather than not. Does it matter how many identicals you have? I doubt that triplets or quads or quints are any less happy than twins on this score. Of course, if you know all your identicals, and if there are hundreds of them, this would introduce awkward problems. But none of these problems has anything to do with uniqueness, or so I am about to argue.

In "Second Chances," Data remarks to Worf, "I have found that humans value their uniqueness—that sense that they are different from everyone else. The existence of a double would preclude that feeling." Most of us would agree strongly that our uniqueness is something we value greatly. Let's first disambiguate the idea: is it numerical uniqueness or qualitative uniqueness that's important? If it's numerical uniqueness, then no one has cause for alarm, since it is a logical truth that each of us is numerically distinct. Even the most identical of identical twins are not *numerically* identical. And even if we cloned you a trillion times, or fissed you into a trillion "descendants," we cannot take away your numerical uniqueness. So it must be qualitative uniqueness that is so important. It is important to each of us that there be nobody else exactly qualitatively similar to us. There is philosophical debate about whether or not qualitative uniqueness is also logically guaranteed; some philosophers hold that if *a* and *b* are numerically distinct, then there is at least one property that *a* has and *b* lacks, or vice versa. If this is true, then nobody else is *exactly* like you. But put this to one side; the point Data seems to be making is that it's not good to have others who are extremely similar to you. But why is this a bad thing, and what is the evidence for it's being so? If anything, humans seem to seek out those who are relatively similar, whether in appearance or temperament or conviction. Few of us revel in a situation where we do not "blend in," "fit," or "belong." Looking at it another way, ask yourself honestly whether or not in your opinion the world would be a better place if more people believed roughly what you believe (I bet you're tempted). Wouldn't replicating your psychology help rather than hurt this objective?

My speculative diagnosis of the commonsense fear of duplication is that it really has nothing whatever to do with uniqueness. When we imagine clones or duplicates, we conjure up pictures of vast armies of creatures all looking and thinking alike. These creatures of our imaginations are not frightening because they are similar but rather because they appear to lack the freedom to determine the path their lives will take. We suppose them to be ready slaves to an iron will, since winning the heart and mind of one of them is winning them all. We imagine them to be like the Borg of *The Next*

Generation series, effectively a collective consciousness with no room for individualism. But in reality, fission descendants will lack autonomy only if the prefission subject lacked it. Once they exist, they are unlike the Borg—winning one of them is not winning them all—since they are psychologically unconnected. Of course, fission (and cloning) offers the *possibility* of creating brainwashed armies, but then so does life as we know it, as human history is testament.

It is worth repeating this point, especially in the case of cloning. Scientists in Scotland recently cloned a sheep from a nonreproductive cell of a ewe. The clone is, of course, genetically identical to the cell donor, and the success of the procedure has terrified those who see the all-too-possible extension to human cloning. But many of the objections to human cloning that reverberated around the world rest on an obvious error. Were we to clone you right now and grow a new, genetically identical human being, there is no reason at all to suppose that this person would be your psychological duplicate. Indeed, since the cloned person would grow up in a different era, he or she would probably be much *less* like you than an identical twin would be.

What if you are a fission twin but don't know it? Again, this doesn't seem so bad—to paraphrase the Mariposan prime minister, it doesn't seem to harm you in the slightest—unless you feel that you have missed out on knowing your twin. Indeed, just as it is perfectly consistent with your present experience that *you now* are an identical twin, it is perfectly consistent with your present experience that *you now* are a fission twin. (The person who was born to your parents ceased to exist at the age of fifteen, having been kidnapped and fissed in the process of information transport; your twin is now in a laboratory five miles underground in Virginia.) Would this matter to you, other than concern for your twin? Does it make you a lesser person? Indeed, for all you know, God is fissing humans all the time; perhaps every five minutes each person ceases to exist and is fissed, with one descendant instantly replacing the original and the other materializing on a twin Earth somewhere (or given to Satan to play with). So persons never last longer than five minutes, and absolutely everyone has not only a fission twin but millions of fission cousins, too. Does this change anything at all for you, given that it is no part of your ordinary experience?

But perhaps it's not your fission products' viewpoints that concern you. Perhaps it's your own viewpoint, now. After all, you might ask, what's the point of having dreams and aspirations if it's not *you* who will achieve them? To answer this objection, think of a spectrum of cases involving someone else's achievement of a particular goal you've set for yourself. (Take a moment to think of some appropriate goal.) At one end of the spectrum is ordinary survival, where (we suppose) you are the achiever. In all the other cases, imagine that someone else is the achiever, and that you will not be around to be involved in their lives. At the other end of the spectrum is the case of someone with absolutely no connection to you whatever. Do you identify with that person's achievement and take personal satisfaction in it? Not at all, I presume. Now move along the spectrum a little, to a case of a disciple or close friend of yours being the achiever. Doesn't knowing that they likely will achieve your aspiration provide some personal satisfaction? Now imagine that the achiever is one of your children, who has half your genetic makeup. Doesn't that provide still more personal satisfaction? (Even parents not directly involved in raising their children seem to rejoice in their children's successes.) Next, suppose that the achiever is your clone, someone genetically identical to you. Aren't you rather more pleased—or, at least, no less pleased than in the case of your child? (Remember, you won't be around to be involved in their lives.) Now suppose that it's your fission descendant, who is genetically identical *and* psychologically continuous with you. Isn't that yet further along the spectrum? Isn't it getting close to the case where it is you? Is there such a big difference? And doesn't the fact that there's roughly *double* the chance of such achievement when there are two survivors rather than one mitigate any such difference? (Not only that, but your fission descendants might achieve two mutually exclusive goals of yours, if they cooperate.)

Personal Growth

The preceding argument is meant to support the idea that personal fission is as good as ordinary survival. So if Riker had known that he was about to fiss, this wouldn't have been the end of the world for him, even though he would cease to exist. If this argument is compelling, then personal survival isn't necessarily a matter of personal identity (or, if you insist that personal survival is personal identity, personal survival isn't a matter of major importance). And personal survival isn't a matter of psychological identity, either. What *is* important, then? That there be a close-enough psychological continuer of you—call this the *mind continuity* view of what is important to a person in his or her survival. When close-enough psychological continuity is unbranching over a time period (that is, when there is no personal fission), then personal identity obtains for that period. Since, as far as we know, this is the case in ordinary survival, it is not surprising that we ordinarily mistake personal identity for what really matters. To repeat, the point is that psychological continuity is what matters in *ordinary* personal survival. If identity of some sort is preserved as well, this is a rather inconsequential bonus. And if identity is *not* preserved (say, if God is constantly fissing everybody), then this is a rather inconsequential loss. What we don't know can't hurt us or our psychological continuers!

Psychological Continuity and Justice

Identity in general is a curious thing: the more one looks at it, the less deep and important it seems to be. If fission is vastly preferable to death, this shows that identity, whether of mind or person or anything else, is not what really matters in personal survival. But then what sense can we make of the commonsense intuitions about justice mentioned earlier? Doesn't it follow that if Riker committed some crime, then both of his fission descendants, being nonidentical to him, get off scot-free? Here's a way to make crime pay: do the deed just before fissing!

Of course, this can't be right. But it doesn't follow from the view that personal identity isn't what matters in personal survival. Start with something simple—Riker's property. Our intuitions about justice here seem clear enough: his two fission descendants have an equal right to a share of this property (an intuition $Riker_1$ clearly felt the force of). It's understandable that $Riker_2$ felt set back in his career, since $Riker_1$ got a promotion based on the actions of Riker, and it seems that $Riker_2$ is entitled to a share of the praise. What applies to Riker's assets seems equally well to apply to his liabilities. If he owed money, then it would seem that each fission twin owes half. This idea is extendable to just about any instance of the normal requirements of justice, and at any rate is already in operation in the world we know. Usually, individuals acting in concert are jointly responsible for the results of that action; the fact that a member of a group is not identical to the group is entirely beside the point.

This insight gives us a way of dealing with the case of Jadzia Dax. Since each Trill is a fusion of two consenting persons, it is useful to think of the actions of the Trill as an analogy for two persons acting in concert. More than that, the fusion is like other unions between consenting persons in which each person takes responsibility for the actions of the other. Jadzia—the innocent party—is the one to focus on here. In accepting the fusion, Jadzia realizes that some of the actions of Jadzia Dax will be motivated by that part of the Trill psychology inherited from Curzon Dax. Moreover, it seems that if Curzon Dax made a promise to someone, then even if Jadzia doesn't know anything about it, she tacitly agrees, in consenting to the fusion, that Jadzia Dax will be responsible for making good on the promise if possible. (This is precisely what happens, and precisely Jadzia Dax's attitude, in *DS9:* "Blood Oath.") Hence Jadzia also tacitly agrees that Jadzia Dax will be responsible for any misdeeds on the part of Curzon Dax. So if Curzon Dax was guilty, then Jadzia Dax will bear the responsibility.

The wonderful thing about the argument just given is that it obviates the need to decide whether Jadzia Dax is identical to Curzon Dax. This is just as well, since the most defensible answer to this question is No. Although there probably is proportionately more of Curzon Dax than Jadzia in Jadzia Dax's psychology (since there were seven previous hosts, including Curzon), there is too much of Jadzia to discount. And though the trill body comes from Curzon Dax, the human body comes from Jadzia. Since it is hard to make the case that Jadzia Dax is identical to Curzon Dax or Jadzia, and she cannot be identical to both, the most defensible answer is that Jadzia Dax is identical to *neither*. Curzon Dax and Jadzia both ceased to exist, and a new person came into existence.

Things are not as comfortable in the case of Tuvix. Parallel reasoning leads to the conclusion that Tuvok and Neelix ceased to exist when the fusion occurred. This leaves us with two difficult questions: When Tuvix fissed into *T* and *N*, were Tuvok and Neelix restored? And did Captain Janeway do the right thing in fissing Tuvix? It's clear that neither *T* nor *N* is identical to Tuvix (by reasoning parallel to that in the case of Riker's fission), hence Tuvix was correct in thinking that he would cease to exist after the fission. But this leaves open the question of whether or not *T* is identical to Tuvok and *N* is identical to Neelix. The reason for thinking they're not identical is the gap when neither Tuvok nor Neelix existed—that is, the time period in which Tuvix existed. But perhaps such a gap is not important. Recall that in *TNG:* "Relics" Scotty's pattern was trapped in the transporter for seventy-five years, but no one doubts that it was Scotty who emerged. However, during that particular gap there was no one else around competing to be Scotty—that is, there were no personal continuers of the pretransport Scotty—so the analogy is not a good one.

Instead, let's consider once again "Lonely among Us," in which Picard beams out from the ship as "energy only" and is later rematerialized from the pattern stored in the transporter memory. As noted in chapter 4, Troi's sensing of Picard "out there" in the nebula suggests that his psychology was continuing, yet when Picard is restored he has no memory of events after the beaming. In diagram form, here's what I think went on, where *b* is the time that beaming occurs and *r* is the time of restoration.

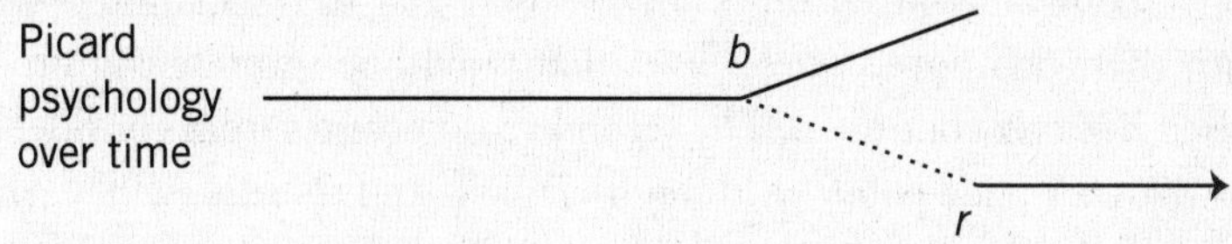

Note that Picard's psychology continues on the upper branch after *b*, but only for a relatively short time. When his union with the energy being fails, this branch of his psychology simply ends. Then at *r*, a psychology is produced which is continuous with the original Picard psychology. I suspect that the closest-continuer schema allows for some backtracking here. There's a discontinuity: between *b* and *r*, the closest continuer of the original Picard psychology is the upper branch, but after *r* it's the lower branch. However, the discontinuity can be overlooked when it's relatively small. (Compare the discussion of bodily resurrection in chapter 4.) This explains why we're tempted to think that the person who finally steps off the transporter pad is indeed Picard.

Now here's the Tuvix situation, where *u* is the time of fusion and *i* is the time of fission.

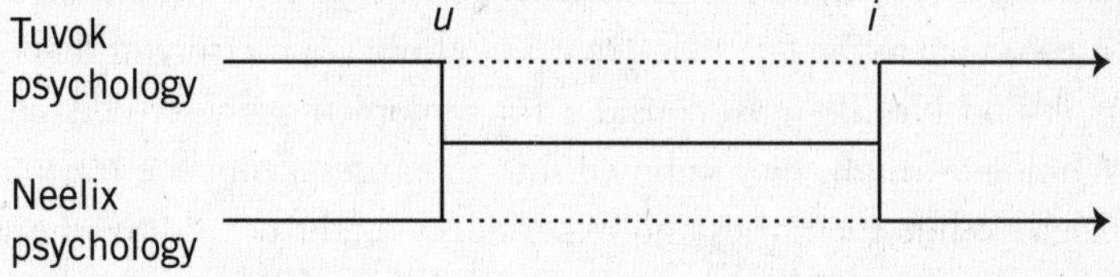

Once again, I think the closest-continuer schema allows for backtracking, and it occurs here along two different tracks. Between *u* and *i*, the closest continuer of Tuvok (upper branch before *u*) is Tuvix, but *T* (upper branch) is the closest continuer of Tuvok after *i*. Since Tuvix is relatively short-lived and the gap small, *T* is identical to Tuvok. By a parallel argument, *N* (lower branch after *i*) is identical to Neelix (lower branch before *u*).

But did Janeway do the right thing in bringing back Tuvok and Neelix? There are two reasons for thinking so. First, neither Tuvok nor Neelix consented to the fusion, nor would they have if asked. One obvious reason for thinking so is that they have separate lives, with their own loved ones—lives that would be severely compromised if Tuvix continued. The second reason comes from considering Tuvix's viewpoint. Although Tuvok and Neelix will each continue in *T* and *N*, it is not as though Tuvix never existed. Each of them has half of Tuvix's body (so just as Tuvix regards Tuvok and Neelix as his "parents," he should regard their continuation in *T* and *N* as his "children," since each has part of his genetic endowment). But more than that, each has half his psychology, with memories of the experience of being Tuvix. So although the consolation of fission is not as great as it is in a case like Riker's—that is, in a case where each fission descendant is qualitatively identical to the prefission subject—it is still nowhere near as bad as death. Although these positive reasons still have to be weighed against Tuvix's desire for continued existence, this desire seems at least counterweighted by consideration of Tuvok's and Neelix's desire not to be fused. I think that on balance Janeway did the right thing; at least, I don't think she did the wrong thing.

I should say at this point that the case of Tuvix makes much less sense to me than that of Riker. Leaving aside the obvious implausibilities—such as the fact that Tuvix's clothing is a mixture of that of Tuvok and Neelix—just consider for a moment how two distinct psychologies might be combined into one, preserving the features of each. While memories and experiences might be additive here, the mental states that drive action—beliefs and desires—are not. There would be glaring inconsistencies in belief, and drastically incompatible desires. So at best the individual resulting from such a fusion would be a person confused about what to think and do, and at worst would be a psychotic mess—perhaps not even a person.

A Fork in the Road

I have interpreted the Riker, Jadzia Dax, and Tuvix cases on the assumption that identity is lost when psychology fuses or fissions. But the philosopher David Lewis has constructed an ingenious challenge to the argument that personal identity is lost in fission cases, and perhaps we can adapt the argument for fusion cases. Lewis questions the assumption that there was one and only one person present before fission, by drawing an analogy with highways. It's tempting to identify highways with road surfaces, but this cannot be right, since sometimes highways *share* a road surface. Indeed, if we ought to identify highways with road surfaces, then by arguments parallel to the one from transitivity of identity we can show that the map is wrong when it shows a highway continuing when the road surface has branched! Lewis argues that we can think of persons as analogous to highways, and what I have called person-slices (such as the person-slice occupying your chair for the last ten seconds) as analogous to road surfaces. When fission occurs, all it does is reveal the fact that two persons shared the prefission person-slice, just as two highways may share a road surface. The number of persons sharing a person-slice depends on what will happen to its continuers—that is, on whether any fissions occur. Persons are, in Lewis's view, four-dimensional spacetime "worms," some of which might intersect by occasionally sharing person-slices.

Hence there never was just one Riker: $Riker_1$ and $Riker_2$ always existed, but no one noticed because $Riker_1$ and $Riker_2$ shared the same person-slices right up until the fission. Applying the same picture to fusions, the rather unrealistic case of Tuvix is like two separate highways coming together briefly and then parting again. Correct or not, Lewis's view is by no means a restoration of the commonsense notion of personal survival and what matters in it. In both Lewis's view and the one I have argued for, the continuation of your psychology is that of a single person over time only if there is no fission. In my view, if you fiss, then you no longer exist but that's not so bad. In Lewis's view, if there is a fission (and will be no more fissions), then there never was a single *you* anyway, since each of the person-slices from "your" birth until fission was in fact shared by two persons. Perhaps that isn't bad, either, but it doesn't seem any better!

Personal Growth

To repeat, the more one looks at identity, the less deep and important it seems to be. Suppose that you are captain of the *Enterprise-D*. While the ship is in space dock, bizarre thieves steal your starship and blow it to pieces. But these are philanthropic wealthy thieves (I said they were bizarre!) and they leave a qualitatively similar ship in the place of your old one. The new ship is identical to the old in both function and appearance. What have you lost? You no longer have the very same starship, but so what? But now change the case. Suppose these thieves, being philanthropists, try to ascertain before the crime whether or not you are completely happy with your starship. Their spies hear you complain about this and that, so they do you a favor. Instead of replacing your ship with a functionally identical one, they make a few improvements here and there. This and a few aesthetic improvements result in differences in appearance, too. What have you lost? A little familiarity, perhaps, but haven't you gained much that offsets this? Suppose further that you are radically unhappy with the old *Enterprise-D,* and the replacement left by the philanthropic thieves is therefore radically different from the original. Wouldn't that give you exactly what you want?

Now suppose you are about to undergo instantaneous total synthetic body and brain replacement—or its equivalent, single information transport. Up to now, we have imagined simply replacing your body with one equivalent in function and appearance. But suppose we make a few changes—a nip here, a tuck there, off with the love handles, away with the cellulite—at no extra cost or inconvenience. Can you honestly say that there's *nothing* about your body you would change, given such an opportunity? A few pounds less? A few inches taller? Indeed, for many of us, getting the body we would like might result in a radical change in function and appearance, a loss of disease and disrepair, perhaps even a change of sex! What have you lost? A little familiarity, perhaps, but haven't you gained much that offsets this?

Is Data Human?

Or suppose instead that you suffer from some particular disability. La Forge was born blind but has prosthetic vision thanks to his visor and some cybernetic implants (just as some nearly deaf persons in our time have had their hearing restored through prostheses). What if we could simply replace a blind person's eyes with identical, functioning ones; or use the transporter, fed with the correct genetic information (as in "Unnatural Selection" and "Rascals"), to rematerialize functional eyes? In *Voyager:* "Lifesigns," the Viidian Danara Pel is suffering the ravaging effects of the "phage." To protect her mind, the ship's doctor transfers her psychology temporarily into a holographic body. But instead of reproducing the diseased body, the holographic projectors are used to create a phage-free body. If this sort of medical care is feasible, isn't that a good idea? It's perfectly consistent with the idea that bodily identity or continuity doesn't matter much in personal survival.

But now ponder psychotherapy for a moment. What's the point of it? To *change* the patient's *psychology,* of course—to rid the patient of unwanted desires, beliefs, memories, attitudes, fears, and so forth, and replace them with desirable ones. Now suppose we offer you such changes by means of a process like single information transport. Since we have to extract and temporarily store your psychology anyway, why not a nip here, a tuck there, off with an unhealthy desire, away with an excruciatingly embarrassing memory? Can you honestly say that there's *nothing* about your psychology you would change, given such an opportunity? A few phobias less? A few IQ points more? Indeed, for many of us, getting the psychology we would rather have might result in a radical change in mental function, a healthier psyche, perhaps even a change of personality! What have you lost? Perhaps *not even* a little familiarity (you might not remember how you were, if that's what you want), and haven't you gained much that would offset this anyway?

Now put the two procedures together, in what I shall call *transporter therapy*. It's like visiting the hairdresser. Before undergoing single information transport, you tell us what you want done, or look through our brochures at pictures and descriptions of various body and psychology styles. Once you have made your choice, we program the transporter, and *voilà*—the new you is materialized. What possible objection could you have to such a procedure? After all, if staying the same is important to you, no one is going to force you to change—you can have the equivalent of just a trim, or nothing at all. But for some of us, choosing according to our deepest desires for change will mean a radical loss of both bodily and psychological continuity.

Notice a progression in the views we have considered in this chapter and the previous one. We started out looking for an immutable soul as a means of preserving what is really important in personal survival. Then we discovered that an immutable soul was unnecessary, and that we can survive change without the loss of personal identity. Then we discovered that it is at least arguable that we can survive even the loss of personal identity. Now we discover that it is at least arguable that we can survive without even significant personal continuity! Indeed, the philosopher Raymond Martin has argued that for many people, what matters primarily in survival is not personal identity, nor is it psychological continuity, but rather *becoming the person they most want to be*. Someday perhaps transport technology such as that in *Star Trek* can put these intuitions to the test. But one remaining question might be whether or not it's rational to undergo such radical transformations. This one I shall leave you to ponder.

The Enemy Within

A standard theme in *Star Trek* is the psychological coup d'état. In episode after episode, some crew member or other is "body-snatched"—taken over by an alien intelligence and manipulated accordingly. Usually the effect involves the temporary suppression of the person's real psychology, as in the *The Next Generation* episodes "Lonely among Us," "Conspiracy," "Clues," and "Power Play," and the movie *Star Trek II: The Wrath of Khan,* but sometimes there is something like peaceful coexistence, as in *TOS:* "Return to Tomorrow," wherein Spock's psychology is temporarily placed in Nurse Chapel's body, alongside her own psychology. And sometimes there is a struggle for ascendancy, as in *TNG:* "The Schizoid Man," wherein Data is invaded by the psychology of the cybernetic genius Dr. Ira Graves upon the scientist's bodily death, and Graves gradually takes over, to predictable dramatic effect.

This theme of more than one person or mind in a single body has increasingly become a part of real life, too. Few of us are unfamiliar with tales of abused children whose personalities fragment into many pieces, resulting in so-called *multiple personality disorder*. (In *TNG:* "Masks," Data is taken over by a variety of different personas!) But this disorder is merely the tip of a very large iceberg, for there is substantial evidence challenging what has been called the *unity of consciousness* assumption, which roughly is the idea that minds and persons come one per customer. More specifically, the assumption states that associated with each normal human organism is exactly one unified consciousness, one mind, and exactly one person.

If *Star Trek* is to be believed, there is plenty of room in a single body for more than one person. But does this occur only when there is some sort of invasion from outside the body? When asked in "Lonely among Us" why her empathic powers didn't detect the presence of the energy being, which temporarily occupied Worf and Dr. Crusher before settling in with Picard, Counselor Troi claims that she normally reads a "duality" in humans, a duality she illustrates by means of the metaphor of coming to a crossroads and being of two minds about which road to take. Is this just an excuse for her failure, or is there some justification for thinking that humans display a psychological duality?

Add to this the strange transporter accident in *TOS:* "The Enemy Within," wherein Kirk undergoes a fission quite unlike Riker's. The two "Kirks" who result are not qualitatively psychologically identical—they are as different as chalk and cheese. One has inherited Kirk's violent, animal, "evil" half, and the other Kirk's cerebral, peaceful, "good" half. Eventually the two halves are reunited. (Notice that this overall process is the exact opposite of what occurred in *Voyager:* "Tuvix.") In diagram form, it looks like this, where *i* is the time of fission and *u* the time of fusion.

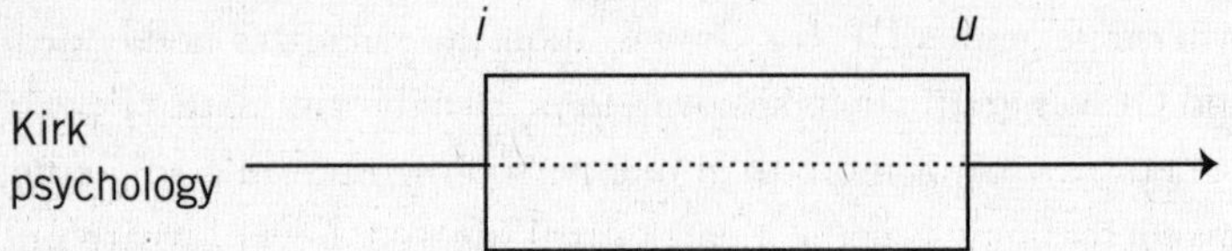

The upper branch between *i* and *u* is *GK* ("Good Kirk"), the lower branch is *BK*, and the person who exists after *u* may be called *K*. First of all, note that neither *GK* nor *BK* is identical to Kirk (by the same reasoning used in the case of Riker's fission), nor is either identical to *K* (by the same reasoning used in the case of Tuvix's fusion). But unlike Riker, Kirk does not simply cease to exist. Since GK and BK are in existence for a relatively short time, and since K is the closest continuer of Kirk before *i*, the closest-continuer schema ignores the gap and counts *K* as identical to Kirk.

But that's not why I introduced the example. How can the transporter split Kirk into two different, working psychologies? Either there's an extraordinary coincidence—that is, somehow the transporter, in dividing Kirk's unified psychology into two, manages to produce two lesser but *viable* psychologies—or it really is a split, which implies that there are already two psychologies present before *i*. Does this mean that Kirk is importantly dual, just as Counselor Troi suggests all humans are?

We Are Not Alone

There's some startling evidence that Troi is correct, but before we examine it we must add something to the discussion of minds and persons in chapters 1 through 3. In the earlier discussion, we were trying to establish *type* identity criteria for minds and persons; that is, we were trying to establish what properties something must possess in order to count as intelligent, or as a person. But we did not inquire into *token* identity criteria; that is, we did not ask how to distinguish one mind from another, or one person from another. To put it a different way, when confronted by one or more minds or persons, how do you know how many there are? How do you count minds, or count persons? The commonsense answer to this question, refined in various ways, is to count living human organisms.

But there are other ways. Suppose you telephone a company and speak to a man named Pete about some business. The next day you call back and ask for Pete. But the man who comes to the phone claims not to know who you are, or anything about your business of the day before. Assuming you believe this man, you likely will conclude that you are in contact with a different Pete, a different person, a different mind. Why? Because you expect that if this man were the first Pete, he would not have forgotten your case so quickly. A person's mental states are private—barring ESP, no one else has the same sort of introspective access to them. The first Pete would have introspective access to memory of the conversation; since the second Pete does not have introspective access to these memories, he isn't the same Pete at all. Now consider the following data.

You've no doubt heard of the left and right hemispheres of the brain. In the 1960s, the psychologist Roger Sperry and his colleagues conducted experiments on patients who had undergone a surgical procedure (*commissurotomy,* or *brain bisection*) that cut the main communication channel (*corpus callosum*) between the left and right hemispheres of the brain. Here's a typical experimental procedure. Suppose we have an opaque screen, through which you can put your hands. On the other side of the screen is a bowl of marbles (which you can't see). The experimenter will ask you to pick up a few in your right hand, ascertain the number, return them to the bowl, and then signal with your right hand the number. Then you will be asked to say the number aloud. The procedure is repeated for the left hand. Other things being equal, you will do very well at this simple experiment. But here is what happens when the subject has had a commissurotomy (call such a subject a *split-brain patient,* or *SBP*). The subject behaves typically for the first half of the experiment, when he or she is using the right hand. When switched to the left hand, the typical SBP will correctly signal the number of marbles picked up, but when asked the number will do no better than someone making an educated guess. Hence, if the number is 4, the subject might say any small number, but will not say something crazy, like 2,034. In another experiment, a subject will have the word "keycase" flashed briefly in the center of his visual field and then will be asked to feel objects out of sight with his left hand to find the one corresponding to the word he saw. Unlike normal subjects, the SBP will choose a key, although when asked to identify verbally what he saw, he will say "case." To cut a long story short, the result of these experiments is extremely robust across a variety of tests. Sperry reports:

> One of the more general and also more interesting and striking features of this syndrome may be summarized as an apparent doubling in most of the realms of conscious awareness. Instead of the normally unified single stream of consciousness, these patients behave in many ways as if they have two independent streams of conscious awareness, one in each hemisphere, each of which is cut off from and out of contact with the mental experiences of the other. In other words, each hemisphere seems to have its own separate and private sensations; its own perceptions; its own concepts; and its own impulses to act, with related volitional, cognitive and learning experiences. Following the surgery, each hemisphere also has thereafter its own separate chain of memories that are rendered inaccessible to the recall processes of the other.

In the marbles case, for instance, the left hemisphere receives information from and controls the movements of the fingers of the right hand, and since in almost everybody the speech center is in the left hemisphere, the left hemisphere has no trouble producing the correct verbal response. Similarly, the right hemisphere receives information from and controls the movements of the fingers of the left hand, and has no trouble signaling the correct number. But speech is produced by the left hemisphere, and it seems that the left hemisphere literally *does not know* the correct verbal response—it does not know how many marbles are in the left hand, and produces an educated guess.

One of the aspects of the marbles experiment disturbing to common sense is that the left hemisphere doesn't simply say *I don't know*. Since there's no reason to suppose that the left hemisphere is lying, this phenomenon appears to be an instance of *confabulation*. As has been pointed out several times already in preceding chapters, one of the commonsense assumptions we must reject is the idea that everyone knows exactly what is going on in his or her own mind. Introspection is not an infallible guide to one's mental life. Indeed, some theorizing mechanisms of the brain are outside of introspective consciousness; the brain is constantly inventing plausible hypotheses about your experience. Here's a simple example of everyday confabulation. Look at the diagram below, which is blank except for a small square and a small dot. Close your left eye, and place the diagram a foot or so away from you, looking directly at the square with your right eye. Now slowly move the page toward you, staring steadily at the square, until the dot disappears. You have discovered the location of your *blind spot*—the spot where your optic nerve passes through the retina. The reason the dot disappears is that you cannot see what is in your blind spot, and your brain fills in that area of your visual field with its best guess at what is there. Since the surrounding page is white, your brain tells you that that area is white, too. Notice that your brain does this without *you*. Indeed, without the experiment you might never have noticed that you have a blind spot in each eye. (To try this out with your left eye, turn the page upside down.)

■ ●

Wilder confabulations turn up in cases of brain pathology. For instance, Korsakoff's syndrome causes subjects to lose their short-term memory. Place a glass in the sufferer's hand and he will invent an impressive story for how it came to be there. He's not lying—he just doesn't know that it's an invention. Probably the same sort of process goes on in the SBP. After all, how can a subject not know what is in his own hand? The left brain probably invents the most plausible story it can which does not threaten the assumption that everyone knows what is in his or her own hands. So the left brain makes an educated guess and explains away the errors.

Sperry is rather cautious in his description of the SBP's behavior. But the philosopher Roland Puccetti brings a three-stage argument to a rather startling conclusion. Ask yourself what the best explanation is of the strange behavior of SBPs. Surely the situation resembles that of your telephone contact with the two distinct Petes. We find in SBPs a radical failure of access between the two hemispheres, and yet each is otherwise a complete mind, with its own beliefs, desires, memories, intentions, and so on. (To reinforce this idea, consider that on one occasion an SBP was observed sitting in front of the television set with a newspaper; every time one hand brought the newspaper up in front of his face, the other hand would bat it away to allow a clear a view of the television.) The obvious evidential conclusion is that we are dealing with two separate minds and two separate persons, each housed in one hemisphere of the brain.

Now ask yourself what the best explanation is of the fact that SBPs house two minds and two persons. There seem to be two possibilities. One is that there was a single mind and person, which split into two when the commissurotomy was performed; in other words, the original person *fissed*. The other is that there were two minds and persons all along, and the operation revealed their existence. Is it plausible that this is a case of fission? Notice that unlike the transport doubling of Riker there is no duplicating procedure here. All that happened is that a surgeon took a scalpel and sliced a bundle of nerve fibers. Is it plausible that this somehow creates at least one brand new mind, and at least one brand new person? Not very. It is far more plausible that cutting the communication channel merely reveals the existence of the two minds, and the two persons, that have been there all along. So we ought to conclude that SBPs housed two minds, and two persons, all along.

Stage three. Ask yourself, Is there anything special about pre-op SBPs? Well, most of them were severely epileptic and the operation was performed in the hope of preventing potentially fatal *grand mal* seizures in these subjects. (In this respect, the procedure was a moderate success; severing the corpus callosum seemed to prevent the spread of seizures from one hemisphere to the other.) But apart from the epilepsy, was there anything unusual about these subjects before the operation? No—they have brains that are structured exactly as yours and mine are; that is, the brains of SBPs prior to the commissurotomy are representative of the brains of the rest of the population. So the obvious, startling conclusion to draw is that *every normal human organism houses two minds and two persons*. As I like to say, each of us is really a pair of Siamese twins, permanently joined at the brain!

Two main objections might be offered to Puccetti's argument. As the philosopher Thomas Nagel points out, the following argument has a conclusion that is inconsistent with an assumption in the very first step. Suppose one comes to the conclusion that an SBP has two minds *by comparing SBPs to normal humans*. Since the behavior of SBPs is not like ours, we conclude that they have two of what we have, hence we conclude that they house two minds and persons. But we cannot then conclude that normal humans have two minds and persons, too, on pain of inconsistency! In the form in which I have presented Puccetti's argument, however, it is immune to this objection. We begin with our conception of a mind, and the token identity criteria for a mind, and we apply these criteria directly to the SBPs' behavior. No assumption about normal human organisms enters into the argument at all, so there is no inconsistency.

The second objection is more promising. If Puccetti is correct, then each of us is just like Data after he has been invaded by Dr. Graves. *We are not alone!* But the internal conflict between Data and Graves manifests itself in behavior, and enables Picard to infer that Data is not alone in there. So if Puccetti is correct, then we ought to observe conflict in normal human organisms—conflict like that demonstrated by the man whose two hands battled over the television and the newspaper. Since we do not observe such conflicts, then Puccetti's conclusion must be false.

The reply is in two parts. First, let's separate mentality into two areas—informational and volitional. Beliefs, memories, and sensory experience are informational, and desires and intentions are volitional. In a human organism with the corpus callosum intact, there is nearly instantaneous exchange of information across the hemispheres (and most of the experiences of the two hemispheres are nearly identical anyway). Hence one would expect each hemisphere to have almost exactly the same informational states, and such states are not going to be a cause of conflict. Turning to volitional states: since both hemispheres share the same interest in the body, there will probably be an impressive intersection of desires and intentions, too. But the match is unlikely to be so close to perfect that conflicts do not occur, so what explains the apparent unity of volitional states? Here Puccetti points to the fact that almost everyone has the speech center in the left hemisphere, and he speculates that the left-hemisphere person—*Lefty*—literally dominates *Righty*. Lefty is a bully, and controls not only speech but most of what the body does in volitional terms. So, for much of the time, Righty is a helpless accomplice in Lefty's actions.

This reply also answers a third objection that may have occurred to you. If there are two of you in there, why does it seem like only one? The answer is, of course, that the *you* in question here probably is Lefty—and you have been in control so long that Righty is practically invisible to you. If you speak your present mind, and Righty hears you, Righty is probably thinking, "*I'm* here, you bully!" Notice a tricky ethical problem that arises if this schizoid view of humans is correct. If Lefty commits a crime in which Righty is unwillingly along for the ride, then punishing Lefty is also punishing the innocent Righty. And perhaps Righty occasionally exacts revenge, taking advantage of a relaxation of control by Lefty to get Lefty into trouble, too!

This all fits well with Troi's claim that she senses duality in humans. Because she is an empath, she can sense the conflict between Lefty and Righty even when it does not manifest itself in behavior. And the "being at the crossroads" phenomenon she describes is probably not unfamiliar—a feeling of conflicting volitions attempting to drive your body.

It might also occur to you to ask why we seem to have two brains. Consider that Klingons, such as Lieutenant Worf, have two of just about everything in their bodies. The advantages of such an arrangement are demonstrated in the *Next Generation* episode "Ethics," when Worf apparently dies and then a backup system kicks in and he recovers. Such wholesale duplication of systems is especially useful in a warrior race, but we have backup systems, too. We have two gonads, two kidneys, and two lungs, and can survive and reproduce if we lose one of the pair. Perhaps the brain really is two brains joined together, and we have two because a brain is so important that it's worth having a backup. The evidence from brain pathology supports this speculation, for a human organism can survive the destruction of one hemisphere. Indeed, if the destruction occurs early enough in life, the organism can function almost completely normally. This is so even if the left hemisphere is the one destroyed: the right hemisphere takes over the production of speech with little or no difficulty if the loss occurs in early childhood.

Ponder for a moment what it would be like to be Righty—of course, all you Righties know what I'm talking about! Wouldn't it be awfully frustrating? Indeed, a lifetime of living in Lefty's shadow might produce some strange psychological characteristics. With this thought in mind, consider some of the more popularly known phenomena that have no easy naturalistic explanation, such as "demonic possession," automatic writing, and hypnosis. In automatic writing (and its related phenomena, such as successful use of the Ouija board), a subject will produce sensible writing that he or she claims to have no control over. Often such writing is done with the left hand, and often, strikingly, the result is "mirror" writing—writing that one has to look at in a mirror to read. (One subject produced five novels apparently through automatic writing.) In hypnosis, there is a phenomenon known as the *hidden observer,* discovered relatively recently by the psychologist Ernest Hilgard in the course of demonstrating hypnotic deafness in a blind subject. One can say to a hypnotized subject, "When I count to three, you will be deaf. You will not hear anything at all, and you will remain that way until I place my hand on your right shoulder." One can then make all sorts of noises and speeches with no reaction from the subject, who after hypnosis will not remember any of them. Hilgard discovered that he could contact "some part of" the hypnotized subject, who heard and remembered everything. Hilgard dubbed this part the *hidden observer*.

Perhaps the existence of Lefty and Righty can explain some or all of these phenomena, perhaps not. It may also explain mediumship and the New Age phenomenon of "channeling," and it may even explain what the psychologist Julian Jaynes claims is the fact that our ancestors literally heard voices in their heads telling them what to do (before Lefties won the struggle for the body?). On the other hand, it certainly cannot completely explain multiple personality disorder, and we may well have to conclude that, as well as divisions in consciousness between the two brains, there might be all sorts of poorly understood divisions in consciousness within each brain. As usual, the more we find out, the less we know.

One thing seems sure, though: the unity-of-consciousness assumption doesn't have a lot going for it! Indeed, just as eliminativists predict that we shall discover there really is no such thing as consciousness (see chapter 3), the whole notion of "persons" and "selves" might turn out to be a fiction. Perhaps there is no real executive control in the brain at all—perhaps things just happen, the way they do in ordinary life. The philosopher Daniel Dennett and the psychologist Nicholas Humphrey liken the self to the head of a government. The head of government has a mainly symbolic function, with little or no actual power, but it may be good for the nation to live under the illusion that someone responsible is at the helm. Similarly, it may be useful for human organisms to *confabulate* the illusion that each of us has a single person at the helm, directing actions in a rational way.

But suppose there really are persons. Then if the unity-of-consciousness assumption is false, the potential ethical implications for punishment and reward are serious, as I mentioned earlier. There are implications for therapy, too. Since we commonsensically regard strict unity as normal and desirable, we naturally suppose that dissociated subjects need to be cured, and we celebrate the reintegration of personalities in multiple-personality cases. However, it is not uncommon for the reintegrated subject to report deep sorrow and feelings of loss, as one would at the death of a loved one. Putting all this to one side, let's suppose that unity really is desirable, and that every human organism really is a set of Siamese twins joined at the brain. Then there is another practical application of the *transporter therapy* I described earlier. We simply scan Lefty and Righty independently, and materialize two subjects, one of whom is Lefty's mental continuer while the other is Righty's continuer. Of course, the prefission subject might object to this separation, but then that is only Lefty talking, and liberation from Lefty is Righty's right. Right?

Which brings us back to Kirk's fission in "The Enemy Within." Perhaps the "good" Kirk is Lefty and the "evil" Kirk is Righty ("evil" Kirk seems to have difficulty with speech, for instance). Wouldn't you go a bit over the top if you were finally unleashed from servitude to Lefty? And wouldn't you resist fusion with Lefty, the return to servitude, as the "evil" Kirk does? Apparently the episode was intended to point up the difference between the higher cognitive functions of the mind/brain and its lower, emotional, animal functions (see Yvonne Fern's *Gene Roddenberry: The Last Conversation*), but it's hard to understand how a transporter accident could produce such a fission. A Lefty/Righty split seems far more more plausible.

Personal Growth

PICARD: "You said yourself that this is only a possibility."

DR. CRUSHER: "But you've been to the future—you *know* it's going to happen."

PICARD: "I prefer to look on the future as something that's not written in stone."

—TNG: *"All Good Things . . . "*

DATA: "One cannot cheat fate."

PICARD: "Perhaps not, Mr. Data, but we can at least give it a try."

—TNG: *"Time's Arrow I"*

"Well, I know this much. We can't avoid the future."

—*Riker,* TNG: *"Time Squared"*

Temporal Distortions

chapter 6

In *The Physics of Star Trek,* Lawrence Krauss counts twenty-two episodes of the original series and *The Next Generation* which involve time travel. Add to this three of the movies and quite a few episodes of the continuing series, including *DS9:* "Past Tense I & II" and *Voyager:* "Future's End I & II." Let's face it, there's a lot of time travel going on in *Star Trek.* Krauss's interest in time travel, naturally enough, is a physical one; he considers whether time travel is physically possible. But many philosophers have wondered whether time travel is even logically possible; that is, does the very idea embody contradiction? If time travel is logically impossible, we can save the physicists a lot of trouble, since nothing can be logically impossible but physically possible.

To this end, several paradoxes of time travel have been put forward. But before we examine any of these, it is useful to get a handle on just what time travel is supposed to be. First, it's not enough to simply have an experience of being in another time (as did Ebenezer Scrooge, in Dickens's *A Christmas Carol,* who saw parts of his past and potential future). This is too much like a hallucination. Looking into a (genuine) crystal ball won't do it, either, for one manifestly remains in the present. One must *go* to another time to be a time traveler.

But time travel is also more than just moving from one time to another. Since you were around a year ago, and you are around now, that alone makes you a time traveler. Time travel is something out of the ordinary, and surely what is involved is some sort of deviation from the passage through time of ordinary lives.

But what sort of deviation? I don't think I will live to see the twenty-fourth century, but I could be wrong. Suppose I'm placed in suspended animation and awaken, rather like Rip Van Winkle, exactly four hundred years from now. It will seem to me as though hardly any time has passed, but this isn't a true case of time travel. Why not? Because I've really been "here" all along, enduring the centuries with a succession of other people; I was just blissfully ignorant of the passage of time. To see the point more clearly, imagine that I have a reliable timepiece implanted in my cranium. The time elapsed on this clock will match the ordinary passage of time external to me (that is, four hundred years). I have overslept and not time traveled (nor has Scotty, in *TNG:* "Relics").

The same goes for the converse case. If I dream or otherwise have the experience of a great deal of time passing even though it has not, then this isn't time travel either. In two *Next Generation* episodes, Picard has this sort of experience. In "Inner Light," an alien mind probe causes him to live about forty years' worth of experiences in under twenty-five actual minutes. In the Capraesque "Tapestry," he is badly wounded, and as he lies dying on the operating table in the *Enterprise-D* sick bay, the omnipotent Q appears privately to him. Picard admits to Q that he regrets the choices he made early in life, and Q gives him the chance to relive some of it. The experience spans (parts of) many years, but Picard never leaves the operating table. In both of these cases, a reliable timepiece in Picard's cranium would have recorded the true passage of time for him, and this would match perfectly the passage of time external to him.

This suggests a condition on time travel. The passage of time for the time traveler must not only seem to be but really be different from the passage of time external to him. The philosopher David Lewis calls this the difference between *personal* time and *external* time. So I time travel to the future only if my personal journey time differs from the external time elapsed. If my journey takes an hour of personal time, and I arrive four hundred years in the future in external time, then I have time traveled.

Is *any* discrepancy of this sort sufficient for time travel? This is a hard question, but I doubt it. Simply by traveling very fast, one can produce a time discrepancy, as any neophyte in physics knows. I might go on a long, very fast journey that takes ten years and return to find that fifty years had passed on Earth. Although this makes acceleration into the future a possibility, it doesn't provide the sort of symmetry that turns up in time-travel plots like those in *Star Trek,* since I can't go into the past in this way. Genuine time travel seems to involve the possibility of a return journey. The time pod operated by the inventor Berlingoff Rasmussen in *TNG:* "A Matter of Time" is typical in this respect—with it, one is free to move about in time, backward and forward. This suggests a condition on the nature of time itself: time must be a dimension, very like the spatial dimensions. Many if not most philosophers nowadays accept this condition, adopting the view known as *four-dimensionalism*. According to four-dimensionalism, other times are just like other places. "Now" is just like "here." Just as some other place exists even though you now are not there, so some other time exists even though you now are not then. Other places are somewhere else, and other times are some*when* else.

Length, Breadth, Height, and Time

In chapter 4, I gave an account of personal identity over time which presupposed four-dimensionalism about persons. *I-now* am just a temporal slice of the four-dimensional spacetime worm that is Richard Hanley, and *you-now* are just a temporal slice of the four-dimensional spacetime worm that is you. According to four-dimensionalism, we should view the entire universe (past, present, and future) in this way, as the mother of all spacetime worms. Consider the following analogy: The universe appears to us ordinary folk as a movie appears to the audience in a movie theater. All we experience at any time is one part of the movie, the "present." We can reconstruct what happened earlier in two ways—by consulting our memories (history), and by making inferences based on what is happening in the present. We can try to predict the future by making inferences based on what is happening in the present. But we cannot check independently the accuracy of these memories or inferences. We are trapped in the present. God is supposed to be outside time altogether (or at least all times are to God as the present is to us), so God has other ways of knowing what the past and future hold. In the movie analogy, God sees all the frames at once. The time traveler is somewhere between God and us. Like us, he can experience only one time, his present, but like God he can examine first-hand what to us are other times—past and future. To stretch the movie analogy a bit, his time machine is a remote control, which allows him to skip back or skip ahead.

Before examining four-dimensionalism more closely, let's consider its chief rival, *presentism,* usually regarded as the commonsense view of time. According to presentism, only the present is real. It is not the case that the past and future exist. Of course, what is past did exist, once (when it was the present), but it doesn't exist any more. It's gone, closed, over, if not forgotten. And the future will exist, but it doesn't exist until it's the present. (One has to be very careful in trying to state the difference between four-dimensionalism and presentism. For instance, the presentist thinks that the future doesn't exist *yet,* but if this just means that it doesn't exist *now,* then the four-dimensionalist agrees. Consider the spatial analogue: I am in Melbourne, and New York certainly exists, but it doesn't exist *here*.) Moreover, unlike the four-dimensionalist, the presentist thinks that there is an important asymmetry between past and future. The past happened in just one way, and we can now state truths about the past. (For example, either Oswald shot Kennedy or he didn't, and that's all there is to it.) But the future is an array of mere possibilities. It isn't fixed, even though as a matter of fact (according to most presentists, anyway) there is only one way that the future will turn out. The presentist sees time as rather like a zipper. The present is represented by the location of the zipper head, the past is the closed-off seam behind the zipper head, and the future gapes open. Time's passage is represented by the motion of the zipper head, moving from one present to the next—turning future possibilities into past facts, so to speak.

But presentism leaves no room for time travel. If the future doesn't exist until it becomes the present by means of the ordinary passage of time, how can one get "then" by any accelerated means? There isn't a "then" to go to yet! And if the past is over, doesn't exist, and never will, there is no "then" at all. Presentism seems to leave the time traveler with nowhere and no*when* to go!

I don't think presentism is true. For one thing, if presentism is true, then there are no particular truths about the future. It's not true that so-and-so will win the men's 100-meter sprint final at the Sydney 2000 Olympics, for instance. It's not true that the 2000 Olympics will be held in Sydney. It's not true that there will be an Olympics in the year 2000. But it's also not true that there won't be an Olympics in the year 2000. It's not true that there will be a year 2000, and not true that there won't be a year 2000. It's true that there's only one way that things will turn out, but it's not true of any one way that *that's* the way things will turn out. (It isn't even true that in the year 2001 it will be true that there was a year 2000, although *now* it's true that there was a year 1900.) Moreover, if there are no particular truths about the future, then no one can know any particular thing about the future, not even God. All in all, I prefer to embrace particular truths about the future, and am inclined to reject presentism on this ground alone.

But suppose I'm wrong and presentism is true. Still, it isn't true of necessity. Four-dimensionalism is logically possible. And if four-dimensionalism is possible, then time travel might be possible too. At least, the existence of the past and future leave the time traveler with somewhen to go. So the question to ask now is, Is time travel possible in a four-dimensional universe? If it is, some puzzling paradoxes need to be resolved.

The Grandfather Paradox

> "History cannot be changed."
>
> —*Spock to Kirk,* TOS: *"Spectre of the Gun"*

This one is well-known among both philosophers and physicists. If time travel to the past is possible, then someone—myself, say—can travel back in time and affect what happens in the past. For instance, I can get a gun and kill somebody. I might kill one of my ancestors—say, my paternal grandfather, in 1920. The trouble is, my father wasn't born until 1929, so if I killed my grandfather in 1920, wouldn't it be true that I would never come into existence? But I must exist in order to kill my grandfather! Since I cannot exist and yet fail to exist (a contradiction), it must be impossible for me to travel to the past and kill my grandfather in 1920. But if time travel to the past is possible, then it surely is possible for me to kill my grandfather in 1920. So time travel (to the past, anyway) must be impossible.

Star Trek firmly embraces this paradoxical plotline. In *The Next Generation*'s final installment, "All Good Things . . . ," Picard's attempt to seal a temporal rift threatens to affect the past by preventing the event that kicked off the evolution of life on Earth. Picard has to undo the damage (and succeeds, of course), but the clear implication is that had he failed, then Picard and everything else in the history of terrestrial civilization would not exist. Once again, this possibility embraces a contradiction: how can Picard cause himself never to have existed? The solution seems to be that the whole plotline is impossible. Fun, but impossible.

Still, while the plot premise of "All Good Things . . ." is impossible (apparently, anyway—I'll come back to this), most of what actually happens in *Star Trek* time-travel episodes is not impossible. For instance, there is a way of resolving the Grandfather Paradox without denying the possibility of time travel, but it's inconsistent with the presumptions in nearly every *Star Trek* time-travel story. Central to most of these stories is the idea of a *chronoclasm.* (I borrow this marvelous term from the time-travel story "Chronoclasm," by science fiction writer John Wyndham.) Roughly, the idea is that there are certain crucial points in history where any changes to "what happened" result in a calamitous "ripple effect" of further changes. In *TOS:* "The City on the Edge of Forever," the *Enterprise* encounters a bumpy patch of space in the vicinity of an uncharted planet, which causes McCoy to accidentally inject himself with a large dose of "cordrazine," inducing a paranoiac mania. The manic McCoy, bent on escape from the *Enterprise,* beams down to the planet, and a landing party follows in pursuit. On the surface, Kirk, Spock, and the others find the "Guardian of Forever," a machine with a portal through which one can see other times and places. While the landing party is watching Earth's history unfold, McCoy suddenly appears and leaps through the portal into 1930. Not a good move. As the landing party watches in horror, Earth's history changes: the Nazis win the Second World War; there is no peaceful twenty-third century, no United Federation of Planets, and no starship *Enterprise* (the landing party hails the ship, with no response). A chronoclasm has occurred, and the burden is on Kirk and Spock, who decide that McCoy must be the culprit, to undo the damage by going back in time to 1930, too. Landing in what appears to be New York City, they meet up with Edith Keeler, who runs a shelter for the homeless. When Spock jury-rigs a computer to read out the immediate future, they discover that Edith Keeler is the key figure in the chronoclasm: She is supposed to die in 1930 in a car accident. Apparently, McCoy will somehow prevent this from happening. In the new future, she will remain alive and, as an ardent pacifist, will persuade the leaders of the United States not to enter the Second World War, unless Kirk and Spock can stop McCoy.

The idea of a chronoclasm, so beloved by the *Star Trek* writers, presupposes that one can travel back in time and act so as to change the past and, by the ripple effect, everything that ensues. Yet if we drop the assumption that the past can be changed, the Grandfather Paradox can be resolved. Should we then drop the assumption? Let's reconsider the paradox. What should be obvious is that since I, the time traveler, exist, I *cannot* succeed in killing my grandfather before my father has been conceived. This doesn't mean that I cannot travel back in time, but only that there are things it's logically impossible for me to do in the past. Which things? Here you might think that the restrictions that logic places on me concern only those matters affecting me directly. But this isn't right. My father was born in 1929, and my grandfather died in 1934. Doesn't this imply that I could go back in time to 1930 and bump off my grandfather a few years early but after my father's birth? This wouldn't threaten *my* existence, after all. There's a simple reason why I cannot do this: *my grandfather died in 1934!* (I suppose resurrection is a logical possibility, but let's eliminate it by supposing that my grandfather died but once.) Since it's impossible for my grandfather to die in 1930 *and* in 1934, I cannot kill my grandfather in 1930. Logic will defeat me just as surely in 1930 as in 1920.

In both the four-dimensionalist and presentist conceptions of time, there is only one past. For instance, why is it true that Kennedy was assassinated in 1963? Because that's what happened. Why isn't it true that Kennedy survived to lead the United States to victory in Vietnam? Because that's not what happened. So in the four-dimensionalist view we are considering, it is logically possible to travel back to the past, but it is not logically possible to travel back to the past and change it. Hence any story in which someone travels to the past and changes it has a logically impossible plot.

But mustn't we therefore concede that time travel itself is logically impossible? After all, if you journey to the past you must affect it merely by being there. If you really are in the past, then of necessity you affect the past, and it affects you. To take the most fundamental of cases, you wouldn't be able to see or hear or touch anything if the world around you didn't causally impinge on your senses, and in doing so you would absorb light, cast a shadow, and so forth. No matter how careful you try to be, if you travel to the past you are *in* the past, and you must affect it. So how can you help but change it?

This objection relies upon a conflation: it is one thing to affect the past, and quite another to change it. Suppose I jump into my time machine and travel back to 1920. The common picture, which I am urging you to resist, looks at time travel in the following way. *Before* I got into my time machine, there was a 1920 without me. I wasn't born until 1957, and that was the first the world saw of me. *After* I got into the time machine and took my journey, there was another, changed 1920, with me in it. This picture hardly seems coherent; I for one have no idea what the italicized "before" and "after" are supposed to mean. Here is a different, more coherent picture: there is only one 1920, and it has me in it. Putting this another way, if I was not around at all in 1920, then it's impossible that a time machine takes me there, and if I was around in 1920, then it's impossible that something like a time machine does *not* take me there! If I was around in 1920, then I affected the past, as did everyone else who was around in 1920. The path that the future took depended partly on what I did in 1920.

Armed with the understanding that there is only one past, we can make consistent sense of "The City on the Edge of Forever." In the end, the chronoclasm is "averted," but in fact it could not have happened anyway, since it *didn't* happen. Because the Nazis lost the Second World War, nothing McCoy could do would have prevented their defeat. But at the same time it's not true that McCoy couldn't have done anything at all back in 1930. That things happened the way they did *depended on the presence of the time travelers*. There was only one 1930, and Kirk, Spock, and McCoy were there. Kirk and Spock didn't just prevent McCoy from saving Edith Keeler, they were instrumental in what in fact occurred. In the episode's denouement, Keeler has already crossed the street safely, and when she sees Kirk and Spock struggling with McCoy she turns and runs back toward them, only to be a hit by a car. It was the time travelers who got her killed! Still, we need to use a bit of license to make the rest of the story consistent. Earth's history does not change after all, so why did the landing party *see* the "changes" when they looked into the portal back on the Guardian's planet? Because the Guardian (in Capraesque fashion) showed Kirk and the others what would have been if (contrary to fact) Edith Keeler had remained alive. Given that Kirk and Spock were around in 1930 too, *something* had to motivate them to follow McCoy through the portal, and this ruse by the Guardian, together with their false belief in chronoclasms, did the trick. If they had had their wits about them, they would never have fallen for the ruse. If the chronoclasm had really occurred, and the Federation and the *Enterprise* therefore not existed, what would explain their presence, in their Federation uniforms, on the Guardian's planet in the first place? In general, it seems a requirement of an interesting time travel story that the travelers themselves be mistaken about what they can do. Only if they think they can make a difference will they even bother to try.

I should mention that the writers of *Star Trek,* as they often do, provide a post-hoc explanation of their error—in this case, allowing an apparent drastic change in history to leave the landing party itself unaffected. I explained this away as a ruse, but a different explanation is offered in *DS9:* "Past Tense I." The senior officers from Deep Space Nine are in orbit around Earth in the *Defiant*. Commander Benjamin Sisko, Dr. Bashir, and Jadzia Dax beam down, but are accidentally transported back to San Francisco in 2024, to the time of some world-changing events. Sisko knows the history: There were deep social divisions, and large numbers of homeless people were forced into walled sections of the city known as "sanctuaries" and run by government troops. In 2024, one sanctuary was taken over by the homeless, who took hostages in the process. One of the homeless, Gabriel Bell, was instrumental in keeping the hostages alive and forcing the authorities to institute social reform, putting the United States on the path toward more enlightened government. With no money or identification, Sisko and Bashir soon find themselves in a sanctuary, and in a fight with some thugs. A man comes to their rescue and is killed. Sure enough, it's Gabriel Bell! *Chronoclasm!* Sisko realizes that he must take Bell's place, and succeeds in doing everything that Gabriel Bell is famous for.

Back on board the *Defiant,* in orbit around twenty-fourth-century Earth, Kira Nerys and Miles O'Brien have figured out that the away team was accidentally sent into the past. But Starfleet command, concerned about contaminating the timeline, issues an order prohibiting rescue attempts. When Kira and O'Brien suddenly lose all contact with Starfleet installations—including sensor readings—like the landing party in "The City on the Edge of Forever," they quickly come to the conclusion that the timeline has been altered; history has somehow been changed, and they may have to take action to restore it. Then Kira asks the obvious question: Why weren't *we* affected? O'Brien offers what I shall call the *chronoton-particle protection hypothesis*. Apparently, the *Defiant*'s "cloaking" device generated "chronoton particles," and the passage of a microscopic singularity polarized these particles, which is what turned the transporter into a time machine. O'Brien hypothesizes that this singularity also "created some kind of subspace bubble around the ship—isolated it from the changes in time."

This is just the sort of "and then a miracle occurred" explanation that should be avoided in making sense of a time-travel story. The chronoton-particle protection hypothesis not only suggests that chronoclasms are possible and that there are different possible timelines, but also that one can be in one timeline and yet not be a part of it. After all, the "subspace bubble" doesn't prevent the influx of ordinary information from the "new" world (that's how Kira and O'Brien discover that things have changed), so the "new" world changes do have an effect on what occurs within the bubble. The bubble is somehow semipermeable to causation, along no principled line that I can discern. I don't buy it, and neither should you! Here's my alternative interpretation: in order to rescue Sisko, Bashir, and Jadzia Dax, O'Brien and company have to find them by looking in time. The only "miracle" that occurs is a coincidence: the total loss of communication with Starfleet combined with faulty sensor readings. This leads the *Defiant* crew mistakenly to suppose that the past has been changed, which prompts them to ignore Starfleet orders and attempt the search and succeed in the rescue.

Another aspect of "changing the past" (if we allow this possibility for a moment) is never satisfactorily resolved in *Star Trek*. The attitude of Starfleet concerning "contamination of timelines"—also known as the Starfleet Temporal Displacement Policy—clearly is a relative of the Prime Directive, a sort of *Don't interfere with history* analogue of it. In *Voyager:* "Time and Again," Captain Janeway invokes this policy. She is part of an away team investigating the remains of a planet. They discover that an enormous explosion has destroyed the entire civilization there just hours before their arrival. Moreover, the blast produced local fractures in time, one of which sends Janeway and Lieutenant Tom Paris back one day in time. They thus find themselves in the awkward position of knowing that all the local inhabitants are doomed, and Paris favors letting them know, in an effort to save lives. Janeway disagrees, specifically invoking the "noninterference in natural development" clause of the Prime Directive. Paris quite rightly balks at the idea that total annihilation is a "natural" developmental outcome, but that is beside the present point. It isn't clear (to me, at least) how far this Temporal Displacement policy extends. Suppose that interfering with history will produce a *better* future—a chrono*bonus*? After all, no one history, one timeline, one future is inherently privileged, so there doesn't seem anything inherently bad about changing things. Perhaps the policy is meant to prevent Starfleet crews from unwittingly making things worse, but if things are (were, will be) already bad enough, isn't it worth a try, every now and then?

What Could I Have Done?

I haven't yet properly disposed of the Grandfather Paradox. The remaining problem is that although I have said that I cannot possibly kill my grandfather in 1920 or 1930, there's a perfectly good sense in which I can. Surely I can train myself to be a flawless shot, and properly maintain my weapon, and lie in wait for my grandfather on a windless day, and pull the trigger at point-blank range. If anybody can kill anybody, then I can kill my grandfather! It must be that a miracle occurs to save him from the lethal bullet. But I do not want to introduce miracles to make time travel possible, so I agree that I can kill my grandfather. But now I'm faced once again with contradiction, for I have claimed that I can kill my grandfather, but also that I cannot.

Fortunately there's a way out, because words like "can" (and so also "could") are ambiguous. I'm sure you'll agree that Michael Jordan can make a three-point basket in the final seconds to win the game. If anyone can do it, Jordan can. That's why the Bulls get the ball to him on the perimeter. This is the *general* sense of "can," which pertains to one's capabilities. But Jordan sometimes misses, and he might well say of such a miss, "I tried to make it, but I couldn't." This is the *particular* sense of "can," which simply refers to success or failure on a particular occasion. Jordan wouldn't contradict himself if he were to say, "I could make it, but I couldn't make it." Similarly, given time travel, I agree that I could kill my grandfather in the general sense of "can," but I deny that I could kill my grandfather in the particular sense of "can." There is no contradiction here.

One World or Many?

You may well have heard of the "many worlds" interpretation of quantum mechanics. The idea roughly is this. At the quantum level, the future genuinely is open (as presentism suggests), but there isn't only one way that the future will go. Rather, every way that the future *can* go is a way that the future *does* go. Every time a quantum "choice" is made, parallel but different universes are produced. As Data puts it in *TNG:* "Parallels," at the quantum level "all things which can occur, do occur." If these quantum choices are reflected in genuine alternatives at the macroscopic level, then perhaps we are wrong to dismiss the idea of more than one past. There would be instead uncountably many pasts.

This is a fascinating idea, but it matters not at all to the present discussion. First of all, the most important feature of four-dimensionalism for our purposes is not the claim that there is a *single* time dimension but rather the claim that time is importantly like space. It is the *spatialization* of time that matters. I wish to argue that time travel is logically possible, by using what I think is the most plausible account of time, but it wouldn't upset me (or change the fact that chronoclasm is impossible) if there were more than one time dimension. Suppose there are indeed "many worlds." Still, the world that includes you and me and this book is a *single* world, a single timeline. There is in this world only one way that the past has gone. Hence my killing my grandfather is not an event in this world—it couldn't be, since here I am. And notice something else—it is very difficult to make sense of personal identity through time in the "many worlds" picture. For instance, there are uncountably many individuals, all in different worlds, all called "Richard Hanley." But these individuals are not identical to each other—rather they are counterparts of each other. So even in another world, it's not true that *I* do anything. The Richard Hanley in that world is some other chap! This identity difference is implicitly acknowledged in *Star Trek* when alternative timelines somehow intersect (as occurs in the original series in "Mirror, Mirror" and its sequels in *Deep Space Nine:* "Crossover," "Through the Looking Glass," and "Shattered Mirror"). You do not get to replace your mirror-universe counterpart from the inside; rather, you are *you,* either miraculously transplanted into your counterpart's place (as in "Mirror, Mirror") or else there along with your counterpart (as in "Crossover," "Through the Looking Glass," and "Shattered Mirror").

Suppose my time machine is a "world jumper," a machine that can take me to an alternative 1920. Couldn't I kill my grandfather—that is, my grandfather's counterpart—in *this* world, since my existence is not, as a matter of logic, threatened by his death? It seems so, in which case my grandfather has no descendants in the world I'm visiting. But this, once again, is not a matter of changing the past. I haven't changed the past in my own world, and (by our previous reasoning) since I was there in the other world to prevent my grandfather from procreating, I haven't changed anything in that world, either. Nor is there any contradiction, since there is no world in which it is true that I do and don't exist, or that I do and don't kill my grandfather.

"Yesterday's *Enterprise*"

I don't yet expect you to be convinced that the idea of changing the past can't be saved: it's too deeply ingrained into our science fiction consciousness. So let's allow that there are alternative timelines—

however this is to be explained—and think about things from the point of view not of the time travelers or world jumpers, but of everyone else. Consider the third-season *Next Generation* episode "Yesterday's *Enterprise,*" which has generated a small interpretation industry among Trekkers. When Picard and company in the *Enterprise-D* investigate yet another anomaly, it turns out to be a temporal rift, and a ship—apparently a Federation starship—appears from out of the rift. Suddenly just about everything on board the *Enterprise-D* changes. The Klingon Worf is no longer a member of the crew, Lieutenant Tasha Yar—who was killed on Vagra II by a creature called Armus, in the first-season episode "Skin of Evil"—is back, and everyone remembers the past twenty-two years as dominated by a long and bloody war with the Klingon Empire, a war the Federation is losing.

The ship that emerged from the temporal rift is the *Enterprise-C,* and it has jumped twenty-two years into the future. Guinan, on board the *Enterprise-D,* somehow knows that something is wrong—for instance, she knows that Lieutenant Yar "doesn't belong here"—and tells Picard. Eventually they figure out what has happened. By leaving the past in the middle of battle, the *Enterprise-C* failed to defend a Klingon outpost from Romulan attack, and *chronoclasm!* Instead of the battle's leading to an alliance between the grateful Klingon Empire and the Federation, the incident provoked full-scale war. Something must be done, and the crew of the *Enterprise-C* are willing to do it: they will return to their own time and defend the Klingon outpost, even though it means certain death. Tasha Yar, who has been told by Guinan that her death—that is, her death on Vagra II—was meaningless, volunteers to go with them. Meanwhile, the Klingons arrive and begin firing on both vessels. The *Enterprise-D* places itself in the firing line—and is apparently destroyed—to protect the *Enterprise-C,* which disappears back into the temporal rift. Suddenly, we see the crew back in their familiar roles on board the *Enterprise-D,* as if nothing ever happened.

This episode cannot be explained away as a single timeline travel story, because the chronoclasmic events really do happen. The altered *Enterprise-D* is a part of the chronoclasm, and the people on the altered *Enterprise-D* are instrumental in returning things to "normal." If they cause anything, then they must exist. But this immediately leads to contradiction: for instance, it is true that Tasha Yar both was and wasn't killed on Vagra II. I conclude that "Yesterday's *Enterprise*" is not a single timeline travel story but rather a case of world jumping.

Here's what *really* happens. There are two timelines—two worlds or universes: one is the world we have been learning about in previous *Next Generation* episodes. Although no timeline is inherently privileged, I'll assume that the world we have been learning about is our world, our timeline (that, surely, is what *Star Trek* invites us to imagine). Our world contains the *Enterprise-D* and her crew; the alternative world contains their counterparts. I shall refer to the inhabitants of the alternative world as alt-*Enterprise-D,* alt-*Enterprise-C,* alt-Picard, alt-Yar, and so on. "Yesterday's *Enterprise*" gives us a glimpse into the alt-timeline. At the beginning of the episode, and again at the end, we see things from the point of view of the people in our timeline, but for the rest of the episode we see things from the point of view of the people in the alt-timeline.

Here's what happens in the alt-timeline. The alt-*Enterprise-C* fails to save the Klingon outpost, leading to twenty-two years of full-scale war between the Klingon Empire and the Federation, a war the Federation is losing. A temporal rift connects the two timelines. (See the following diagram, which shows the two timelines running in parallel, with twenty-two years between time *a* and time *b*.) It connects to our timeline at the time and place of the battle over the Klingon outpost (at time *a*) and to the alt-timeline at the time and place of the alt-*Enterprise-D* (between *b* and *c*). The *Enterprise-C* flies through the rift into the alt-timeline, arriving at time *b*.

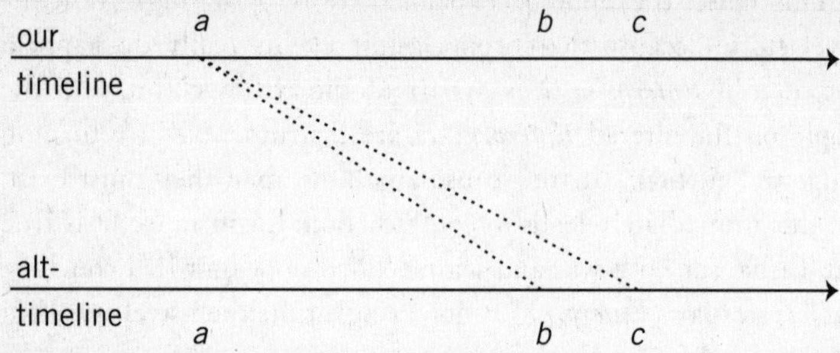

On board the alt-*Enterprise-D,* alt-Guinan—who must have some sort of world-jumping ESP ability—convinces everyone that a chronoclasm has occurred. This is a mistake, of course. But it inspires the crew of the *Enterprise-C,* and alt-Yar, to return to our timeline, and it also inspires the crew of the alt- *Enterprise-D* to sacrifice themselves and their vessel to enable the return (at *c*). The alt-*Enterprise-D* really is destroyed, and alt-Picard and crew with it.

Here's what happens in our timeline. The *Enterprise-C* saves the Klingon outpost, and alt-Yar plays a crucial role in its defense. Without her advanced—twenty-two years advanced—tactical knowledge, the nevertheless doomed *Enterprise-C* would never have lasted long enough to save the Klingon outpost. It would have suffered a fate similar to that of the alt-*Enterprise-C*. So the glimpse into the alt-timeline shows us what would have happened in our timeline, if there had been no temporal rift. Moreover, the actions of the people in the alt-timeline saved their counterparts in this timeline from a similar fate.

This is a perfectly consistent story, which would be a great interpretation of "Yesterday's *Enterprise*" if we could explain away a few things. At the beginning of the episode, the *Enterprise-D* encounters a temporal rift and sees a ship come out of it. Either this is a different temporal rift altogether from the one the *Enterprise-C* goes through (and it's a different ship), or else the one temporal rift *also* connects our timeline at *b* with the alt-timeline at *b*, and the *Enterprise-C* leaves *a*, pops out into our timeline again at *b*, immediately pops back in, and world jumps to alt-timeline *b*. This leaves one loose end: when the *Enterprise-D* crew sees the other ship come out of the temporal rift, we watch the bridge and crew *transform* into the alt-*Enterprise-D* bridge and crew. We *see* Picard become alt-Picard—dramatic license, perhaps?

A later episode of *The Next Generation* supports the world-jumping interpretation of "Yesterday's *Enterprise*." In "Redemption I & II," there is a Romulan officer named Sela, who bears a striking resemblance to Tasha Yar. Indeed, she claims to be Tasha Yar's daughter. But she is twenty-three years old, and Picard calculates that Tasha would have been a young child at the time that Sela was born. How is this possible? The story Sela tells Picard is that when the *Enterprise-C* was destroyed, some Federation personnel were taken prisoner by the Romulans, including Tasha Yar. In exchange for the safety of the other captives, Yar agreed to become the consort of a Romulan general, and subsequently gave birth to Sela. Later, when Sela was four, Yar tried to escape, and was executed.

Sela has some other news for Picard. Her mother told her that it was Picard himself who sent Yar back in time. Picard is reluctant to believe her story, but that's understandable, because he doesn't remember doing any such thing. Nor could he, since it wasn't him but alt-Picard. Sela's story rings true precisely because no one in this timeline but the crew of the *Enterprise-C* knew of the events depicted in "Yesterday's *Enterprise*." Sela's mother, of course, was not Yar but alt-Yar. Yar could not have been executed by the Romulans *and* killed on Vagra II by Armus. The existence of alt-Yar in our timeline clinches the fact that the alternative timeline is real.

Identity in Crisis

I claimed that we cannot appeal to the "many worlds" view to make sense of the assumption of past-changing activity of time travelers in *Star Trek,* partly because of the problems it raises about identity. However, there are problems about identity in the four-dimensionalist view, if we allow backward time travel. For instance, in *TNG:* "Time Squared," Picard meets himself! That is to say, there is a meeting between the "present" Picard and his "future" self, a self who arrives by shuttlecraft from six hours into the future. If time travel to the past is possible, then surely it's possible for the time traveler to journey back to his own past and so bump into his past self, just as Picard does. Of course, the *Enterprise-D* crew, and especially Picard himself, find it difficult to accept the credentials of the interloper, despite Troi's assurance that it is indeed Picard who arrives in the shuttle. Consider Worf's reaction to discovering that the shuttlecraft in which the "other" Picard is found appears to be the very same shuttlecraft (NCC–1701D, U.S.S. *Enterprise-D,* Shuttlecraft 05) as the one sitting next to it in the shuttle bay: "How is this possible!" Worf exclaims. *Two* Shuttlecraft 05s? *Two* Picards?

Surely Picard cannot be in two different places at once, and that means it's impossible for Picard to travel back in time and meet himself. So time travel (at least to the past) must be impossible. But in fact, there is no impossibility here. Remember that according to four-dimensionalism, the person that is Picard is a four-dimensional object consisting of an aggregate of temporal parts, each of which is a time-slice or person-slice. Without time travel, different slices of a person never meet, because each persists over a different time interval. But with time travel to the past, it is possible for two or more slices of the same person to persist over the same time interval, hence it's possible for two slices of the same person to be in different places at once and even to meet each other. Note that it's not the case that the very same person-slice is wholly in two different places at once—that would be impossible—but rather that the very same person (Picard) is *partly* in two different places at once, by virtue of having different temporal parts in each place. (Just as, by standing with one foot on either side of the border, a person can be partly in two different states at once, by virtue of having different spatial parts in each state.) One temporal part is the present Picard (call him $Picard_1$), and the other is the future Picard (call him $Picard_2$). $Picard_2$ is six hours older in Picard's personal time than is $Picard_1$. Thanks to backward time travel, they both exist in the same external time but at different locations (even when they are in the same room, they're in different parts of the room).

Unfortunately, it's not possible to make consistent sense of all that happens in "Time Squared"—at least not on the assumptions that there is a single timeline and $Picard_2$ exists and is a time traveler. One problem is that the past is changed in order to avert a disaster (a *chronobonus* this time). The shuttlecraft records (which tell the crew that the craft is from six hours into the future) indicate that the *Enterprise-D* was destroyed by an "intelligent energy vortex." $Picard_1$ eventually realizes that $Picard_2$ made a mistake in trying to avoid the vortex, and so does something different, flying straight into the vortex and thus saving the day. Now you might try to get around the impossibility by saying that it was the *future* that was changed, but remember that in four-dimensionalism there is no real difference between the past and the future, so this is just as impossible. (Have another look at the quote from Riker at the beginning of this chapter.) Here's another way to think about it. Remember that $Picard_1$ and $Picard_2$ are different temporal parts of the same person. So anything that either of them does is done by the one and only Picard, and logic requires that it cannot be the case that Picard does and does not do the very same thing. It cannot be the case that he both avoids the vortex *and* flies into it.

There's another problem with the story, too. In order to get his own way, so to speak, and fly the *Enterprise-D* into the vortex, $Picard_1$ finds it necessary to kill $Picard_2$! Though this is not in itself impossible (whereas, for Grandfather reasons, it's impossible for $Picard_2$ to kill $Picard_1$), I hope you can see that it's improvident. In killing $Picard_2$, a later temporal part of the same person, $Picard_1$ ensures that there will be no personal continuers of himself after $Picard_2$ (putting aside the fission possibilities raised in chapter 5). So, Picard commits a sort of delayed suicide. However, the story continues with Picard in it; so another, more personal disaster is somehow averted (another chronobonus). Moreover, none of the other things that $Picard_2$ experienced happen to $Picard_1$ and his continuers. Worse still, once the *Enterprise-D* flies through the vortex, earning the chronobonus, the corpse of Picard, and the contemporaneous slice of Shuttlecraft 05 simply disappear! Do they go somewhere (or somewhen) else, or do they cease to exist? What is the causal explanation of their disappearance? A gigantic "temporal eraser"? (A similar "erasure" occurs in *TOS:* "Yesterday Is Tomorrow"—indeed, it's the *Enterprise* that gets "erased," from the skies over Nebraska.)

Toward the end of "Time Squared," Riker suggests that maybe none of what they have experienced was real, and if the story is to be consistent I think we must agree with this appraisal. Among the vortex's fantastic powers is its ability to produce a mass hallucination; perhaps the vortex wanted to spare the *Enterprise-D* and concocted a plan to persuade Picard to abandon his usual instincts and fly into it.

Causal Loops

We are accustomed to thinking of cause and effect as having a necessary temporal asymmetry—namely, a cause must always precede its effect (or, at least, an effect can never precede its cause). An example of normal causation would be the present event of someone tying my shoelaces together causing the later event of my falling down and hitting my head. Reverse causation, wherein an effect precedes its cause, is certainly counterintuitive, but if time travel to the past is possible, then so is reverse causation. Indeed, reverse causation seems inevitable, given backward time travel. Suppose that while I'm sitting in the time machine in the year 2000 about to travel back to 1920, someone ties my shoelaces together. I arrive in 1920, attempt to step out of the time machine, and fall down and hit my head. Therefore an event in 2000 causes an event in 1920, a case of reverse causation. Similarly, in "The City on the Edge of Forever" McCoy's manic behavior is caused by the accidental injection of "cordrazine," which takes place in the twenty-third century, but some of McCoy's manic behavior occurs in 1930.

Reverse causation is no less plausible than backward time travel itself, so we ought not to reject the possibility of backward time travel on this ground. But the possibility of reverse causation generates another paradox, since it seems to allow for *causal loops.* The simplest type of causal loop involves two events, A and B, where A causes B and B causes A. There are several opportunities for causal loops in *Star Trek*. For instance, in "Time and Again," there is the following apparent sequence of events. After Janeway and Paris, on the surface of the devastated planet, get caught in the temporal fracture that propels them back one day in time, their disappearance prompts their crewmates to mount a rescue attempt. It is this rescue attempt that causes the explosion that destroys the planetary civilization; and this same explosion also creates the temporal fracture that traps Janeway and Paris and propels them back in time. This sequence would be an excellent example of a causal loop if the writers had left it alone, but the whole sequence is "erased" at the end of the episode when the explosion is prevented and a chronobonus is earned. There is a genuine causal loop in another *Voyager* episode, titled "Parallax" (see the section on "loopy loops," later in this chapter), and there are a few in the most coherent time-travel story in the *Star Trek* canon, *TNG:* "Time's Arrow I & II."

The story in brief: In the twenty-fourth century, scientists discover some five-hundred-year-old artifacts, including a revolver and a watch belonging to Samuel Clemens (aka Mark Twain), in a cavern a mile beneath San Francisco. Most startling of all these artifacts—especially to Data—is Data's disembodied head! There are temporal disturbances in the cavern, which appear to have their source in the Devidia system. The *Enterprise-D* journeys to Devidia II, where Data beams down with the away team. They discover a temporal rift, but it's too dangerous for humans to enter, so Data is sent through, and arrives in 1893 San Francisco. Among the local inhabitants is Samuel Clemens, and also Guinan, the long-lived alien bartender on the *Enterprise-D.* Clemens begins trailing Data, out of a mixture of curiosity and suspicion. Several of the *Enterprise-D* crew members, including Picard, eventually follow Data through the temporal rift into 1893, in pursuit of two Devidians, nasty time-traveling aliens who prey on the city's inhabitants like vampires, except that they extract "neural energy." Everyone concerned ends up in the cavern, where Data struggles with one of the aliens, and there is an explosion that decapitates Data, hurling his headless body through the temporal rift and back into the twenty-fourth century. Picard and Guinan are left in the cavern, but Clemens leaps through the rift before it closes. On the other side of the rift, Clemens and Data's body are brought onto the *Enterprise-D,* where La Forge reattaches Data's head (the one that's been lying around for five hundred years). Upon awakening, Data discovers a warning message that was tapped into his head by Picard in 1893, in binary code (actually a pretty laborious way of writing a message, but never mind). Picard has learned from one of the aliens that if the *Enterprise-D* blasts the alien operation on Devidia II with photon torpedoes, it will—via the temporal rift connecting Devidia II to 1893 San Francisco—cause the destruction of the Earth (chronoclasm!), and his warning saves the day. Finally, the only way for Picard to return to the future is by means of a one-person time-travel device taken from the Devidians. But Clemens has brought this device with him to the twenty-fourth century. Clemens uses it to go back to 1893, and Picard uses it to return to the twenty-fourth century.

One causal loop involves the history of Clemens's watch. When Clemens comes aboard the *Enterprise-D* in the twenty-fourth century, he sees his watch on La Forge's desk, picks it up, and pockets it. Then when he returns to the 1893 cavern, he puts his watch down while he helps the injured Guinan. She is taken away, and Clemens picks up the watch, then thinks better of it and leaves it there, knowing it will be found five hundred years later (I shall have something to say about this decision shortly). So the act of leaving the watch in the cavern is (part of) the cause of its being found five hundred years later. Its discovery is (part of) the cause of its being picked up by Clemens in the twenty-fourth century. And Clemens's retrieval of the watch is (part of) the cause of his leaving it behind five hundred years earlier, since if he hadn't picked it up it wouldn't have been in his pocket in 1893. This is a causal loop.

Another causal loop concerns Picard and Guinan. On board the *Enterprise-D* en route to Devidia II, Guinan insists to Picard that—contrary to Starfleet policy—he must join the away team, too. Picard is puzzled, and the conversation continues:

GUINAN: "Do you remember the first time we met?"
PICARD: "Of course."
GUINAN: "Don't be so sure. I just mean, if you *don't* go on this mission, we'll *never* meet."

In external time, Picard and Guinan first meet in 1893. This meeting is (part of) the cause of Guinan's persuading Picard to join the away team. And Guinan's persuading Picard to join the away team is (part of) the cause of their meeting in 1893.

I submit that there is nothing particularly puzzling about such causal loops. But a new puzzle emerges once we recognize that if time travel is possible, then some rather strange causal loops are possible. These loops display *explanatory closure;* hence I shall call them *closed* loops. I have found two strong candidates for closed loops in the *Star Trek* canon. In *TOS:* "Tomorrow Is Yesterday," the *Enterprise,* in escaping the pull of a black hole, is thrown back in time to the skies over Nebraska in the 1960s. Badly damaged, the ship is detected by radar and pursued by an air force fighter. Not wishing to destroy the plane, Kirk orders the use of the tractor beam, but this crushes the fragile airplane, and they must beam the pilot, Captain John Christopher, aboard. At first, Kirk thinks it best to prevent Christopher from returning, since their historical records show that Christopher made no significant contribution to history and there is concern that he will pollute the timeline with his knowledge of the future. But then they discover that Christopher will have a son who will be instrumental in Earth's program of space exploration, so Christopher must after all be returned. Spock tells Christopher that his son's name will be Sean Jeffrey Christopher. On the assumption that Christopher and his wife didn't have "Sean Jeffrey" already picked out for their first male child, there is a causal loop here: the event of naming the boy Sean Jeffrey causes that name to be recorded in history, which causes Spock to learn the name, which causes him to tell Christopher the name, which causes Christopher to name the baby Sean Jeffrey. The puzzling thing about this causal loop is that no one *thinks up* the name "Sean Jeffrey." So where did it come from? Although we can completely explain each event in the loop by reference to other events in the loop, there is no explanation of the loop itself.

But perhaps the unexplained appearance of a name doesn't trouble you. My second example comes from *Star Trek IV: The Voyage Home*. Earth in the twenty-third century is about to be destroyed by a massive cylindrical object, and Spock figures out why. Some far-off intelligence has been communicating with humpback whales; but the humpbacks are gone—hunted to extinction—and the cylinder has been sent to investigate. (Why it has to destroy anything is not explained.) Kirk and his crew travel back to twentieth-century San Francisco with the plan of finding a mating pair of humpbacks to bring to the twenty-third century. But to do so they must convert their ship—a Klingon Bird of Prey—to carry a *lot* of seawater, and twentieth-century technology will not suffice. Scotty and McCoy (suitably disguised) visit a Plexiglas factory and Scotty supplies the factory manager with the formula for lightweight, transparent aluminum in return for some of the product. When McCoy questions this apparent contamination of the timeline, Scotty asks, reasonably enough, "How do you know *he* didn't invent it?"

Let's grant what must be the case: history records the factory manager as the inventor of transparent aluminum. Once again, we have a causal loop, and the strange thing about this causal loop is that no one actually *invents* transparent aluminum. Scotty got the formula from his knowledge of twenty-third century engineering materials; he gave it to the factory manager; and because he gave it to the factory manager, it ends up being a twenty-third century engineering material. Although every event on the loop is explained, the loop itself is unexplained, yet a significant technology is brought into being as a result. However, philosophers are used to the idea that some significant things have no apparent explanation. It may well be, for instance, that there is no explanation for why anything exists at all. Perhaps the universe began with a Big Bang, but there may be no explanation at all for why there was a Big Bang. Explanations have to end somewhere! (Even if there is an infinite chain of explanations, there may be no explanation of the fact that there is an infinite chain of explanations.) Weirdness is one thing, impossibility quite another, and if there are closed causal loops, we must expect the weird.

Loopy Loops

The causal loops I have so far described fit comfortably into the metaphysical picture of four-dimensionalism, and that's because each event occurs only once. (For example, in "Time's Arrow" Samuel Clemens picks up his watch in La Forge's lab and pockets it once, and only once.) Now consider the following conversation from "Time Squared."

WORF: "There is the theory of the Mobius: a twist in the fabric of space where time becomes a loop, from which there is no escape."

LA FORGE: "So when we reach that point, whatever happened will happen again. The *Enterprise* will be destroyed, the other Picard will be sent back to meet us, and we do it all over again. Sounds like someone's idea of Hell to me."

Although the crew avoids any such loop this time, sure enough they get caught in one in "Cause and Effect," going through the same sequence of events four times. The first three end with the destruction of the *Enterprise-D* in a collision with another ship, but on the fourth they have learned their lesson and escape from both the destruction and the loop. In *The Physics of Star Trek* Lawrence

Krauss mentions this episode with apparent approval as involving a "closed timelike curve," but although I'm no physicist, this cannot be all there is to it. Granted, the *Enterprise-D* can go on a journey and return to the same point in space and time, but this would be time travel; in doing so, the ship would age, and what returns would be a later, different time-slice of the ship and the people on it. So each time around, the crew would have a different set of experiences. Moreover, if a ship returns to the same region in space and time, then there are at least two time-slices of the ship present at that time. It's not the case that there's one time-slice, then next time around there are two, and so on. When the crew first encounters the loop, there ought to be three other *Enterprise-D* slices in the loop, too, and not just the *Bozeman,* the ship that the *Enterprise-D* crashes into. But this revised scenario is impossible anyway, since the *Enterprise-D* is destroyed the first time through. Hence there are no later time-slices of it to return to the same point in spacetime.

Here's my quick-fix rewrite. Have the *Enterprise-D* narrowly escape collision with another ship. Then the narrow escape happens again, but is seen from a different perspective. Then a third time, the crew sees two other ships narrowly miss colliding. And so on. Slowly but surely, the crew figures out that they are caught in a temporal loop and have just missed colliding with themselves!

But perhaps I'm missing something. The premise of "Cause and Effect" is that each time through the loop the *same* time-slice of the *Enterprise-D* is going through the same events. That is, each time the events of the loop are played out, time is "rewound" and the whole series of events plays out again and again. Such loops involve not reverse causation but reverse *time*. Even if temporal reversal is possible, what happens in "Cause and Effect" isn't possible. Worf discovers that while they've been trapped in the loop, seventeen days have passed for the rest of the nearby universe, so external time wasn't reversed, only the local time (roughly, the personal time of the *Enterprise-D*). So far, so good. The trouble is, the crew members keep experiencing déjà vu, which tips them off to their predicament. This is impossible, given time reversal; indeed, that anything at all is remembered implies quite the opposite—that the second, third, and fourth times through the loop are *later* in local time than is the first. You can't have temporal reversal *and* déjà vu! And of course the escape from destruction is yet another chronobonus, so the episode is doubly impossible.

Then there is the "Mannheim Effect," witnessed in *TNG:* "We'll Always Have Paris." Picard, Riker, and Data are standing in front of the empty turbolift, about to go to the bridge. Data says, "Incidentally, Captain, the effects of the time distortions are now being felt in the Ilakom system." The trio enter the turbolift, Picard says "Bridge," and the turbolift appears to start up. When the door opens, the trio—call them trio_A—see themselves (trio_B) outside the door. As trio_A stare in disbelief, here's the conversation:

DATA_B: "Incidentally, Captain, the effects of the time distortions are now being felt in the Ilakom system."
PICARD_A: "It's *us,* before we stepped into the turbolift!"
PICARD_B: "It's happening again."
DATA_B: "I feel no disorientation."
DATA_A: "Nor do I."

Then we see the turbolift doors close on trio_A, as trio_B continue talking:

RIKER_B: "What was that?"
DATA_B: "I believe what could be termed as the Mannheim Effect is becoming more pronounced."
RIKER_B: "This is where we started. If *we* are *us*—"
DATA_B: "Oh, we are *us,* sir. But they are also us. So, indeed, we are both us. At different points along the same time continuum."

Trio_B then wait anxiously as the turbolift doors open to reveal . . . an empty turbolift. They enter, and Picard_B says, "Bridge."

This is one of the few occasions when the *Star Trek* writers really messed things up—so much so that I wonder whether or not the sequence was meant as a joke. Clearly this series of events is intended as a causal loop in a single timeline, and the statements of both Picard_A and Data_B bear this out. Later in the episode, Data says to Picard, "The time distortions occurred along the same continuum, as a preview—or a reprise—of a specific point in time." I'm afraid this *cannot be right*. The problem is that the writers haven't stuck to the events as they occurred previously. Each member of trio_A ought to be a later temporal stage of each member of trio_B. But when trio_B are outside the turbolift, and Data_B says "Incidentally, Captain," and so on, is the turbolift empty? Impossibly, the answer is yes *and* no! Does Picard_B say "It's happening again?" No and yes! Does Data_B say, "I feel no disorientation?" No and yes! Do trio_B enter the turbolift immediately after Data says "Incidentally, Captain . . . "? Yes and no! And so on. Worse still, when trio_B continue their conversation, it's as though *they* are later temporal stages of the members of trio_A, since it's Riker_B who says, "This is where we started." (Compared with this, the fact that the turbolift went somewhere without going anywhere is a minor difficulty.) As loops go, the Mannheim Effect is a multiply impossible doozy!

Philosophers have toyed with yet another loopy kind of loop. It doesn't turn up in *Star Trek,* but we can produce one with a little license. There is a perfectly consistent causal loop in *Voyager:* "Parallax," where a sequence of events goes like this. Janeway receives a garbled message on an emergency frequency. This causes her to head toward a singularity, where the crew detects the presence of a ship. Janeway sends a message to the ship on an emergency channel. And this is the message that Janeway received in the first place. That is, Janeway has unknowingly sent a message back in time to herself! Let's play with the loop a little by automating it. A similar loop would have occurred if Janeway had ordered a device built which could receive messages, and also send messages to itself back in time. In order to trigger the sending of the message, the device is designed to send the message if and only if it receives it (it has a switch that's activated by the receipt of the message). Such a device surely is possible, if it is possible to send messages back in time. But suppose Janeway orders a change in design: instead of being activated by the receipt of the message, the switch is *de*activated by the receipt of the message. If the first device is possible, then so is this one, surely. Given that the device can't help but receive the message if it sends the message, then the second device is designed to send the message if and only if it doesn't send the message! But surely such a device is impossible. Something has gone wrong, and some philosophers have suggested that the problem should be resolved by denying the possibility of backward time travel—by messages or anything else.

This reaction seems too hasty. Although we can *describe* such a self-inhibiting device if backward time travel is possible, that doesn't mean that it's possible to build one. Consider an analogy. I can describe a mill in which water drops from the top of a waterfall to a waterwheel at the bottom. I can describe a mill in which water flows by the force of gravity alone from a waterwheel to the top of a waterfall. I can also describe a mill in which both of these obtain, and there is only one waterfall, and only one waterwheel. I have just done it. There is even a visual description of this mill: M. C. Escher's *Waterfall*. Yet, as I'm sure you will agree, we cannot build such a mill. This doesn't demonstrate that one of the components of the mill is impossible, but only that the combination of the components is impossible. By the same token, that the self-inhibiting device is impossible doesn't demonstrate that one of its components (that is, the sender of time-traveling messages) is impossible.

Knowing What Will Happen

I suggested earlier that misconception on the part of time travelers is often necessary to make the plot of a time-travel story work. But do some stories require sheer ignorance? Consider "Time's Arrow" once again. When Data's head is reattached to his body, the five-hundred-year-old message from Picard is discovered. But we know that Data's head can function without his body (this happens in

TNG: "Disaster"), so La Forge might well have got Data's head working right away, in which case the message would have been retrieved *before* Picard left on the away-team mission. Now suppose that only part of the message is retrieved before Picard has to leave—that part identifying it as a warning from Picard. Thus Picard knows there's a warning but doesn't know the contents (let's suppose he also knows somehow or other that the message will turn out to be a complete one).

In our revised version, Picard is in a rather queer position. Consider his reasoning when he is in the cavern and discovers from the alien the danger to Earth from the photon torpedo blast the *Enterprise-D* is likely to unleash. In the original story, it was this knowledge that motivated Picard to send the message to the future. But in our revised version Picard already knows that the message is received in the future, so surely he doesn't need to go to all the trouble to send it, does he? But if he doesn't send it, then who does? So he must send it. Imagine all this going through Picard's mind; perhaps he is bound to come to the realization that he must send the message, and simply will resign himself to it. He will adopt a fatalistic attitude, if he is wise, and get on with the job. If he is not wise, then perhaps he will be paralyzed into inaction.

The problem with this sort of foreknowledge, according to some philosophers, is that it threatens one's freedom. If you already know what you will do, then there seems to be no possibility of rational reflection about it, and so no room for genuine, effective deliberation. Picard thinks he knows what he will do, so he cannot freely choose to do it. There is a genuine risk that time travel will remove one's freedom by compromising effective deliberation.

The *Star Trek* writers, to their credit, seem more or less aware of one side of this problem. In "Time Squared," for instance, when the log from the "future" shuttlecraft is recovered, Picard (the Picard of the present, or Picard$_1$) expresses apprehension about playing back a log which from his point of view hasn't yet been recorded. Then Dr. Pulaski opines that Picard$_1$ is afraid that doubt might paralyze him when the time comes for action—doubt generated by his foreknowledge that the *Enterprise-D* will be destroyed. Riker has something of the same problem in "Time's Arrow," when he is trying to extract information—about Picard's predicament in the past—from Guinan, five hundred years after the events of 1893.

RIKER: "You were there in the cavern. You know what happened. What am I supposed to do?"
GUINAN: "If I told you what happened in that cavern, it might affect any decision you'd make now. I can't do that. I won't."
RIKER: "*Not* telling me may affect my decision. Did you think of that? . . . I can't sit around and hope it all works out. I've got to *do* something!"

It seems that a little knowledge of the future is a dangerous thing, and one is better off—in the sense of *freer*—when one is ignorant of what will occur, and what one will do. Or so argue some philosophers—though I doubt that freedom, or effective deliberation, is necessarily compromised in such situations.

Effective Deliberation in the Face of Foreknowledge

DATA: "It seems clear that my life is to end in the late nineteenth century."
RIKER: "Not if we can help it."
DATA: "There is no way anyone can prevent it, sir. At some future date I will be transported back to nineteenth-century Earth, where I will die. It has occurred. It *will* occur."

—*"Time's Arrow I"*

In chapter 3, I argued that free action is that which issues from a well-functioning will, and that a will roughly is a faculty composed of a belief generator, a desire generator, and a deliberator. A well-functioning will engages all three subfaculties in producing action, given that all three subfaculties are themselves well functioning. Now, in a minor sense one's deliberation is effective if one's deliberator is *engaged*—that is, if one's deliberator plays a causal role in producing the action under consideration (putting it another way, if the operation of one's deliberator *makes a difference* to which action is produced). I trust it is obvious that actions produced by a free will are effective in this minor sense.

For our purposes, the major sense of "effective" is that one's deliberation is effective if it *makes a salient difference to what happens,* and not all freely produced actions are effective in this sense. If one's actions are ineffective, then the deliberation that produced them is also ineffective. Here's an example of ineffective deliberation adapted from Dan Dennett. Suppose I have imprudently jumped off a tall building without a parachute or other means of stopping my fall. I can deliberate all I like on the way down, but none of it, or any action that results from it, makes a jot of difference to what happens. I will die, no matter what I decide, so I might as well give up deliberating and resign myself to my fate.

It may be that when one knows in advance that one's actions and one's deliberations will be ineffective, then deliberation (and freedom of action) is compromised. But it seems to me that one can know perfectly well what one will do in advance and yet genuinely deliberate, when one has good reason to think that the deliberation will be effective. For instance, suppose I know myself really well. I know that I will put off relatively unpleasant duties until the last minute. But I also know that I am too conscientious not to complete a duty on time. Now I am confronted with an unpleasant duty; the example that springs to my academic mind is a pile of essays to be graded by next Wednesday. Hence I know that I will grade the papers next Tuesday night. Note that I know *what* I will do, and *when* I will do it. Yet isn't it odd to say that come Tuesday night I don't genuinely deliberate about whether or not to grade the papers, and don't freely act when I sit down and grade them? It will not do to claim that I act freely in grading the papers because I already decided *in advance* to grade the papers on Tuesday night. Why not? Because it undoubtedly takes an effort of will on my part to get myself to grade the papers, and this effort of will occurs *on Tuesday night,* not days beforehand. For the papers to get graded by me, there must be effective deliberation by me on Tuesday night.

Applying this line of reasoning to the revised case of Picard in the cavern, the fact that he knows he will send the message does not prevent him freely from doing so. Of course, it will be an unpleasant duty, but not because it's pointless. When Picard through an effort of will forces himself to send the message, he knows that his deliberation is effective, since it is that very deliberation which brings about receipt of the message in the twenty-fourth century. The attitude that Picard must adopt in the meantime is a philosophical one in the ordinary sense of this term—a resigned acceptance of his lot. Indeed, it is likely that such an attitude, far from threatening freedom, is *essential* to it, in cases of foreknowledge of what one will do.

We learn a lot from Data in this respect (see the epigraph). When the *Enterprise-D* is on route to Devidia II, Riker tries to talk Data out of joining the away team, thinking they can prevent Data's decapitation this way, but Data knows better and refuses to allow foreknowledge to cripple his deliberative process; indeed, he seems to regard his foreknowledge as providing a reason to join the away team. Clemens, too, takes the philosophical attitude when he decides to leave his watch in the cavern. He reasons thus: the watch will be found here in the twenty-fourth century, therefore I must leave it here. And leave it he does.

All Good Things . . .

I'm really fond of the final installment of *The Next Generation,* in which Q has Picard chasing his tail through time, trying to avert the retroactive destruction of all life on Earth, which he himself has caused in his efforts to prevent it. This story has just about everything in it. The Grandfather Paradox threatens when Picard seems to be in danger of bringing about his own nonexistence. There is an identity paradox when three *Enterprise-Ds* (all with a Picard on board) meet in a temporal rift. There is a nice little causal loop when Picard discovers in his future that he has a neurological disease, originally diagnosed by Dr. Crusher. This causes him to seek medical advice in an earlier time, when Dr. Crusher discovers the neurological defect that will later cause the disease (see the dialogue at the beginning of the chapter). Moreover, if we take the story really seriously, then there is a *closed* loop, since Picard in restoring life on Earth brings about his own existence, leaving his existence with no explanation. Also, Picard sometimes seems unable to act because he knows what will (or did) happen; and there is even some local time reversal (enabling Geordi La Forge to recover his sight).

Unfortunately, practically none of this story can be taken at face value, because it isn't a time-travel story at all. Recall the intitial conditions we laid down—to be a time traveler one must actually *go* somewhere or somewhen. But although Picard has the experience of moving about in time—shifting mainly between the present, twenty-five years into the future, and seven years into the past—he doesn't actually do so. To the others around him, he seems only to become distracted for a moment or two. Perhaps what occurs is not time travel, but internal communication between time-slices of Picard. Even if this is what occurs (with a little help from Q), there's still no way to make consistent sense of everything that happens.

First, there is the alleged chronoclasm. If there really was a rift between time and "antitime," then there really *was* such a thing. (It's clearly visible in the heavens when Q takes Picard back to the nascent Earth.) So how can things be returned to normal, without explicit contradiction? Not only this, but in each of the three different time periods Picard allegedly shifts between, the *Enterprise-D* is destroyed in the temporal rift. Clearly, for Grandfather reasons, only the twenty-five-years-ahead time-slice of the *Enterprise-D* can be destroyed, and that really would be the end of Picard and company. Then there's the internal inconsistency in the story: the rift between time and "antitime" travels *backward* in time, increasing in size as it goes (that's why the nascent Earth is threatened). But twenty-five years on, Picard, Dr. Crusher, La Forge, and Data go looking for the rift and can't find it; they return a little later and it's there. In the meantime, they've helped to cause the development of the rift—by looking for it with an inverse tachyon pulse—but surely the rift won't be present *later* than when it was produced, if it's moving *backward* in time. Then there's the other internal inconsistency: at one point Q shows Picard how his actions have prevented life from forming on the nascent Earth. So why hasn't everything changed—the chronoclasm gone all the way—already? Suppose we invoke the chronoton-particle protection hypothesis, somehow keeping things together around Picard in three different time periods? But we can't, because when Picard asks Q at the end of the episode whether or not humanity has been saved, Q says, "You're still here, aren't you?"

All in all, I have to agree with Dr. Crusher's suggestion to Picard: "I want you to allow for the possibility that none of this is real." What's occurred is all a fantasy induced by Q as another test of Picard's mettle, so it's no surprise that Picard records in his personal log that he's the only one who remembers any of it. None of it happened anywhere but in Picard's mind! However, even Data throws away everything he knows about time by the end of this episode. Here is some conversation from the final scene:

DR. CRUSHER: "I was thinking about what the Captain told us all about the future. . . . Why would he want to tell us what's to come?"

GEORDI: "Sure goes against everything we've always heard about not polluting the timeline, doesn't it?"

DATA: "I believe, however, that this situation is unique. Since the anomaly did not occur, there have already been changes in the way this timeline is unfolding. The future we experience will undoubtedly be different from the one the Captain experienced."

RIKER: "Maybe that's why he told us. Knowing what happens in the future allows us to change things now, so that some things never happen."

In any account of time I have presented here, Riker's surmise borders on nonsense. Perhaps there are some accounts of time in which Riker's surmise makes sense, or is even true, but I doubt it. Of course, I haven't canvassed every philosophical account of time. In some views, time is essentially psychological, and in others, there's no such thing as time at all! But we don't have time for that now. On that note, "All Good Things . . ." must come to an end.

The Future

epilogue

In these last years of the second millennium, science is under attack on many fronts. Religious conservatives accuse scientists of blind faith in the dogma of Darwinism; New Age thinkers charge that the naturalistic materialism of science is a superstition that must be abandoned if we are to make progress; feminists question the phallocentric nature of the entire Western intellectual tradition, including science; nonwhites question the Eurocentric nature of science; and postmodernists would reject everything about it, if only the concept of rejection were not itself infected with Western intellectual bias. Even many ordinary people have a modicum of contempt for science, blaming it for the production of a great deal of the mess in which we find ourselves. The more conservative critics regard science the way the twenty-fourth century Federation regards the Klingon Empire—as an ally with whom you have an uneasy truce, but whose attempts at expansion require vigilance. The more radical regard science as they would the Borg—any involvement with it will end with your assimilation.

Insofar as there is a coherent antiscience thesis that these groups have in common, it is in two parts. First, all parties are of the view that science necessarily is limited in scope. Second, there is a deep suspicion that somehow science has everyone fooled into thinking science *isn't* limited in scope— that is, science has bluffed itself and everyone else into thinking that science holds the key to everything important. Hence the project the crusader must undertake is to put science in its proper place. Thus we shall see not a return to the Dark Ages that preceded the scientific revolution but rather a new and even more enlightened age, in which the proper alternatives to science may be freely pursued.

I am in total agreement with the claim that science necessarily is limited in scope (of course, I think that philosophy takes up much of the remaining slack). But there my agreement with the critics of science ends. There are some deep and difficult issues about the nature and scope of science which many good minds are pursuing, such as whether or not the successful application of a scientific theory gives us adequate reason for believing it. But many trenchant popular critics of science speak either from profound ignorance both of science and philosophy or—what is worse—from a passing but jaundiced familiarity. For example, some will insist that scientific claims are restricted in principle to what can be tested by repeated experiment, hence science necessarily (not to mention conveniently) is silent on, say, biblical history.

My personal view is, if anything, in polar opposition to that of the populist critics. I find the criticisms and warnings about science running wild ironic, since I share elements of the *Star Trek* vision; if we can pursue science relatively untrammeled by superstition, I think we have a chance of not merely technological but genuine human progress. (*Star Trek* has its warnings, too. One common theme is that the more advanced societies have lost something valuable which we comparatively primitive humans have in abundance—be it childlike innocence, boundless curiosity, or intense emotions. Another is that scientists have a strong tendency to pursue their research at all costs.) When one contemplates the extent of popular belief in alien abductions and visitations, psychic phenomena, and so forth, and the plethora of misinformation on these subjects generated by the media, one might despair of the prospects for any progress at all. The scientific enterprise is an all too human one, and has its limits, but there seems a fundamental and dangerous inconsistency in refusing to apply it where it has something important to tell us.

Critics of science often claim that scientific and technological progress is useless or worse unless accompanied by philosophical progress. Who would disagree? But many of these critics offer philosophical *re*gress—either a return to traditional superstitions or a modern woolly headed relativism. If philosophy were no more than a corrective to such thinking, it would be a worthwhile undertaking. But philosophy can do more. Much of this book has been devoted to the ways in which consideration of possible scientific futures can inform present philosophy; my vision of the future includes the hope that philosophy will increasingly inform science. There is not as much evidence of this as I would like in the *Star Trek* future. Central characters often display considerable ignorance when it comes to philosophical issues—an ignorance out of step with other projected developments. Practically everybody on board a Federation vessel seems to understand and be able to fix or jury-rig any piece of starship technology, and any time there's a high-powered discussion in theoretical physics the whole crew seems to understand it. Scientists quibble over the details and positively wince at the technobabble, but it must be said that *Star Trek* has at least earnestly attempted to project science and technology centuries into the future. However, on philosophical issues the general level of competence among the crew is that of the ordinary late-twentieth-century denizen of the Western world.

My point is not to condemn the *Star Trek* writers—far from it, for *Star Trek* at least raises philosophical issues in the first place; moreover, to appeal to a general audience one obviously must present characters with attitudes that the audience can identify with. But within these constraints, it is possible to present a more philosophically realistic future. Accelerating scientific and technological developments—such as genetic engineering, the increased ability to keep people alive long past the point when it is worthwhile, brain transplants, cloning, better and better interactive computers, and the like—will challenge even the ordinary person to confront his or her cherished metaphysical beliefs. And sometimes the rational response will be to abandon those beliefs. It is often said that we are conducting a huge physiological experiment on ourselves by subjecting our essentially Stone Age physical constitutions to the modern Western diet, with no good idea of the result. We are also conducting a huge psychological experiment by subjecting our comparatively primitive worldviews to the modern information explosion. My hope for the future is that our worldviews can adapt more readily than our bodies can, and fortunately there is reason to believe this. The entire advantage of being creatures largely driven to behavior by beliefs and desires is that we are in principle flexible, able to respond relatively quickly to changes in our environment. If the inertia of centuries of superstition can be overcome, we may yet have a future worth looking forward to—a time of peace on Earth and goodwill toward men—perhaps even a future like that depicted in *Star Trek*. We could do a lot worse.

In addition to the references in the text to contemporary philosophers, the views I have expressed are indebted to the work of particular philosophers, especially in two cases: the argument of chapter 5 owes substantially to Derek Parfit, and that of chapter 6 owes to David K. Lewis. I have listed all contemporary sources in the order of their relevance to the text.

Part I: New Life, New Civilizations
Chapter 1: Prime Suspects

Singer, Peter. *Applied Ethics*, 2d ed. Cambridge: Cambridge University Press, 1993.

Quine, Willard V. O. *Word and Object.* Cambridge, MA: MIT Press, 1960.

Dennett, Daniel C. *Elbow Room: The Varieties of Free Will Worth Wanting*. Cambridge, MA: MIT Press, 1984.

Chapter 2: Insufficient Data

Turing, Alan. "Computing Machinery and Intelligence." *Mind* 59 (1950).

Weizenbaum, Joseph. *Computer Power and Human Reason.* San Francisco: Freeman, 1976.

Chapter 3: Pro Creation

Farrand, Phil. *The Nitpicker's Guide for Next Generation Trekkers.* New York: Dell, 1993.

Stampe, Dennis, and Martha Gibson. "Of One's Own Free Will." *Philosophy and Phenomenological Research* 52 (1992).

Sober, Elliott. *Core Questions in Philosophy*, 2d ed. Englewood Cliffs, NJ: Prentice Hall, 1995.

Searle, John. "Minds, Brains, and Programs." *The Behavioral and Brain Sciences* 3 (1980).

Boden, Margaret A. "Escaping from the Chinese Room." In *The Philosophy of Artificial Intelligence*, edited by Margaret A. Boden. Oxford: Oxford University Press, 1990.

bibliography

Cole, David. "Artificial Intelligence and Personal Identity." *Synthese* 88 (1991).

Part II: Matters of Survival
Chapter 4: To Beam or Not to Beam?

Nozick, Robert. *Philosophical Explanations.* Cambridge, MA: Harvard University Press, 1981.

Jackson, Frank. "What Mary Didn't Know." *Journal of Philosophy* 83 (1976).

Lewis, David K. "Knowing What It's Like," Postscript to "Mad Pain and Martian Pain." In *The Nature of Mind,* edited by David M. Rosenthal. Oxford: Oxford University Press, 1991.

Chapter 5: Personal Growth

Parfit, Derek. *Reasons and Persons.* Oxford: Oxford University Press, 1984.

Lewis, David K. "Survival and Identity." In *The Identities of Persons,* edited by Amelie Oksenberg Rorty. Berkeley: University of California Press, 1976.

Martin, Raymond. "Identity, Transformation, and What Matters in Survival." In *Self and Identity: Contemporary Philosophical Issues,* edited by Daniel Kolak and Raymond Martin. New York: Macmillan, 1991.

Sperry, Roger. "Hemisphere Disconnection and Unity in Conscious Awareness." Address presented to American Psychological Association in Washington, D.C., September 1967.

Nagel, Thomas. *Mortal Questions.* Cambridge: Cambridge University Press, 1979.

Puccetti, Roland. "Two Brains, Two Minds? Wigan's Theory of Mental Duality." *British Journal for the Philsophy of Science* 40 (1989).

Hilgard, Ernest R. *Divided Consciousness: Multiple Controls in Human Thought and Action*. Expanded ed. New York: Wiley, 1986.

Dennett, Daniel, and Nicholas Humphrey. "Speaking for Ourselves: An Assessment of Multiple Personality Disorder." *Raritan: A Quarterly Review* 9 (1989).

Chapter 6: Temporal Distortions

Lewis, David K. "The Paradoxes of Time Travel." *American Philosophical Quarterly* 13 (1976).

Earman, John. "Implications of Causal Propagation Outside the Null Cone." *Australasian Journal of Philosophy* 50 (1972).

Dennett, Daniel C. *Elbow Room: The Varieties of Free Will Worth Wanting*. Cambridge, MA: MIT Press, 1984.

index